THE GUITAR

THIS IS A CARLTON BOOK

Copyright © 1998, 1999, 2003, 2004
Carlton Books Limited

This edition published in 2004 by
Carlton Books Ltd
20 Mortimer Street
London
W1T 3JW

A CIP catalogue for this book is available
from the British Library.

ISBN 1 84442 692 0

Contributing author: Mike Flynn
Project Editor: Amie McKee
Designer: Michelle Pickering
Picture manager: Steve Behan
Art director: Clare Baggaley
Production: Lisa Moore

Printed and bound in Dubai

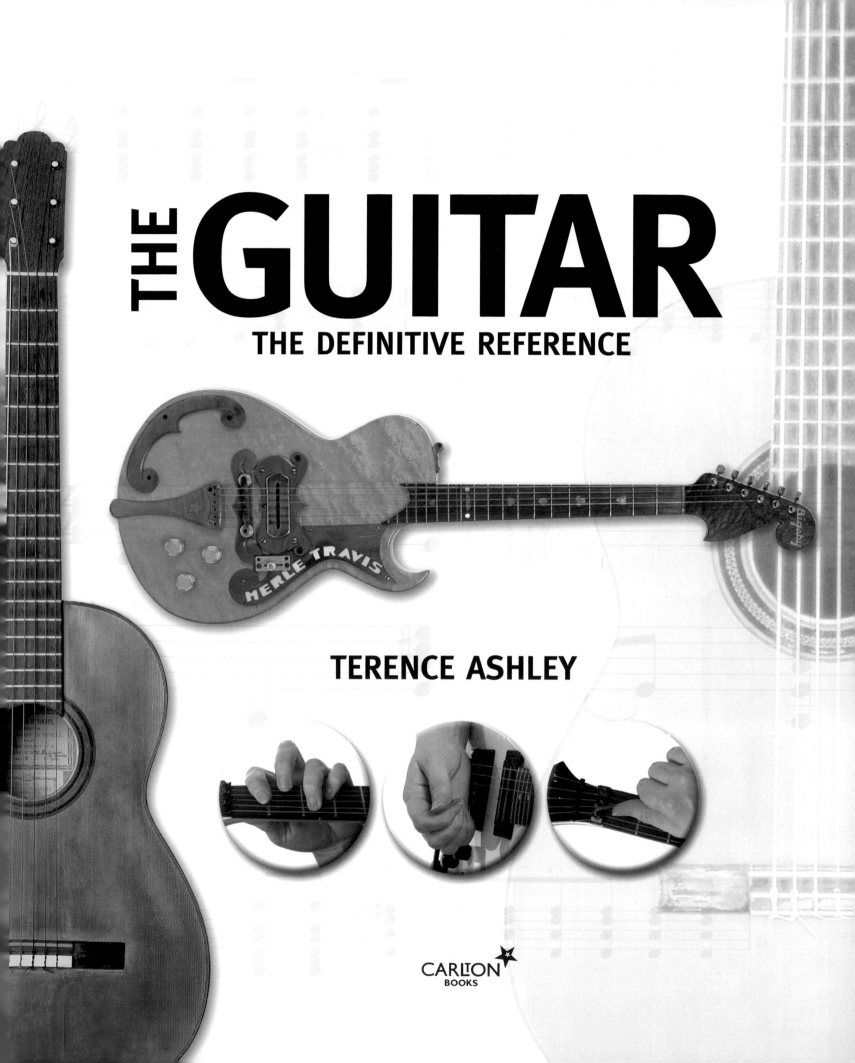

THE GUITAR

THE DEFINITIVE REFERENCE

TERENCE ASHLEY

CARLTON
BOOKS

CONTENTS

THE GUITAR

FIFTY GREAT GUITARISTS

PLAYING THE GUITAR

INTRODUCTION

Welcome to the guitar – the world's most popular musical instrument.

For the beginner, even taking your initial step into a music store can be quite overwhelming when faced with the huge range of paraphanalia which is associated with the modern guitar. As well as having to choose from a huge range of nylon-string, steel-string, solid-body electric, semi-acoustic and electro-acoustic guitars, there is also the mind-boggling mass of electronic hardware to become acquainted with, while considering the merits of valve and solid-state amplifiers. (Or, for that matter, with a new generation of amp simulators, deciding whether you even need an amplifier at all.) And as for the plethora of inscrutably named sound processing effects, what does it all mean?

But don't panic, help is on hand to guide you through this seemingly daunting maze.

The Guitar modestly aims to be the ultimate compendium of this great instrument. Divided into three distinct sections, this book will hopefully provide you with a thorough understanding of the history and evolution of the guitar, and a knowledge of the many different types of instrument used in modern guitar music – this is critical if you are to make suitable choices when you first step into that music store (or log on to eBay). Controversially, we'll also be discussing 50 of the best, most influential, or most interesting guitarists in history. One of the best ways we as musicians can develop is by listening to and understanding the work of others.

Finally – and above all – this book aims to teach you the fundamentals of the instrument. We're not concentrating on specific styles, just the basics that will enable you to make decisions on your own. Afterwards you should have a good understanding of the fundamentals of music theory and sight-reading of standard musical notation and tablature. You should also be able to play any of the most commonly used open-string chords, and many more complex barre chords. You will also be taught single-note techniques that will enable you to play melodies and perform solos.

So why is this book any different from other, similar titles you might have already tried? The main reason is that most guitar tutorial books are written by people who seem to want you to STUDY the instrument. They don't understand that you might just want to be able to strum the chords to your favourite tunes or write your own music. And so many of them seem geared to one specific style of music. You'll find no such prejudices here. We make no claims to be arbiters of good taste – whether it's classical, rock, jazz, folk, thrash, pop, avant-garde or metal that interests you, *The Guitar* will point you in the right direction.

Try to think of this book as a kind of "virtual friend". We're going to teach you the basics of playing the guitar in as informal a manner as possible. We're not going to be enforcing any hard-and-fast rules here: if you don't like what we have to say, feel free to ignore it! We want to arm you with the tools to allow you to think and play for yourself. Throughout the book, lessons and techniques are shown using a variety of different audio-visual aids – you can study finger diagrams, photographs, charts, notation and tablature.

So, get ready for the rollercoaster ride ahead. At first you'll find it a tough and frustrating business – the muscles in your fingers will ache and you'll want to smash your guitar each time they refuse to obey your commands. But no matter how great the challenge, please don't let it become torture. You only live once, and the precious time you spend doing anything should be enjoyable and satisfying, otherwise it's just not worth bothering. As the legendary Les Paul told me a few years back: "You don't work the guitar, you play it." Wise words indeed.

Have fun.

TERENCE ASHLEY

London, January 2004

PART 1

THE GUITAR

From the middle of the 1950s, the guitar – especially in its electric form – became one of the coolest cultural icons of the period, conjuring up notions of rebellion and freedom. Although it's quite true that the instrument's widespread popularity in classical and popular music has been relatively recent, the guitar has a heritage that can be traced back well over 4,000 years.

So let's take a journey through the guitar's colourful history, and see how the instrument evolved and shaped different forms of music throughout the ages. You'll also discover how they are made, how they produce sound and which of the modern alternatives is most appropriate to the kind of music you want to play. Finally, the chapter concludes with a timeline of 25 of the most important guitars from the past 500 years.

THE BIRTH AND EVOLUTION OF THE GUITAR

The origins of the world's most popular musical instrument are shrouded in mystery, a mystery made all the deeper by scholarly disagreement over what actually constitutes a guitar. Further confusion is added to this by the fact that, until relatively recently, the guitar and many of its predecessors were instruments on which folk music was played. As such, they were considered of little interest or consequence by those strata of polite society from whom we learned the lessons of history.

No one can be certain just when the guitar, or guitar-like instruments, arrived in Europe, although it is fairly safe to assume that the instrument did not originate there. That said, investigations of its origins are often muddied by the almost random way in which some historians have given the name "guitar" to almost any instrument from the Middle East or Far East which bears even a passing resemblance to this instrument. This was often done without any knowledge of how the instruments were constructed, tuned or played. While it is true that some of them possessed strings, a neck and frets, they may well have been played with a bow, or may even have been made solely for use as artefacts in religious or cultural ceremonies.

While we know for certain the history of the guitar in the period following the Renaissance, it has become a rather tired cliché to claim that the guitar is merely a development of the European lute. To do so ignores its rich history and its non-European origins.

ANCIENT ANCESTORS

Some people point to an ancient Greek instrument called the *kithara* as a possible ancestor of the guitar, although any similarity to the modern instrument appears to be in name only. It is also true that certain long-necked lutes found in what used to be Mesopotamia bear a passing resemblance to the guitar, as do a number of lutes found in Egypt from a slightly later period.

These instruments possess flat backs and sides and in this respect resemble the modern guitar more so than the lute. That said, not all guitar-shaped instruments had flat backs. In order to narrow down the number that might be considered as precursors to the modern guitar, this chapter concentrates on those stringed and fretted instruments which, from the front, most resemble the modern guitar: those which are said to have a waisted look. (It was not until the twentieth century that the fashion for wasted guitarists began.)

The earliest recorded instrument with the classic pinched-waist look also dates from ancient Egypt. This instrument bore a closer resemblance to a long-necked lute, but it did possess a guitar-shaped resonating body. The shape did not persist in later designs, however, so it cannot really be counted as a true ancestor of the guitar.

The next earliest example of a guitar-shaped instrument was found in Central Asia. It dates from the earliest days of the Christian era and, although it was probably a form of lute, its

THE KITHARA RESEMBLES
THE GUITAR IN NAME ONLY.

gittern had three or four pairs
of strings, called courses, which
were attached at the base of the
instrument – near the bridge –
and again at the peg box. The
space beneath the fretboard was
hollowed out, making it easier
for the musician to reach the
strings. The earliest known
example of the gittern appears
in a carving which dates from
the first century AD and it
continued to be depicted for at
least the next thousand years.
There is an example in a carving
(of a musical angel) in London's
Westminster Abbey, which dates
from around the year 1250.

A brief check of the accounts
of court from this period can also
be very enlightening as to the

shape resembles most closely that of the guitar. This design
persisted in the region for around four hundred years but then
disappeared, not to be seen again until the eleventh century. By
then there were already a variety of guitar-shaped instruments in
use in Europe, and a number of these had names suggesting they
were among the first true ancestors of the guitar.

THE GITTERN

The gittern was a plucked instrument constructed with parallel
sides, a flat back, a fretted neck and gut strings – a description that
could almost describe the modern classical guitar. The back, sides
and neck of the only known surviving example of the instrument
are carved from a single piece of wood. Paintings and carvings from
this period show, however, that there were several variations on the
basic design. Early gitterns normally had at least two sound holes,
rather like a violin, but these had been replaced by the thirteenth
century with a single rounded hole decorated with a "rose," a piece
of wood carved ornately to resemble a rose. The tuning pegs were
placed at the end of the fretted neck on the peg box, which was
usually carved ornately and set back at an angle to the neck. The

extent of the popularity of the gittern, which by now was known
by a variety of similar names, such as *gitar*, *quitarra* and *guiterre*.
A *gitarer* was employed to play at the Feast of Westminster in
1306. In France, the Duke of Normandy had a musician on his
staff called Jean Hautemar, who
played the *guitare latine*, an
instrument which scholars
have since identified as the
gittern. The name was used
deliberately to signify that
the instrument's origins were
European (Spanish, to be
precise), rather than the *guitare
morisca* – the name given to
the guitar-like instruments
believed to have originated
in the Middle and Far East.

The original medieval
gittern had slipped out of
fashion in Northern Europe

THE LUTE AS DEPICTED IN ASIAN ART.

It is a tragedy that no living person has ever heard music that was composed originally for the gittern. None survives and we can only guess at what the instrument might have been used for. Although it was possible to pick out melodies on the instrument, and occasionally strum a few chords, it was most likely used to provide a rhythmical drone to accompany dances. We are given just a hint of how the instrument might have sounded by a character in *Ralph Roister Doister*, a play from the early 1500s, who says: "Anon to our gitterne, thrumpledum, thrumpledum, thrumpledum thrum."

While it is true to say that the gittern was essentially a box and a neck

by the beginning of the fifteenth century – to be replaced by the lute – but the name persisted and was used to describe all manner of guitar-shaped instruments. The fact that the gittern was believed to have originated in Spain alongside the lute may partly explain the belief that the guitar was merely a development of it. In Southern Europe, the gittern continued to be popular and the instrument eventually evolved into the *viola da mano*, or *vihuela*.

Even the English king Henry VIII found time to play the gittern. In the inventory of his instruments, drawn up after his death, was found "Foure Gitterons with iiii cases to them: they are caulled Spanish Vialles [vihuelas]." It is not beyond the bounds of possibility that "Greensleeves," a top Tudor tune normally credited to the king, may actually have been composed on this instrument.

The gittern also warrants a mention in Chaucer's *The Canterbury Tales*. In *The Pardoner's Tale* there is mention of the instrument being played at something resembling a raucous pub gig:

In Flandres whilom was a compaignye
Of yonge folk that haunteden folye
As riot, hasard, stywes, and tavernes
Wher as with harpes, lutes and *gyternes* [gitterns]
They daunce and pleyen at dees bothe day and nyght.

carved from a single piece of wood, with another piece laid over the resulting hole to create a sound box, instruments of the lute family were beginning to show signs of the more sophisticated building techniques that were eventually to be applied to the classical guitar.

THE LUTE

As early as the tenth century, the body of the Arabic *al ud* (from which we get "lute") was being delicately fashioned from thin strips of wood, which were carefully steamed to bend them into a shape that even now we would recognize as the back of a lute. It was to be several hundred years, however, before European craftsmen mastered the techniques

THE DELICATE EARLY LUTES
SURVIVED ONLY IN PAINTINGS.

needed to perform this operation and began to apply them to the lute, using strips of maple or sycamore cut into shape. These were moulded to form the characteristic shell-like back. The strips were held together on the reverse of the shell by a similar strip of wood and attached at the front of the shell to a wooden block, to which the neck was joined. Until around the middle of the eighteenth century, the neck was simply held in place with a large nail.

The neck of the lute was rounded at the back to accommodate the player's hand and shaved until the optimum point between strength and playability was reached. A fretboard made from a separate piece of wood was then added. The peg box was set back from the neck at quite a sharp angle, and tuning pegs made of hard wood were inserted into holes drilled in the side of the box.

The soundboard, which fits over the front of the instrument, was usually made from a single flat piece of pine, into which was carved the rose-patterned sound hole. The soundboard was very thin – around 2 mm (0.08 in) – which is all the more remarkable considering the relatively crude tools with which these instruments were made. (Such was the delicacy that no lutes from before about 1500 have survived intact to the present day.) The bridge – to which the strings were attached – was glued to the surface of the soundboard. Tension from the strings tended to cause the thin wood of the soundboard to warp in the direction of the neck. This was combated by fitting the underside of the soundboard with supporting struts.

Fitting supporting struts to the underside of the soundboard had the double benefit of strengthening the lute and improving the quality of its sound. The struts effectively divide the soundboard into separate, smaller areas. This raises the natural resonant frequency of the instrument, causing the soundboard to produce more of the supporting harmonic frequencies of the fundamental notes played. In non-technical terms, this use of struts made the lute stronger and yet sweeter sounding. It also had the added benefit of introducing an "edge" to the sound, which enabled it to be heard above other larger and louder instruments when played as part of an ensemble.

THIS QUEEN ELIZABETH I LUTE WAS MADE BY JOHN ROSE IN 1580.

THE VIHUELA

As lute-building techniques developed, the range of the instrument was increased by fitting it with extra pairs of strings, or "courses," as they were known. By the end of the fifteenth century, some were being built so that six courses could be fitted. But the lute was not the only instrument to benefit from these improvements. In fifteenth-century Spain, it had been passed in popularity by the *vihuela*.

The earliest accounts of the vihuela date from the thirteenth century and describe a Spanish instrument that was smaller than a lute and fitted with a flat back. But things had changed somewhat by the fifteenth century, when the vihuela would be instantly recognizable to any guitarist, who might be forgiven for thinking that it was simply an old guitar. In shape and structure it resembled the guitar in many ways. A glance at even the oldest surviving examples reveal a distinctive guitar-like body (much larger than the lute's) and a long, guitar-like neck. The body is not as deep as that of the modern guitar and the narrower waist, a common feature of the guitar family, is only slightly pinched in. The vihuela's long neck extends far beyond the body to the peg box, which was set back from the fretboard at a much flatter angle than that of the lute.

The fretboard was fitted with 10 frets, which at this stage were made of gut. They could be moved around to suit the mode or key in which a piece of music was being played. The instrument was fitted with six pairs (or courses) of strings, with each pair tuned in unison. These were attached to a fixed bridge and heard via the guitar-like sound hole.

THE FOUR-COURSE GUITAR

The vihuela achieved its peak of popularity in the middle of the sixteenth century, when it was considered to be the instrument of choice among the musical élite. However, its days were numbered. By the end of the century, it had been all but replaced by the guitar. This did not please everybody, as can be seen from the work of one Sebastian Orosco, who wrote shortly after the turn of the century:

"…since the invention of the guitar there are very few who study the vihuela. This is a great loss because…the guitar is nothing but a cow-bell, so easy to play, especially when strummed, that there is not a stable-boy who is not a musician of the guitar."

And so it was that during this period the very first guitars – in name and design – appeared. There can be no doubt that the design of the early guitar was based heavily on that of the lute and the vihuela, and although some have argued that these first guitars were merely simplified versions of these instruments, it is clear that a new instrument was beginning to emerge.

It was known as the four-course guitar, so called because it was fitted with four pairs of strings. It had a waisted front, flat back and sides, and a fretted neck. The first mention of its "invention" appeared in a work by Johannes Tinctoris in which he claims, in 1487, that it was "invented by the Catalans," the inhabitants of a region that is now in north-east Spain. This appears to indicate that this instrument – which many argue was the first true guitar – originated in Europe, but one cannot ignore the influence of the lute and vihuela, which provided the inspiration that led to the design in the first place.

The typical sixteenth-century four-course guitar resembled the modern classical guitar in many respects, although anyone acquainted with today's instrument would be struck immediately by the small size of its ancestor. There were also other, more subtle differences. In common with lutes of this period, the four-course, and later five-course guitar was fitted with a rose over the sound hole. The frets were made of gut, which would be tied around the neck. The number of frets the guitar possessed would vary depending on the type of music played. Simple strumming required no more than a

ROVING MINSTRELS WERE A COMMON SIGHT IN EUROPE.

AN EARLY FIVE-COURSE VIHUELA.

handful of frets, whereas more complex music called for a greater number.

The four-course guitar was tuned in such a way that the intervals between the courses were laid out as a perfect fourth, a major third and another perfect fourth. This arrangement corresponds to the top four strings of the modern classical guitar, although during this period the guitar was tuned a tone lower, to C-F-A-D rather than D-G-B-E.

The five-course guitar appeared in the sixteenth century, and was essentially the same instrument with an extra course. Although this usually meant adding strings in the bass register, there were a number of guitars constructed with additional strings in the treble register, above what is now the top E string on the modern instrument. Like the four-course guitar, the five-course version was small by today's standards (about 80 cm in length – 31.5 in) and had the variable fret arrangement. It seems that it originated in Spain and was probably produced to satisfy the demands of slightly more ambitious pieces composed for the guitar at this time.

One of the most noticeable and striking features of the guitars made after 1600 is the incredibly ornate manner in which they tended to be decorated. Although the guitar was still overshadowed by the lute, which continued to be the most popular plucked instrument throughout the Baroque period (circa 1600–1750), the sheer effort and care involved in creating the beautiful designs with which guitars of this period were decorated suggests a great love for the instrument among those who possessed them. These designs were achieved by staining the woods that were used in the guitar's construction. Sometimes the maker might dispense with wood altogether and create extraordinarily intricate inlaid designs from tortoise-shell or ivory. Among the most outstanding examples of guitar makers' art of this

period are those by the Voboam family, based in France, Joachim Tielke in Germany and the Sellas brothers in Italy. Then as now, some makers went way beyond the bounds of good taste in their choice of adornments for the instruments, in contrast to the subtle beauty of guitars created by Antonio Stradivari, better known for his work as a violin maker.

By this time the techniques that one would normally associate with playing the classical guitar were beginning to appear. Up to this stage, the guitar had been played with techniques developed for the lute and the vihuela. This usually involved the little finger of the right hand resting on either the bridge or the soundboard of the guitar, while the player plucked at the strings using a pinching motion with the thumb and the first two fingers of the right hand. As the instrument grew in size, the right arm rested on the top of the guitar body and the right hand floated free over the strings. This meant that the player could achieve different qualities of sound by plucking the strings at different locations. If the strings were plucked near to the bridge, the guitar produced a bright, almost metallic sound; if played over the sound hole, it was much warmer and softer.

STRADIVARIUS, THE VIOLIN MAKER, ALSO MADE BEAUTIFUL GUITARS.

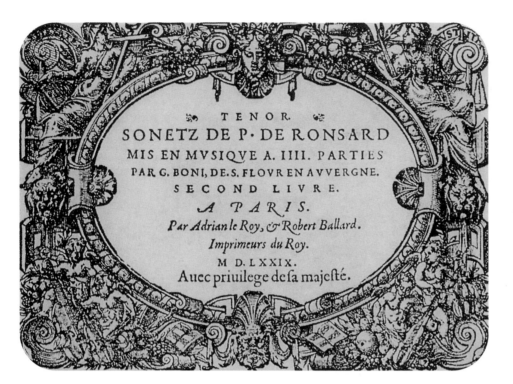

in its own right and was not merely some freakish variant of the lute family. One of the first known tutor books for the guitar had been written by the Frenchman Adrian Le Roy in around 1550, and translated into English by James Rowbotham. Corbetta himself is believed to be the author of a book called *Easie Lessons On The Guittar For Young Practioners* (a sort of seventeenth-century *Play In A Day*), which appeared in 1677. Other tutor books published around this time include *The False Consonances Of Musik* by Nicola Matteis and *Instrucción* by Gaspar Sanz.

As the general level of musicianship rose among guitar players, so too did the quality of the repertoire for the guitar, until it eventually came to rival the lute in terms of the complexity and beauty of the compositions written for it. And so it was that, with the nineteenth century peeking out over the distant horizon, guitarists could begin to look forward to the first golden age of the classical guitar. Improvements in the design and construction of the instrument were to have a profound effect on the way the guitar was perceived by composers, performers and the world at large. From its humble origins as an instrument of peasants, the guitar was to grow until it would eventually dominate the world's stages. Truly, a star was about to be born.

Most of the music played on the guitar at this time was, however, still strummed, so the guitar was still not considered a fit instrument for a serious soloist. This did not in any way affect its popularity. The fact that the guitar could be "mastered" in a relatively short period of time made it all the more appealing to people who wished to create music without the bother of having first to undergo a long period of training. This perhaps explains why it was so popular in royal circles, where the affairs of state must have left a busy monarch with little time for the complexities of the lute.

Francesco Corbetta was one of the first guitarist to achieve an international reputation, which he used to gain a position as guitar teacher to King Louis XIV of France. His first book of music, *La Guitare Royalle* (1674), was dedicated to the king and was filled with simple pieces that could, for the most part, be easily strummed by monarchs with short attention spans. Corbetta very sensibly failed to mention to the king that he had already dedicated the book to King Charles II of England three years earlier. Charles was an enthusiastic player whose lack of any real talent was more than made up for by his royal status, which contributed to the guitar becoming extremely fashionable in England at this time – even though diarist Samuel Pepys loathed and despised the sound of the thing.

Several tutor books began to appear during this period, testifying to the fact that the instrument was becoming established

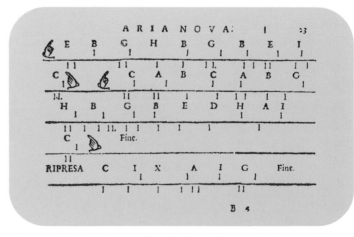

EARLY GUITAR NOTATION RESEMBLES A MODERN CHORD CHART.

EARLY MUSIC FOR THE GUITAR

Early guitar music was nearly always written down as tablature, although in a variety of different styles dependent largely on the country in which the music was produced. Tablature, still used today by some guitarists, is a method of notating music by means of numbers (representing frets) and horizontal lines (representing guitar strings). Because the earliest guitars had only four courses, with each pair of strings tuned in unison, early guitar tablature displayed only four horizontal lines, which can be thought of as corresponding to the modern five-line stave or staff.

The Spanish placed any notes that were to be played on the top (highest-sounding) string on the lowest line of the stave, reasoning that, in physical terms, the highest-sounding string was the one nearest the ground. The French and the Italians, however, placed the highest-sounding string at the top of the stave on the grounds that the top notes should go on the top line. Anyone fearing that the French and the Italians might have been forming some sort of unholy musical alliance against the Spanish will be heartened to hear that while the Italians and the Spanish used numbers to indicate which frets were to be fingered, the French used a visually appealing but slightly confusing system of letters: the letter A indicated that the string was to be played open (unfingered), while the letter B indicated that the note at the first fret was to be fingered, and so on. The rhythm to be played was indicated above the stave but applied only to the fastest-moving parts. It was left to the discretion and good taste of the individual musician to decide just how long the other notes should be held.

The first printed music for the four-course guitar appeared in 1546. It was a collection of six pieces written by Alonso Mudarra and titled *Tres Libros*. Three years later four short dances, arranged for guitar, were included in a collection of pieces for the lute written by Melchiore de Barberis. To include pieces for the guitar in collections of other works for fretted string instruments was a fairly common practice at the time, as seen in the inclusion of nine compositions for guitar in a collection of pieces for the vihuela by Miguel de Fuenllana, called *Orphénca Lyra* and published in 1554. The fact that these pieces were included almost as an afterthought is indicative of the degree of interest in the guitar in the countries where these works were produced (Spain and Italy). Over in France, however, it was an entirely different story.

The guitar exceeded the lute in popularity in sixteenth-century France and so guitar music was deemed worthy of publication in its own right. Between 1551 and 1555, nine books of tablature for the instrument were published in Paris alone. These included four books by Adrian Le Roy.

On the whole, the guitar music published at this time did not make too many demands on the player – after all, the instrument really had only four strings. The lack of strings limited the amount of harmonic variation that was available to the composer and, as a result of this, chords tended to be implied by the music rather than stated. Only rarely did guitar music published during this period approach that composed for the lute or the vihuela. Generally it seems that the guitar was a popular instrument because it was perceived as being easy to play and could be mastered in a short space of time. This meant that there was an enormous demand among players for the kind of dull, simplistic material that so often clogs up compilations of guitar music of this era.

At an even simpler level were those books of guitar music that were created for the strummers. These provided easy-to-play chord sequences for those whom talent had neglected. This style of playing was named *rasguedo* (meaning chordal strumming) while the more demanding finger-picking style was called *punteado*. Surprisingly, at this time the *rasguedo* style tended to be favoured by players of the five-course guitar, while the *punteado* style was the preserve of the four-course guitarist.

THE CLASSICAL GUITAR

The eighteenth century reached its end with America electing its first president, Britain in the throes of the world's first industrial revolution and Napoleon Bonaparte seizing power in France. But of far greater importance was the fact that, while all this was going on, the five-course guitar had evolved into the six-string guitar.

THE SIX-STRING GUITAR

History is remarkably vague on the details at this point – it's almost as if it happened while no one was looking – so investigations into the origins of the modern classical guitar are temporarily reduced to the level of hearsay, conjecture and supposition. We know that the six-string guitar appeared first in France or Italy, although the Germans may have some claim to having added the sixth string in the bass – our modern E string. There had been guitars built before with six courses, and others built with five single strings, but none of these was tuned like the modern instrument and so cannot truly be considered the first "real" six-string classical guitar.

Over the next 30 or 40 years, the guitar ceased to have much in common with the lute, and instead began to take on the form that we now recognize as the modern guitar. The changes that this transition required – to the way the instrument was constructed – were many and varied. Starting at the head, the peg box as we know it was dispensed with, and usually replaced by an ornately carved design which served the double purpose of making the guitar even more beautiful, and allowing the maker to leave his distinctive mark upon the instrument. This also led to a degree of restraint in other areas of decoration, and the guitar gradually became less garish until the simple beauty of the wood, and the art of the maker, were allowed to shine through.

THE GUITAR CAN EVOKE A VARIETY OF SUBTLE MOODS.

The wooden pegs that had been used to tune the instrument were replaced with machine heads, a simple metal screw-type worm and gear mechanism that is still in use to this day. A separate fingerboard was added and though this initially lay flush with the soundboard, it was later raised so as to allow the inclusion of extra frets. The fretboard itself was no longer fitted with adjustable gut frets. Guitars from the very early eighteenth century were fitted with frets made of hard woods such as ebony – or even hard bits of elephant, such as ivory. These were both later replaced with much more hard-wearing frets made of metal. The relationship between the neck and the body of the guitar changed, allowing the neck to be fixed to the body at the twelfth fret. The soundboard, on the surface at least, changed little, but the rose design over the sound hole was swept away and the hole left open. It became standard for guitars to be built with flat backs, taking the instrument even further away from the lute both in terms of its design and the way in which it was constructed. The raised fretboard meant that the strings had to be raised also. To this end, the bridge was made higher and a proper bridge saddle was introduced.

Striking as these changes were, they were as nothing compared to the mysteries unfolding under the surface of the instrument,

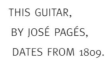

THIS GUITAR,
BY JOSÉ PAGÉS,
DATES FROM 1809.

for it was at this stage that the guitar makers began their truly ground-breaking work.

Fan struts, literally struts fixed under the soundboard and arranged in a fan-like pattern, were first used on six-course guitars built by José Pagés and Josef Benedid in the late eighteenth century. These builders, based in Cádiz, introduced fan struts to the lower half of the soundboard (below the sound hole), and added cross struts that ran perpendicular to the neck on either side of the sound hole. This greatly improved the quality of the sound and was taken up by other makers during this period, the most notable of whom were René François Lacôte, who was based in Paris, and Louis Panormo, who was based in London.

The new guitar design led to changes in the way the instrument was played. Guitar tutor books from this time reveal that the practice of resting the little finger of the right hand on the soundboard (a remnant of the lute players' technique that had been handed down to guitarists) was largely abandoned. It was replaced with the "floating arm" technique, which allowed the guitarist's right arm to pivot from the elbow, but the strings were still plucked using only the thumb, index and middle finger of the right hand. It was not until later – in the nineteenth century – that the practice of using the ring finger along with the other fingers was introduced.

(It was not until the 1980s that plucking the strings with the little finger of the right hand became a common sight – although not among classical guitar players, whose technique was by then frozen in time and dictated by the music colleges.)

The strings were usually struck using the *tirando* technique, whereby the fingers of the right hand return to a raised position above the strings after they have been plucked. The *apoyando* stroke, bringing the fingers to rest on the string next to the one just plucked (rather as a modern electric bass player might strike a string) was known but seldom applied at this time. Some players, such as Dionysio Aguado, plucked at the strings with their fingernails, whereas others, including the great Fernando Sor, used the tips of their fingers.

Even the great players of this period were known to use the thumb of the left hand to fret notes on the bottom E string. This was made possible by the fact that the neck of the classical guitar was getting thinner all the time. Nowadays, fingering classical guitar music with the thumb of the left hand is an offence punishable by two weeks in banjo class, but at this time playing techniques had yet to be formalized.

There were also many variations in the positions guitarists adopted while playing their instruments. Some played standing up, wearing the guitar on a strap around their necks. Dionysio Aguado even had a special stand made called a triodion, on which he would balance his instrument.

A DAZZLING ARRAY OF INSTRUMENTS IN A MASTER CRAFTSMAN'S WORKSHOP.

THE GOLDEN AGE

This was the first golden age of the guitar. Here was an exciting new instrument that had the potential for enormous popular appeal. It enabled one to play music that could challenge the world's greatest virtuosi and yet at the same time the most cloth-eared sections of society could experience the joy and pride of being able to provide a simple, strummed accompaniment to a popular song.

As the reputations of the great players of this period spread, so too did the popularity of the instrument. For several years, Fernando Sor pursued a career as a touring soloist, thrilling audiences with the brilliance of his playing and no doubt inspiring many others to take up the instrument. Among those who took their inspiration from Sor was the great violinist Niccolo Paganini, who briefly abandoned the violin in favour of the guitar before finally returning to his original choice.

Even England was not immune to the charms of this new instrument. After Sor's visit in 1815, the popularity of the instrument rose enormously, as was evident from the outpouring of tutor books that accompanied his departure from England. As is often the case when a new instrument appears, the quality and scope of the tutor books varied wildly. Players willing to spend a little more time learning the guitar found that they could take on the simple, cliché-ridden pieces that were all but spewing forth from the hands and minds of journeymen composers — the equivalent of today's "hack" songwriters. Not that guitar composition was restricted to men alone. In England the leading

FERNANDO SOR

guitar composer and performer by the end of the century was one Catharina Josepha Pelzer, who had a reputation for churning out the kind of music that allowed the guitar to be used in what *Grove's Dictionary Of Music* calls "a facile way."

It was left to the great guitarists of the day to produce the serious tutor books. Fernando Sor's book of studies still sends shivers down the spine of any player who has been compelled to learn it from cover to cover. Contained within its pages are a series of pieces, each progressively more difficult than the last, and each devoted to an aspect of the techniques required to play like one of the greats. Nor was Sor alone in producing such a work. Today it is still possible to walk into a quality music shop and leave with a copy of Matteo Carcassi's tutor book, which contains some excellent technique-building exercises as well as any number of pieces with which one can demonstrate the newly acquired techniques.

Likewise, it was left to the great players to produce the truly challenging music for the guitar. Guitar greats Fernando Sor and Mauro Giuliani were responsible for establishing much of the guitar repertoire in the nineteenth century, and their music is still played today. Although their works do not stand up well in comparison with the works of the truly great composers, of this or any other period, they have much to recommend them — and Beethoven, a contemporary of both Sor and Giuliani, though never much of a guitarist, was reputed to have stolen the theme for the *Moonlight Sonata* from Sor.

Ultimately, however, composition for the guitar in this period often suffered because of the limitations imposed upon it by the instrument itself, and the poor imaginations of the composers. One has to wait until the twentieth century, and the work of the great Latin-American composers such as Villa-Lobos, for the guitar's true potential to be realized — and this was helped in no small part by improvements in the design and construction of the classical guitar that occurred in Spain in the latter half of the nineteenth century.

HEITOR VILLA-LOBOS, ONE OF THE GIANTS OF TWENTIETH-CENTURY GUITAR.

THE FATHER OF MODERN GUITARS

The name of Antonio de Torres Jurado is well known to any serious student of the classical guitar. More than any other maker before or since, he modernized the instrument, vastly improving its tone and at the same time increasing the sheer amount of sound that could be produced on it. This enabled guitarists to be heard as part of larger ensembles and also to play in larger concert halls. The richness of tone inspired ever more composers to write for the instrument and thus helped to increase its repertoire.

Torres was responsible for increasing the overall size of the guitar, and determined that the scale length – the distance from the nut, at the top of the neck, to the bridge, near the back of the soundboard – should be 65 cm (25.6 in). He took the fan-struts idea of Pagés and Benedid and improved on it, placing seven struts, laid out in the shape of a fan, behind the sound hole – to distribute the vibrations from the bridge better – and a further two struts at a tangent to the fan. Torres also introduced a bridge saddle to which the strings were tied after passing over the bridge, an arrangement that is still the norm for guitars built today.

As the lute makers of old had discovered, by using struts it was possible to "break up" the surface area of the soundboard. This had the double benefit of introducing extra rigidity to the thinnest part of the guitar (allowing the delicate soundboard to be made even thinner) while also raising the resonant frequency of the instrument. This meant that far more of the supporting harmonics of the fundamental note were produced when the strings were plucked, producing a noticeably richer tone on the instrument. The increase in size of the guitar also made it a lot louder. Put simply, the extra space inside the body increased the amount of air being shifted as the soundboard vibrated, causing a louder sound to be emitted.

Antonio de Torres was the father of the modern classical guitar. Many very fine instruments have been built since his death, but they all owe a debt to Torres' pioneering work. He was succeeded in Spain by a generation or two of very fine guitar makers, men such as Manuel and José Ramirez. The Ramirez company survives to this day, and continues to make some of the most sought-after instruments in the world.

MAKING THE TWENTIETH-CENTURY GUITAR

The renewed interest in the classical guitar in the twentieth century saw the arrival of new, non-Spanish guitar makers on the scene. The quality of their work is such that it can now be said with some degree of certainty that the best classical guitars are no longer made in Spain. Chief among these new makers are Hermann Hauser in Germany, Robert Bouchet in France, David Rubio and Paul Fisher in England and father-and-son partnership John and William Gilbert in America.

These makers are able to take advantage of a range of woods that would have been undreamed of in Torres' day. A typical modern quality classical guitar maker might choose to use Brazilian or Indian rosewood for the back and sides of the instrument and Brazilian rosewood for the neck. The sides and the soundboard would be anchored to a piece of South American mahogany or cedar wood and the fingerboard would be made of ebony from Ceylon. The head might well be decorated with a veneer of South American snakewood and the all-important soundboard made from Alpine spruce, which is specially grown at high altitude.

THE MODERN CLASSICAL
GUITAR STILL RESEMBLES
THOSE PRODUCED BY TORRES.

FLAMENCO MASTER PACO PENA COMBINES TECHNICAL SKILL WITH PASSION.

Once all of this wood has been seasoned – a process which involves storing it under controlled conditions while it dries out and ceases to move around – the maker can begin construction of the instrument, a process which usually takes well over one hundred hours of intensive, hands-on work. The first stage in this process involves creating the characteristic shape of the neck. Slots are cut into the sides of the base of the neck, at the point where the twelfth fret will be once the fretboard has been added. The sides of the instrument, which are around 2 mm (0.08 in) thick, will have been given their waisted shape by steam-bending them and clamping them to a mould. Once this process has been completed, one end of each side will be placed in one of the slots on the neck and the other end fixed to a solid block of a hard wood such as mahogany or cedar. This piece of wood, called the end block, provides a vital anchor point for the various components that go to make up the body of the guitar. The back of the instrument is then attached. It usually consists of two pieces of matched hardwood,

which are cut into shape and joined down the middle. At one end the pieces connect to the end block and at the other they are fixed to what is known as the "toe" of the neck. A thin strip of wood called a cleat is then fixed along the join on the inside of the instrument. This runs for the entire length of the back of the body and serves to seal the join between the two pieces of wood that make up the back of the instrument. The back is then fixed to the sides by means of a strip of wood which has been "kerfed" (slit or scored) to make it more pliable and therefore easy to fit inside the contours of the instrument.

The soundboard, with its various struts already attached, is then fitted to the rest of the body of the guitar, once again being joined at the neck and to the end block, as well as to the sides of the instrument. Then the fingerboard is fitted to the neck and body, the bridge is glued on to the soundboard and the ornate "purfling" around the perimeter of the body is fixed on. (The rosette around the sound hole is normally attached when the soundboard is being

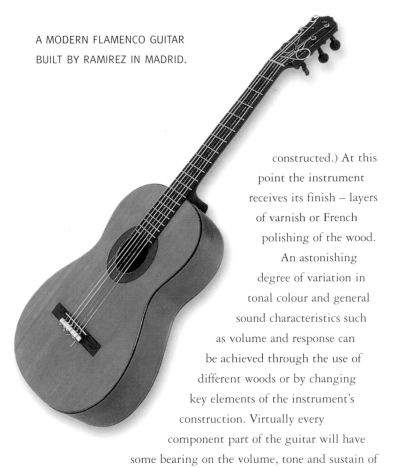

A MODERN FLAMENCO GUITAR
BUILT BY RAMIREZ IN MADRID.

constructed.) At this point the instrument receives its finish – layers of varnish or French polishing of the wood. An astonishing degree of variation in tonal colour and general sound characteristics such as volume and response can be achieved through the use of different woods or by changing key elements of the instrument's construction. Virtually every component part of the guitar will have some bearing on the volume, tone and sustain of the finished instrument. The flamenco guitar, for instance, bears a superficial resemblance to the classical guitar, but is made using different woods, has a thinner soundboard, a shallower body and is generally of a much lighter construction. This is for creating the particular tonal characteristics that one associates with the flamenco guitar – warmer tone, greater attack and a stronger but shorter sustain. The guitar maker's art is in achieving a balance between these properties in order to produce a fine instrument. Learning how to combine and control all of these elements constitutes a life's work, and so even those guitarists who can afford a instrument made by an established and respected guitar maker may have to wait quite some time before getting their hands on one.

In terms of outward appearance, the guitar has changed little in the last hundred years. However, beneath the surface of the soundboard all kinds of changes have been taking place. Torres's struts are still there, but they now run in parallel along the grain of the soundboard. By strengthening the internal bracing, it has been possible to cut down the amount of vibration occurring within the body of the instrument, allowing more of the guitar's sound to be heard as it is projected more efficiently than ever before.

MODERN PLAYING TECHNIQUES

The changes in the way the guitar has been constructed, and therefore the way it sounds and responds, has led to a number of changes in the way the instrument is played. These can roughly be dated as beginning around the time when Torres launched his guitars at the world, although the actual changes in technique can be credited, in the first instance, to Francisco Tárrega, one of the world's leading guitarists toward the end of the nineteenth century. Tárrega, by means of the floating-arm technique mentioned earlier, established the *apoyando* stroke. This had the double benefit to the player of being louder than the conventional *tirando* stroke (which was used almost exclusively at this time) and also of helping to bring out more of the richer qualities of these new instruments. The Torres guitar was bigger than had been the norm up to this point and as such fitted more comfortably across the left thigh – before, guitarists would just as often sit with the instrument placed over the right thigh. It became standard practice to sit with the classical guitar over the left thigh and remains so.

Although Tárrega did not play the guitar using the finger nails of his right hand, several of his students did and so this technique was passed down to succeeding generations of guitarists. At this time, however, the right hand position had not been formalized and it was not until the twentieth century that Andrés Segovia established the practice of playing with a relaxed right hand and striking the strings with the left-hand side of the fingernails. Interestingly, a very small number of concert players favor the right-hand side of the finger nail and so adapt their techniques accordingly.

ANDRÉS SEGOVIA – A TRULY GREAT CLASSICAL GUITAR PLAYER.

THE AMERICAN TRADITION

The evolution of the modern classical guitar tradition can be traced back to European folk and other "low-brow" musical forms, all of which created a view among the upper classes that the guitar was a "common" instrument not worthy of serious attention. Although it now has broad parity with other traditional classical instruments, its greatest asset has been its enduring significance as an unashamedly populist instrument – indeed, the guitar was at the very heart of much of the non-classical music of the twentieth century, from folk, country, and jazz to rock and pop.

This line of popular heritage stems mainly from developments by European immigrants in the United States. For while a classical revolution was taking place in Spain during the nineteenth century, history was also being forged in America, where two distinct styles were being developed by two of the most significant figures in guitar history: C F Martin, maker of guitars with traditional, flat soundboards, and Orville Gibson, who developed archtop guitars with curved fronts in the tradition of violin making.

THE MARTIN FLAT-TOP TRADITION

Hailing from a long line of musical instrument makers, Christian Frederick Martin was born in 1796 in Germany. At the age of 15 he left home for Vienna where he became an apprentice to the noted luthier Johann Stauffer. By all accounts Martin was an eager, motivated worker who within a few years had become a master craftsman and factory foreman. In about 1820, after marrying, he returned to his home town to open up his own guitar-manufacturing business. However, shortly after his return, Martin quickly became embroiled in a bitter dispute between rival guilds. The Martin family had been long-standing members of the cabinet makers' guild, whose craftsmen had traditionally built lutes and guitars. In an effort to restrict

CHRISTIAN FREDERICK MARTIN –
FATHER OF THE AMERICAN GUITAR.

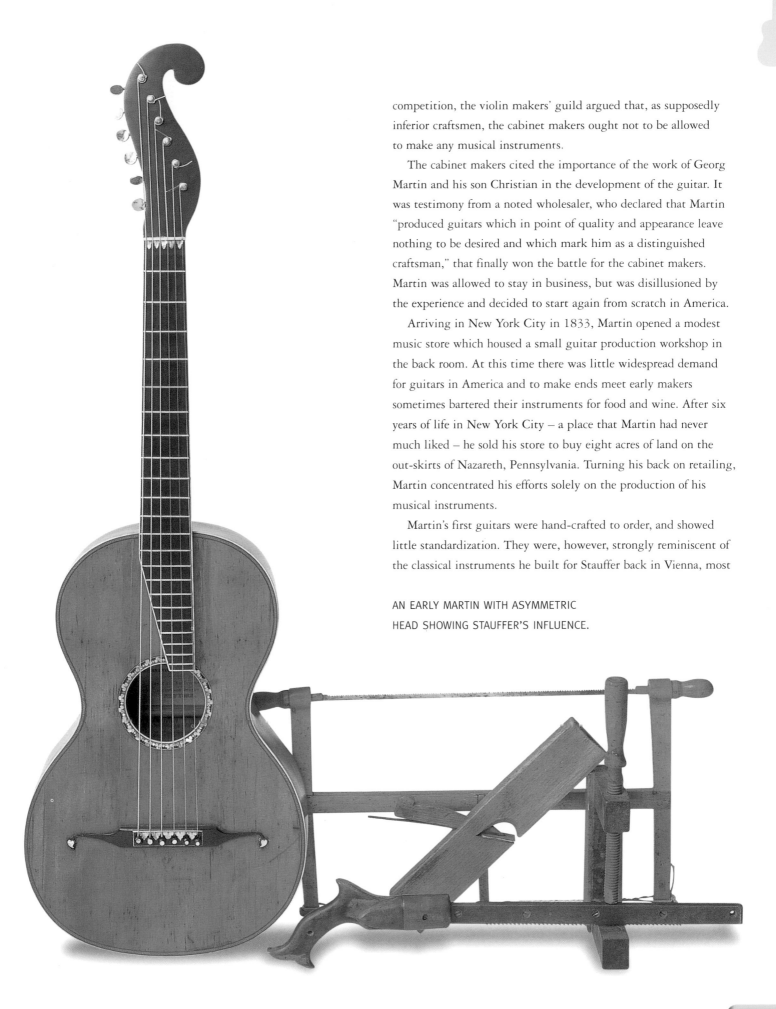

competition, the violin makers' guild argued that, as supposedly inferior craftsmen, the cabinet makers ought not to be allowed to make any musical instruments.

The cabinet makers cited the importance of the work of Georg Martin and his son Christian in the development of the guitar. It was testimony from a noted wholesaler, who declared that Martin "produced guitars which in point of quality and appearance leave nothing to be desired and which mark him as a distinguished craftsman," that finally won the battle for the cabinet makers. Martin was allowed to stay in business, but was disillusioned by the experience and decided to start again from scratch in America.

Arriving in New York City in 1833, Martin opened a modest music store which housed a small guitar production workshop in the back room. At this time there was little widespread demand for guitars in America and to make ends meet early makers sometimes bartered their instruments for food and wine. After six years of life in New York City – a place that Martin had never much liked – he sold his store to buy eight acres of land on the out-skirts of Nazareth, Pennsylvania. Turning his back on retailing, Martin concentrated his efforts solely on the production of his musical instruments.

Martin's first guitars were hand-crafted to order, and showed little standardization. They were, however, strongly reminiscent of the classical instruments he built for Stauffer back in Vienna, most

AN EARLY MARTIN WITH ASYMMETRIC
HEAD SHOWING STAUFFER'S INFLUENCE.

EARLY MARTIN
GUITARS WERE HAND-
CRAFTED TO ORDER
SUCH AS THIS ONE
FROM C.1837.

notably in the headstock design which positioned all the tuning pegs on one side. Although this approach was abandoned after C F Martin's death in 1873, the idea influenced later solid-body designers such as Paul Bigsby and Leo Fender. An unusual feature of the early Martin guitars was the adjustable neck, the tilt of which could be altered by means of a clock key fitted into the heel – the joint between the neck and the body. During the 1890s, when steel strings began gradually replacing those made from gut, this system was dropped because steel strings exerted greater stress on the neck fixture.

During the 1850s C F Martin made one of his most important design innovations – the development of the cross-bracing system fitted to the underside of the soundboard. This was a pattern of struts which gave the instruments a distinctive treble tone. By the turn of the turn of the century the majority of steel-string guitar makers used variations on this system.

THE NEXT GENERATION

After the death of C F Martin in 1873, the company continued successfully under the guidance of successive generations of the family. It was under the presidency of Martin's grandson, Frank Henry, that some of the company's most innovative products were developed, perhaps the most significant being the Dreadnought guitar style.

In 1916, Frank Henry Martin developed a large-bodied instrument with a man named Harry Hunt, who worked for the Ditson music store in New York. Named after the British First World War battleship, the Ditson Dreadnought was built with a wide waist and narrow sloped shoulders. The new instrument was capable of producing a vastly greater volume and bass response, making it an ideal accompaniment for vocalists. In spite of Martin's role in its development, the first Dreadnoughts were available exclusively from the Ditson store. In 1928 Ditsons went out of business and Martin designers began to experiment with their own Dreadnought models. Strengthening the neck and replacing the traditional classical fan-bracing system with Martin's own "X-brace," they built the prototype D-1 and D-2 models. The first genuine Martin Dreadnoughts – the classic D-18 and D-28 styles – went into general production in 1935.

Perhaps the most famous Dreadnought model is the legendary Martin D-45, the first of which was made as a one-off for "singing cowboy" Gene Autry in 1933. Although production of the D-45 was discontinued in 1942, this instrument carved out a reputation among folk and country artists alike, and in 1968, after a

renaissance of the acoustic guitar, production of the D-45 resumed. Since this important innovation virtually every significant guitar manufacturer has produced its own alternative to the Dreadnought, such as the Gibson "Jumbo" models of the late 1930s.

F H Martin made a further influential innovation in 1929 with the introduction of the Orchestral Model. This line of instruments (prefixed with OM) featured a neck that joined the body at the fourteenth fret, rather than the traditional twelfth fret, which, by increasing the guitar's range, was intended to make it a more versatile instrument. This quickly became a standard design feature of American-built guitars.

From the 1930s onwards, Martin enjoyed continued prosperity establishing a world-wide reputation for its flat-top acoustic instruments. Part of the company's success was due to limiting production to the highest quality instruments, creating an aura of exclusivity which remains to this day. Indeed, by the early 1960s demand for Martin guitars was so great that there was a waiting list of three years for new models. This inevitably opened up the market to rival companies such as Guild and Epiphone who were able to thrive during the 1960s steel-string boom period.

SINGING COWBOY GENE AUTRY PLAYED A MAJOR ROLE IN POPULARIZING THE GUITAR.

THE MARTIN D-45 WITH ITS "DREADNOUGHT" BODY.

OTHER FLAT-TOP GUITAR MAKERS

Martin designs defined the US flat-top steel-string tradition, and although there were other successful manufacturers producing flat-top instruments before the Second World War, such as Washburn, they were largely overshadowed by Martin. However, one significant design innovation came about in Europe: the Selmer Maccaferri. The Paris-based Selmer company had a long history of instrument-making, and in 1931 they joined forces with Italian designer Mario Maccaferri. The resulting instrument was unique in that it featured an internal sound chamber suspended from four fixed points inside the top of the large-bodied instrument. The chamber enabled the guitar to produce greater volume and a warmer tone.

Selmer Maccaferris are instantly recognizable from the Art Nouveau styling of the body and the unique "D"-shaped sound hole. Although only around 280 of the instruments were made at the time, they have become well known as a result of their use by the guitarists in the Quintet du Hot Club de France, whose soloist was the legendary Django Reinhardt. A number of custom guitar makers still produce replicas of this classic instrument.

Since the war, although every major guitar manufacturer has produced flat-top steel-string guitars, the most significant rival to Martin has been Guild. Formed in 1952 by former Epiphone craftsmen, Guild guitars have been widely played in the fields of folk, pop and rock music.

THE SELMER MACCAFERRI,
AS IMMORTALIZED BY
DJANGO REINHARDT.

AMERICAN FOLK AND COUNTRY TRADITIONS

From the late nineteenth century onwards the guitar was at the heart of most new American folk music forms. The oral storytelling folk traditions had been brought over to the continent by European settlers during the previous century and were often Celtic in origin. By the end of the nineteenth century, especially in the Southern states, some of these forms had blended and evolved to create a unique new voice. During the 1920s, the first record companies began to take an interest in this new "country" music, bringing novel sounds for the first time to the ears of the more affluent and sophisticated city dwellers.

The first country guitar player to reach a large audience was Jimmie Rodgers. As a youth, he had been taught to play the guitar by black railroad workers. Although he died young in 1933, in his short lifetime he left a legacy that would be carried on by a new generation of popular guitarists. Also important in both the development of country music and the popularity of the guitar were the Carter Family, who introduced many traditional gospel-country songs that are now known as standards. At this time, country music was often tagged as "hillbilly" after the derogatory term applied by city dwellers to rural Southern whites.

The popularity of the guitar spread widely during the 1930s as the "singing cowboy" stars like Gene Autry and the other "singing cowboy" Roy Rogers glamorized the instrument among young movie-goers. This period also saw the birth of a number of sub-genres, such as western swing, which combined the rhythms of jazz dance music with the hillbilly sound. At the same time in the South-West, the honky-tonk tradition evolved, making stars out of fine singer-songwriters such as Hank Williams. In other parts of the US, unique localized traditions integrated the new country sounds into their own cultural heritage: bluegrass picking styles emerged from the Appalachian mountain regions; Cajun music came about from the self-contained communities of the French-speaking settlers in Louisiana.

During the 1950s country music became more mainstream with the widespread availability of television and the phonograph. During this decade Nashville, Tennessee, became the indisputable home of country music, broadcasting the Grand Ole Opry television shows. The Opry tradition had slowly expanded from regional radio in 1926 to become a nationwide television spectacular, introducing the American public to singing stars like Jim Reeves as well as pioneering pickers such as Merle Travis and Chet Atkins, who was central to the next phase of development in country music – the Nashville Sound.

Since the 1960s, country and western music, as it is widely known, has spread its popularity throughout the world, recent stars like Garth Brooks and Dwight Yoakam being among the most successful performers in any musical genre.

Although the showbiz excesses of the Grand Ole Opry are one leg of a heritage that began with Jimmie Rodgers and the Carter Family, a stark alternative was provided by Woody Guthrie who introduced politics and social commentary, and gave birth to a new American folk tradition. A left-wing activist, between 1936 and 1954 he is reputed to have written over 1,000 songs. When the protest movement erupted in the early 1960s, prime movers like Pete Seeger, Bob Dylan and Phil Ochs found fame with music rooted in the Guthrie tradition. Dylan, in particular, went on to exert a major influence on much of the popular music of the 1960s and 1970s.

GIBSON AND THE ARCHTOP TRADITION

Although it was Christian Frederick Martin and his ancestors who established the US as the source of most important innovations to the non-classical guitar, it was Orville Gibson who founded the company that would not only provide an alternative tradition to the flat-top acoustic guitar, but would also play a crucial role in the transition to the electric era.

Born in 1856, the son of a British immigrant, Orville Gibson was not only a skilled woodcarver but an accomplished mandolin player. During the 1880s he began to produce a new range of intricately carved mandolins using methods of construction more usually applied to violins. The principal difference between Gibson's mandolins and others was the curved tops with the bridge and saddles positioned across the highest point of the curve. During the decade that followed, Gibson applied the same ideas to his guitars, which became known as "archtops." In 1902, backed by a group of businessmen in Kalamazoo, Michigan, the Gibson Mandolin-Guitar Manufacturing Company was founded.

The first widespread success was the Style O guitar, launched in 1908. Its body shape was similar to that of Gibson's famed mandolins, and the bass side of the upper bout was carved into an ornate scroll. This model is noteworthy in the history of the American guitar because it features a perpendicular cutaway near the fifteenth fret – probably the first production instrument to feature such a device. The greater access this provided to the upper register made the Style O a great success.

Gibson continued to innovate during this period, one of his more fascinating experiments being the harp-guitar – a Style O-type guitar with 12 additional bass strings, each tuned to a different note. Although this particular idea failed to take off, by the time of Orville Gibson's death in 1918, the company that bore his name enjoyed a reputation second only to Martin.

EARLY JAZZ GUITAR

While the flat-top instruments dominated the country and folk fields, it was the archtop models that dominated the jazz world during the pre-electric era. With the development of louder guitars like the Gibson L-5, the banjo found itself with a greatly reduced role. Nonetheless, because it was unable to compete with the volume of brass and reed instruments – such as the trumpet, clarinet or saxophone – the guitar was still heavily restricted to vamping chordal rhythms. It was in chamber settings that the potential for the guitar as a solo instrument gradually became evident. The player largely credited with this development was New Yorker Eddie Lang, whose work with violinist Joe Venuti exhibits the earliest examples of a sophisticated single-note style.

Surprisingly, perhaps, the Gibson company flourished in the years following the death of the founding father, introducing a number of developments that would have a major impact on the future of the guitar. Many of these pioneering progressions were the work of Lloyd Loar, who joined the Gibson company in 1920. In his early days with the company Loar was one of the first instrument designers to experiment with magnetic pick-ups – but this development would not come to fruition for another decade. In 1924 he was crucial in the design of a succession of legendary production archtop guitars. The first of these models was the highly successful Gibson L-5 with its two violin-style "f-holes" – an instrument that all but replaced the very popular banjo's role in dance bands.

The Gibson archtop tradition continued in 1934 with the birth of the Super 400, Gibson's top of the range archtop instrument. It was during the 1930s, spurred on by successful developments at Rickenbacker, that Gibson began to give serious attention to the electrification of its guitars – a process that would flow quite naturally from their success as the creators of the archtop guitar.

OTHER ARCHTOP MAKERS

The success of the Gibson L-5 was so significant that many other guitar makers followed suit. Gibson's most important rival during the 1930s was probably Epiphone. Founded in New York in 1928 by Epominondas Stathopoulo, the son of a Greek immigrant, Epiphone first built banjos but then established a solid reputation with the Emperor and Deluxe models, both of which found widespread use among jazz musicians. When Stathopoulo died in 1942, much of the company's early promise disappeared. Many of their finest craftsmen left and in 1957 the company was sold to Gibson. Since then the Epiphone brand has become something of a lower-cost diffusion range for Gibson guitars.

Among the most highly rated of all the archtop makers was John D'Angelico who established a small workshop in New York City during the 1930s. Finely hand-crafted instruments, his two models – the Excel and the New Yorker – could be described as Art Deco in styling, with the two-bar trapeze tailpiece, pickguard and machine heads all exhibiting an intricate "stepped" design. Not only are they among the most beautiful guitars ever made, but the warmth and clarity of their tone also attracted players of the calibre of Chet Atkins. Following D'Angelico's death in 1964, his assistant Jimmy D'Aquisto continued the tradition with his own range of New Yorkers.

BIGGEST-SELLING COUNTRY ARTIST OF THE 1990S, GARTH BROOKS.

THE SOLID-BODY ERA

It's pretty well impossible to imagine what much of the popular music produced over the past fifty years would sound like had the electric guitar never been developed. But although a common image of the electric guitar only really drifted into the public consciousness with the first generation of rock and roll stars of the 1950s, the electrification process can be traced back to at least thirty years earlier.

EDDIE LANG IS CONSIDERED BY MANY TO BE THE FATHER OF JAZZ GUITAR.

By the end of the 1920s, the steel-string guitar – especially the louder models like the revolutionary Gibson L-5 – had become a well-established feature in a majority of jazz and dance bands. It was from this point that a new tradition of exceptionally gifted jazz guitarists emerged. Eddie Lang in the US was the first player to demonstrate the potential of the guitar as a solo instrument outside of the classical sphere. Indeed, in the eyes of many critics he was largely responsible for inventing the single-note solo in jazz. A few years later, on the other side of the Atlantic, Django Reinhardt also stunned his audiences with single note runs of staggering complexity.

As the popularity of this new generation of players grew, so too did the demand for louder instruments. Most of the early experiments revolved around increasing the size of the body or new design innovations, like the National guitars, which used an aluminium resonating panel. In spite of these efforts, however, soloing could only cut through in small-group situations. A new solution was needed.

THE FIRST ELECTRIC INSTRUMENTS

Although it's generally accepted that Gibson's Lloyd Loar had experimented with pick-up design in the early 1920s, the first significant breakthrough came in 1931 when Paul Barth and George Beauchamp joined forces with Swiss-born Adolph Rickenbacker to form their own Ro-Par-In

THE GROUND-BREAKING
RICKENBACKER FRYING PAN.

Although the Frying Pan had hardly set the music world alight, within a year Rickenbacker and his two colleagues had introduced the first genuine electric guitar. Known simply as the "Electro-Spanish," this instrument was a basic hollow-bodied arch-top design fitted with the same horseshoe magnet pick-up that had been used on the Frying Pan models. As with many great innovations, the Electro-Spanish was not a huge commercial success and was only produced in limited numbers between 1932 and 1935. Nevertheless, it holds a significant place in the history of the electric guitar and was a major influence on many of the models that followed, especially the first generation of electric instruments produced by Gibson.

company (which would later became the Electro String Company, home to the famous Rickenbacker brand name). Beauchamp, himself a well known guitarist, had already played an important role in the design of the National resonator guitar and also worked with Barth in an attempt to produce an electrical amplification system. Their experiments came to fruition in 1931 with a pair of lap-steel "Hawaiian" guitars – the A22 and A25 models. Commonly known as "Frying Pans" because of their shape, these instruments were powered by a pair of large horseshoe magnets with six individual pole pieces that passed under each of the six strings. Although these models were not technically guitars in the conventional sense, they were nonetheless the first commercially produced electric instruments.

The Frying Pan first went into production under the Ro-Pat-In brand name. The body and neck of the prototype models were made from a single piece of maple, but by the time they were made available to the public cast aluminium was used instead. This was not an entirely successful development as the use of aluminium apparently resulted in problems keeping the instrument in tune. Later in the decade Rickenbacker made lap-steel guitars from strong bakelite plastic which proved to be more successful. Variations on the Frying Pan design remained in the Rickenbacker catalogue until well into the 1950s.

PIONEERING THE ELECTRIC GUITAR

It may seem strange to imagine that a lap-steel instrument was used to pave the way for the electrification of the guitar, but during this period the conventional "Spanish" guitar was only just beginning to establish itself as a popular musical instrument.

ONE OF RICKENBACKER'S
FIRST PRODUCTION
ELECTRIC INSTRUMENTS.

PRODUCTION ELECTRIC GUITARS

After Rickenbacker's early triumph, the period leading up to the mid-1930s saw most of the brand-name guitar manufacturers trying out their own experiments fitting magnetic pick-ups to acoustic guitars. None of these instruments sold in any great quantities until Gibson launched its first electric guitar in 1935.

Marketed in their trade catalogue as "another miracle from Gibson," the ES-150 was the first electric guitar to go into large-scale production. A revamped version of the popular budget L-50 archtop, the ES-150 hit the mark when it captured the imagination of jazz guitarist Charlie Christian. More than any other musician, it was Christian who was responsible for establishing the electric guitar as a serious musical proposition.

The Gibson ES-150 had a hollow mahogany body with a spruce top and featured traditional Gibson-style "f-holes," a long pickguard and bakelite volume and

THE GIBSON ES-175 FROM THE LATE 1940S – STILL POPULAR IN JAZZ CIRCLES.

AS PIONEERED BY JAZZ GIANT CHARLIE CHRISTIAN, THE GIBSON ES-150 IS WIDELY VIEWED AS THE FIRST CREDIBLE ELECTRIC GUITAR.

tone controls. The narrow "bar" pick-up was positioned at the foot of the fingerboard which created a smooth, mellow tone that – partly through the recordings of Charlie Christian – established the archetypal jazz guitar sound which has endured ever since. In 1940 the bar pick-up was replaced by a larger rectangular unit – the forerunner of the famed P90 pick-up. The ES-150 remained in production intermittently until 1956.

OTHER HOLLOW-BODY ELECTRICS

Throughout the 1940s Gibson continued adding models to their range, sometimes making magnetic pick-ups an optional feature for standard Gibson archtops. Notable models were the ES-300 produced from 1942 which featured a single pick-up mounted diagonally in front of the bridge. This could not only give the guitar a harder treble tone but the slanting of the unit also accentuated the ratio between treble and bass. This idea was taken up by Fender on their first solid-body electrics at the start of the following decade.

Another Gibson model to find favour with jazz musicians was the ES-175, produced from 1949, which featured a unique sharpened "Venetian" cutaway. Echoes of the ES-175 shape could be seen three years later when Gibson launched its first solid-body instrument – the Les Paul Gold Top.

After the successful emergence of the first solid-body instruments, the vogue for hollow-body guitars understandably diminished. However, Gibson and other guitar makers such as Rickenbacker and Gretsch continued to produce hollow-body electrics throughout the 1950s and 1960s. Many of the most popular models remain in production to this day.

SOLID BODIES

By the end of the 1940s the idea of the electric guitar had long passed the novelty stage, finding itself not only in large dance bands, but at the centre of burgeoning musical styles, as could be heard in the music of the early electric R&B guitarists like Muddy Waters and Elmore James, or emerging country stars such as Chet Atkins and Merle Travis.

However, a fundamental problem of the early electric guitars – which were, after all, little more than acoustic guitars with pick-ups fitted – was that if the amplifier volume was too great, sound from the loudspeaker would cause the body of the guitar and strings to vibrate on their own.

This created a howling noise referred to as "feedback". Whilst rock players in the 1960s learned to harness this sound as part of their playing styles, to the early electric players it was simply a nuisance. The logical solution to this problem, it seemed, was to increase the body mass of the instrument – without a working soundbox its capacity for vibration would be greatly reduced. During the 1940s a number of unrelated parties therefore set about designing and building a solid-body electric guitar.

No one can say without doubt who got there first, but there are a number of candidates whose research work was unquestionably important. Designer-engineers Lloyd Loar and O W Appleton are well known to have experimented with solid bodies and magnetic coils. In the early 1940s, country-jazz guitarist Les Paul created his own "Log" guitar using a Gibson neck attached to a solid piece of pine on which the pick-ups and bridge were mounted – the bouts from an Epiphone hollow-body archtop were added to the side to give it a broadly normal appearance. Although this was not a true

THE GRETSCH WHITE FALCON – ONE OF THE MOST ATTRACTIVE HOLLOW-BODY GUITARS EVER MADE.

THE FENDER FACTOR

Whilst these pioneers all played a crucial role in the development of the solid-body electric guitar, it was the foresight and ambition of one man that would establish the instrument as the most significant in the second half of the twentieth century. That man was Leo Fender.

In 1946, the Fender Electrical Instrument Company was founded, producing electrified lap-steel guitars and amplifiers. Two years later, Leo Fender – with one of his employees, George Fullerton – set about creating the production-line solid-body electric guitar that became a legend. Their design first saw the light of day in April 1950 as the Fender Esquire – later renamed the Broadcaster and finally the Telecaster.

THE BATTLE OF THE BIG THREE

At first the Fender Telecaster was not a massive commercial success and it was treated by the musical trade as a novelty item. Nonetheless, the fact that the Fender factory at Fullerton was turning Telecasters out in reasonable quantities prompted Gibson to produce a new Les Paul model in 1952.

With its dramatic opulent finish, the Les Paul Gold Top was an altogether more luxurious beast that made Fender's Telecaster look spartan by comparison. Fender was sufficiently worried by the threat it posed that he felt compelled to design his own "luxury" model, the Stratocaster, arguably the most famous electric guitar ever made.

Although their fortunes varied along the way, the Fender Telecaster, Gibson Les Paul and Fender Stratocaster guitars are now viewed as classic designs, immediately recognizable to guitarists and music-buying public alike. The two Fenders have remained in production ever since, differing little from those groundbreakers that first rolled off the production line almost 50 years ago.

The Les Paul – during its early life, at least – experienced mixed fortunes. Sales of the Gold Top had peaked by 1956 and two years later Gibson, fearing that the gaudy decoration may have been too

solid-body instrument, Paul's experiments had been aimed at preventing feedback.

A more significant claimant was engineer Paul Bigsby, who in 1948 produced a solid-body instrument designed with country guitarist Merle Travis. Bigsby and Travis had first collaborated three years earlier when the guitarist had requested some improvements to the vibrola (an alternative tremolo device) on his Gibson guitar. Bigsby came up with a completely new design for a vibrato arm – commonly (though wrongly) known as a tremolo – which was widely used over the next 20 years.

This Bigsby-Travis guitar represented an important development for a number of reasons. The shape of the body and headstock was clearly influential – some of the lines were echoed in the early Fender guitars over the next decade. Also influential were the thinline bird's-eye maple body and the fact that it featured a "straight-through" neck. Since at least a dozen of these instruments were produced, it could reasonably claim to have been the first "production" solid-body electric guitar.

ostentatious, replaced it with the more conservative-looking Les Paul Standard. The Les Paul design, in its various manifestations, has remained in production ever since. The late-1950s Standards are now such prized collector's pieces that they are more likely to be found resting in a bank vault than performing in a smoky blues club.

Although many other guitar makers did produce excellent solid-body instruments during the 1950s and early 1960s there was a clear rivalry between Gibson and Fender from the outset. Indeed, besides the three best-known models, they made most of the other noted solid-body guitars of the period – Fender's Jazzmaster, Jaguar and Musicmaster models, and Gibson's SG, radical Flying V and Explorer. This perceived dominance of the market was often played out with a sense of the old masters versus the new kids on the block, the rivalry filtering through to players themselves who would ally themselves to one camp or the other.

THE SUPPORTING PLAYERS

Although it may sometimes have seemed so, the history of the electric guitar has by no means been a two-horse race. There have been many other quality American manufacturers over the years, classic names such as Gretsch, Rickenbacker and Epiphone producing fine models into the 1960s; Kramer, Guild and Ovation in the 1970s and 1980s; and Jackson, Charvel and Paul Reed Smith into the present decade. Noted European makers such as Selmer, Vox, Hoffner and Burns have also left their own distinct marks on guitar history. However, in recent years, the greatest strides have been made by makers based in the Far East, who have successfully turned around a reputation for producing cheap imitations of classic American designs.

For Fender in particular the copy issue became a problem in the early 1980s. Until then, although many a novice had started on a cheap unplayable plywood "Stratocaster", these copies had been

THE STRATOCASTER – PERHAPS THE MOST FAMOUS GUITAR OF THEM ALL.

THE GIBSON DOUBLE-NECK REACHED
A PEAK OF POPULARITY IN THE 1970S.

too poor in quality to pose any serious threat to the genuine makers in the US. However, during the mid-1970s, some felt that a decade of corporate CBS management had gradually eroded Fender's production standards. During the following decade the world suddenly woke up to the realization that the copies being manufactured by companies like Tokai were not that far behind the originals in terms of quality, and at only a fraction of the price represented excellent value for money.

Change came about in 1985 when Fender underwent a management buy-out and began a new two-tiered approach to production. This initiative saw the quality of their standard US models increase noticeably while they simultaneously produced their own Squier range of instruments in Japan. Later, as production costs began to rise in Japan, less industrialized countries were used for manufacturing, creating a complex multi-tiered system by which the top-range instruments were produced in the US, standard quality instruments in Japan, and budget models in Korea and Mexico. This proved to be both successful and popular with Fender buyers, reinstating a consistency in quality among the top models and allowing novices or those with little money to own genuine, well-made Fender guitars – even if they weren't the real American thing.

JAPANESE ORIGINALS

From the 1970s, some of the better-known Japanese guitar makers began to build up a reputation for their own designs.

The Yamaha SG2000, built between 1973 and 1988, was perhaps the first guitar to prove to the world that instruments to equal the American masters could be made in Japan. Other highly regarded Japanese brand names have included Tokai, Westone and Aria, the last of which introduced their own tiered production system, creating cheaper instruments in developing Far Eastern countries.

Perhaps the most successful Japanese guitar manufacturer of recent times has been Ibanez, whose already strong reputation was further boosted by well-publicized associations with such guitar gods as Steve Vai and Joe Satriani. Ibanez has a vast range of guitars available and some of the top-end models outrank their US counterparts, both in quality and cost.

HYBRID GUITARS

When the electronic fuzz and wah-wah effects caught on during the mid-1960s, it was hardly surprising that some manufacturers would think that what the modern guitarist really needed was a guitar with built-in sound effects. During the 1960s and 1970s guitars found their way onto the market with hot-wired effects like distortion, delay and tremolo. The British Shergold company even produced the Modulator guitar to which a variety of plug-in effect modules could be attached as required. Perhaps the most dramatically useless idea was a guitar built by Guyatone in Japan which featured a primitive drum machine with five preset rhythms. Very handy!

More successful were the attempts to create hybrid instruments. Probably the first such example to go into production was a guitar-organ built by Vox. This British company had already achieved worldwide success not only with its AC30 amplifier, but the Continental organ, which was used by numerous pop groups in the mid-1960s. In 1966, in true Frankenstein style, Vox installed the circuitry from a Continental into the body of a standard Vox Phantom guitar. Featuring ten controls and six switches set into an already small body, the guitar-organ was heavy and looked extremely cluttered. It was also mains powered, a fact that might well have deterred some safety-conscious players. Although it may have "worked" successfully, the Vox guitar-organ, and others that followed in its wake, are now little more than footnotes in recent guitar history – but the idea was far from forgotten.

During the 1970s, the synthesizer, like the organ during the previous decade, became the hippest new noise on the block. It was clearly only a matter of time before someone thought to create a hybrid guitar synthesizer. However, unlike those producing some of the crankier designs of the previous decade, the most enthusiastic purveyor of this new type of instrument was also one of the leading Japanese technology companies – Roland.

The first models to go into production were the GS-500 and GR-500 in 1977. Both units were required for the system to work. The GR-500 was essentially a standard Roland synthesizer without a keyboard; the GS-500 was a regular solid-body guitar which was connected to the first unit. This system, like the improved models that followed, was no gimmicky toy, but a serious modern musical instrument that could reward any musician prepared to rethink his or her playing technique.

During the 1980s, from these beginnings, a number of complex and sophisticated hybrid instruments were unleashed by bold, forward-thinking or just plain mad inventors. Among the most noteworthy were the Synthaxe and Stepp "guitars," both of which could be used to control external MIDI sound modules, such as synthesizers, samplers or drum machines. These have been impressive but were too costly for most even to contemplate. Players of the calibre of Pat Metheny and Allan Holdsworth have demonstrated some of the possibilities of these systems.

One of the main reasons why all of these ideas failed to catch on in a big way was that the guitar itself was viewed as part of the technology. An important aspect of the guitarist's psyche that most of the synth-based manufacturers had failed to take into account was the relationship between the player and his or her own guitar. With this in mind, Roland's next move was the introduction of the MIDI pick-up. Attached in front of the bridge of any standard instrument, it could be connected to a conversion unit, via which it was possible to trigger external MIDI sounds with a high degree of accuracy. But in spite of this considerable technical achievement the MIDI guitar remains a minority pursuit. Indeed, it's probably true to say that without Roland's continued persistence, the idea wouldn't have even made it into the 1990s.

WHAT NEXT?

The electric guitar has dramatically altered the music of the past half-century. Indeed, most of the music it inspired would not even have been possible without the development of magnetic pick-ups, amplification and sound processing effects. But since the Fender Broadcaster first hit the production lines in 1950, how many genuine innovations have been made to the guitar itself? Admittedly, every major manufacturer has experimented with new shapes, from Ted McCarty's Flying V and Explorer designs in 1958 – both of which proved to be way ahead of their time – through the double-necked Gibsons that emerged in the early 1970s, to the dramatic Steinberger "headless" guitars moulded from graphite, that were first built in 1982. It is also true that Ovation's bowl-backed acoustic guitars created a new benchmark in the production of steel-string acoustic guitars. However, viewed from the new millennium, it does seem rather strange that the most popular and desirable guitars remain those which are based not only on designs but also the materials first used a half a century ago.

There have also been many attempts to overhaul the sound and even the role of the guitar in the past, but interesting though some of these ingenious experiments have been, they have never achieved widespread popularity, though thankfully this has never stopped some of the most creative minds from trying to break new ground.

The recent reluctance of many guitarists to abandon tradition and embrace new technology may be partly due to the limiting fashionability of using the latest gadgetry. But one clear advantage that modern guitarists do have over their keyboardplaying counterparts is the knowledge that their own instrument won't suddenly be out of date (or even have lost that much of its value) within the space of just a few months. But then again, perhaps it's something altogether simpler: maybe those early pioneers such as Leo Fender just got it right first time.

HOW THE GUITAR WORKS

All acoustic stringed instruments follow a similar principle to create and project sound. Each time the finger or plectrum touches the string the vibrations disturb the surrounding airwaves. However, this in itself cannot project sufficient volume or produce a pleasant tone. The strings are passed from the nut to the bridge, which is fixed to the top of the guitar body – the soundboard. The energy created by the vibrating string is passed from the nut or frets into the soundbox via the bridge saddle – this is the point at which each string comes into direct contact with the body. The soundbox acts as an acoustic chamber, vibrating in sympathy with the strings. This projects the sound, most of which emerges through the sound hole.

FACTORS AFFECTING SOUND

There are two main factors that govern the way a guitar sounds: the materials used and design of the instrument. These elements play a crucial role in both the volume projected and quality of tone. Nevertheless, there remains no definitive formula for the perfect guitar design. For one thing, not all players like the same kind of sound; equally, some acoustics are better suited to different styles of music.

A more complex factor is the nature of wood. No matter what practical steps a luthier takes to standardize production, no two pieces of wood – even if they have come from the same tree – have identical characteristics. Therefore no two guitars are exactly the same.

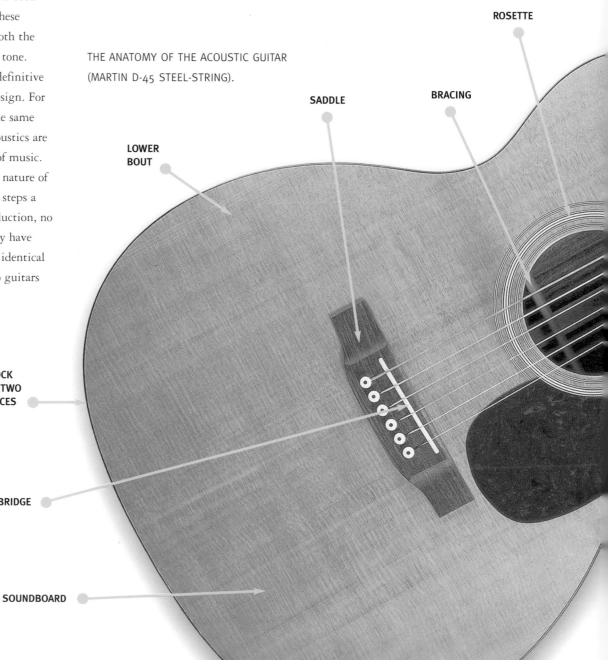

THE ANATOMY OF THE ACOUSTIC GUITAR
(MARTIN D-45 STEEL-STRING).

ROSETTE

BRACING

SADDLE

LOWER
BOUT

END BLOCK
JOINING TWO
SIDE PIECES

BRIDGE

SOUNDBOARD

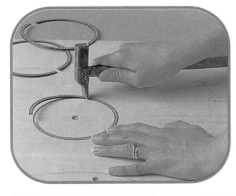

PREPARING THE DECORATIVE ROSETTE THAT FITS ROUND THE SOUND HOLE.

BINDING THE INLAY ROUND THE EDGE OF THE SOUNDBOARD.

HEADSTOCK

CAPSTAN

MACHINE HEAD

NUT

FRET

BASS STRINGS

MARKER DOT

FINGERBOARD

TREBLE STRINGS

PICK GUARD

UPPER BOUT

HEADSTOCK WITH SIX MACHINE HEADS (SOMETIMES CALLED TUNING PEGS).

BRIDGE SADDLE SHOWING STRINGS HELD WITH BALL-ENDS FIXED BY BRIDGE PINS.

NECK HELD IN PLACE BY NECK BLOCK.

DESIGN FACTORS

Makers like Gibson, Martin and National expended great energy in the 1920s, producing instruments which could produce a higher volume. This they largely achieved by increasing the body shape and size. However, the tone of the instrument can be affected by numerous factors, not least the bracing used on the underside of the soundboard and on the back. Bracing fulfils two functions: it is a necessity for giving strength to the body, and for preventing the wood from distorting. However, by their very existence, the bracing struts exert an impact on soundwaves moving around within the body, which alters the tonal characteristics.

A number of different bracing systems have been used by different makers. Most classical designs use a fan-bracing system, the type that was pioneered in Spain at the start of the nineteenth century by the respected luthier Pagés.

The stronger cross-bracing system was developed by the manufacturer Martin in the 1920s when the dominant use of steel strings forced guitar makers to produce instruments capable of withstanding greater degrees of stress.

MATERIALS

A variety of materials have been used in the construction of acoustic guitars through the ages, but manufacturers have generally settled on a fairly restricted range of woods.

The main consideration for a luthier is that whatever wood is used must have been allowed to "settle," which means that it has to lose most of its natural moisture. This can be achieved naturally

BRIDGE DESIGN

As the point at which the strings come into contact with the soundboard, the bridge plays a vital part in transferring to the soundbox the energy that creates the amplified sound. The actual contact point is between the string and the bridge saddle – a small, narrow piece traditionally made from ivory which sits on the bridge unit. Nowadays, saddles are often made from plastic, although most makers agree that this considerably affects the tone of the instrument.

There are two distinct types of bridge unit used on acoustic guitars: flat-top instruments generally have fixed bridges, while archtops usually incorporate a floating bridge design (see picture).

The fixed bridge is glued firmly to the surface of the soundboard and cannot be moved back and forth – if the intonation of the guitar is poor, it can only be remedied by the removal and reapplication of the whole unit. Because of its high density, ebony is the most effective material for the fixed bridge, as for the fingerboard, transferring the string vibration without "soaking" or dampening the sound, which would result from using softer woods. Walnut, rosewood and mahogany are also commonly used alternatives. Strings are secured to the bridge unit using bridge pins which slot vertically behind the saddle trapping the strings in place.

The floating bridge design makes use of a tailpiece which is secured with a screw or bolt to the bottom side of the guitar. This secures the strings in place at the ball-end. The bridge unit is not actually fixed to the soundboard but is clamped in place by the tension of the strings when they are tightened. As the bridge floats freely, it is possible to move the unit back and forth to alter the intonation.

Some floating bridge units (and, rather less commonly, some fixed bridges) also include a height adjustment screw, which allows the overall action of the strings to be raised or lowered.

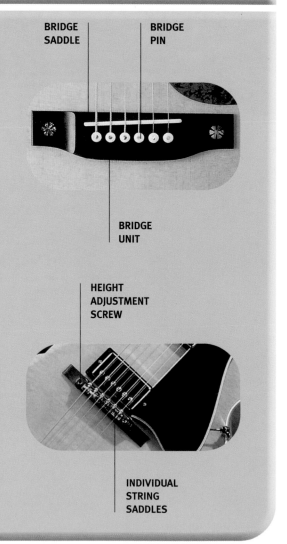

BRIDGE SADDLE

BRIDGE PIN

BRIDGE UNIT

HEIGHT ADJUSTMENT SCREW

INDIVIDUAL STRING SADDLES

using a process known as "seasoning," whereby the wood is stored and allowed to dry out over a long period of time – sometimes a number of years. The top-quality luthiers generally insist on using woods treated in this way. The increasingly common alternative, however, is to use kiln-dried timbers. In this process the wood is placed in enormous kilns which can dry it out within a matter of weeks. If timber was used straight from the tree, it would lose its shape as it dried out naturally – not ideal for a precision musical instrument.

Different types of wood have different properties capable of creating a wide variation in tonal characteristics. Therefore all acoustic instruments are built from a combination of different timbers. The soundboards of most reasonable quality instruments are crafted from European or Canadian spruce, but on expensive instruments the slightly thicker cedar is sometimes used. Cheap acoustic models are generally made from laminated timbers or plywood, which often results in lack of tonal definition. For the back and sides (the ribs), rosewood, maple or mahogany are most commonly used, although some makers have successfully introduced African walnut and sycamore. The struts and bracing are usually made from spruce.

A wider variety of material has been applied in the construction of the guitar neck. Brazilian mahogany is rated by many luthiers as the best, although as a protected wood it is increasingly difficult to obtain. A cheaper alternative is maple. Fingerboards are commonly carved from rosewood, although on the more expensive models ebony is prized as a more attractive, dense and hard-wearing wood.

A notable exception to acoustic manufacturers' preference for wood has been the Ovation company, the most significant makers of acoustic guitars to emerge since the Second World War. Their guitars are revolutionary not only because of their bowl-shaped bodies, but because they are made from materials such as fibreglass, carbon fibre and plastics.

SKILFUL FIXING OF THE NECK TO THE BODY IS CRUCIAL FOR STRENGTH AND TONE.

MACHINE HEADS

On the earliest instruments, the string tension which defines the tuning of the guitar was controlled by friction pegs. One peg per string was fitted to the headstock. The string was wound around the peg until in tune and then the peg was pushed firmly into the headstock to hold it in place. Indeed, on early guitars the headstock was known as the "pegbox."

At the beginning of the nineteenth century guitar makers began using mechanical machine heads (or tuning heads, as they are sometimes known). These systems replaced the tuning peg with a capstan fitted to a gear wheel. The tuning head is linked to a "worm" gear which causes the capstan to rotate but stay firmly in position after adjustment.

HEADSTOCK WITH VERTICAL CAPSTANS.

SLOTTED HEADSTOCK STYLE TYPICAL OF CLASSICAL GUITARS.

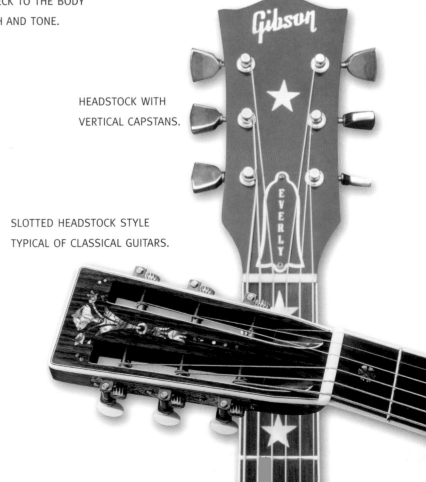

ANATOMY OF THE ELECTRIC GUITAR

Like its acoustic counterpart, there are many approaches to the construction of the solid-body electric guitar. Although most instruments have similar features, the materials used for today's guitars can differ greatly. Most bodies are made from kiln-dried hard woods, such as mahogany, ash, maple, walnut or alder. Necks are usually narrower, but otherwise differ little from those of acoustic instruments, although greater access to the upper frets provides greater flexibility for lead playing, and some fingerboards are capable of a full two-octave range per string.

One major area of contention among guitar makers revolves around the way in which the neck is fixed to the body. The Fender approach, used by most other manufacturers, is to bolt the neck to the body. This makes construction more straightforward and also allows the angle of the neck to be tilted to fit a player's own preference. Gibson guitars have the necks glued permanently to the body. Other manufacturers favour "straight-through" necks, with the body centre – on which the bridge and tailpiece are mounted – and neck carved from a single piece of wood, and the treble and bass bouts glued on separately to the sides. Makers and players argue the merits of all three systems, although most would agree that the straight-through method is capable of producing the greatest sustain.

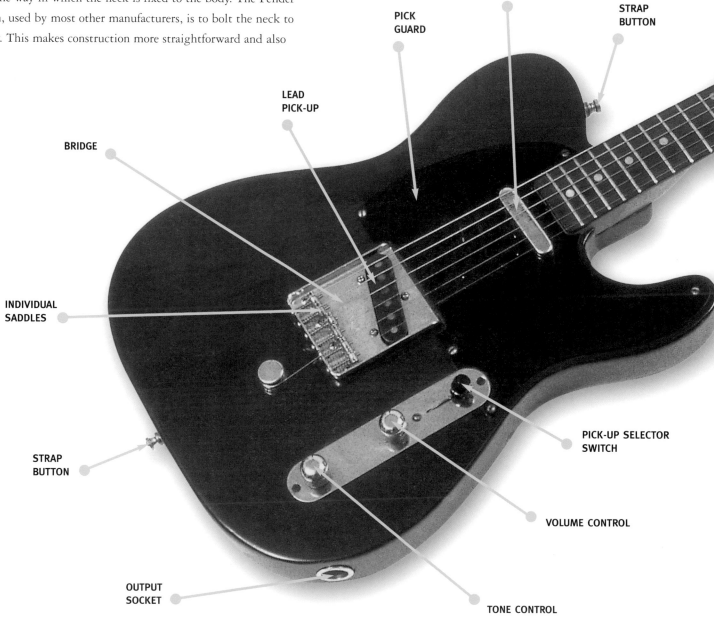

RHYTHM
PICK-UP

PICK
GUARD

STRAP
BUTTON

LEAD
PICK-UP

BRIDGE

INDIVIDUAL
SADDLES

STRAP
BUTTON

PICK-UP SELECTOR
SWITCH

VOLUME CONTROL

OUTPUT
SOCKET

TONE CONTROL

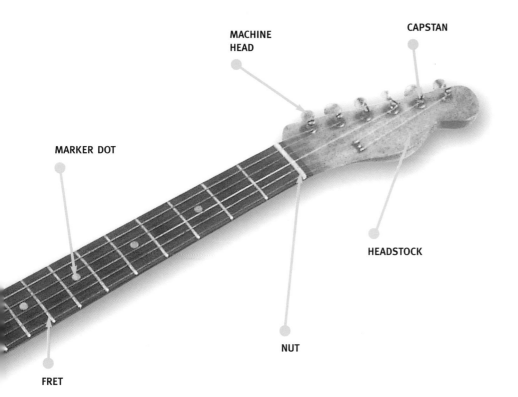

MACHINE
HEAD

CAPSTAN

MARKER DOT

HEADSTOCK

NUT

FRET

JOHN ABERCROMBIE PLAYS A REVOLUTIONARY
STEINBERGER GUITAR.

ALTERNATIVE MATERIALS

Since the aluminium resonator guitars were first produced in the early 1930s, makers have sought out alternative materials to the traditional hardwoods used in guitar production. In some cases it was a genuine search for improvement; in others it was to find ways of reducing production costs. Danelectro solids of the 1950s were notable not only for their extraordinary shape and 32-fret fingerboards, but the fact that the bodies were built from hardboard glued around a wooden frame. These guitars tend to be more sought after by collectors than by players

During the 1960s Dan Armstrong experimented with making plastic-bodied instruments and achieving greater levels of sustain. The 1970s saw a revival of interest in metal, with Veleno producing guitars entirely from aluminium. Kramer aroused a good deal of interest with their aluminium necks, but while nobody who heard these guitars doubted the improvements in volume and sustain, many players didn't like the "cold" feel of the neck.

The most successful materials experiment came in the 1980s when American engineer Ned Steinberger attempted a radical overhaul of traditional guitar design. Initially working with bass guitars, Steinberger produced unique small-bodied, headless instruments from a carbon-based epoxy resin which he referred to as "graphite." It seemed to have everything going for it: it was twice the density of wood – therefore producing greater volume, sustain and an even tone – had ten times the strength of wood, but was also extremely light. Some of the success of these outstanding instruments was undoubtedly due to visual appeal as much as sound and, excellent though they are, sadly they are too often viewed as a relic from one of the less distinguished decades. As the novelty of the shape wore off, Steinberger began producing more conventional-looking instruments and at the end of the 1980s his company was taken over by Gibson.

As the Earth's natural resources become ever more scarce there is an inevitability that instruments made from the most sought-after woods will become increasingly costly. As a result, more and more guitar makers in future are likely to turn their attentions toward synthetic alternatives.

TWENTY-FIVE GREAT GUITARS

We'll end this part of the book with a timeline of fifty of the most significant guitars ever to have been made, from the five-course instruments of the late 16th century, to such hi-tech contemporary pieces as the Parker Fly.

FIVE-COURSE GUITAR ▼
Late 16th century

The first guitars were four-course instruments. They had waisted fronts, flat backs and sides and a fretted neck. And although much smaller, in many respects they resemble a modern classical guitar. The first mention of the guitar's "invention" appeared in 1487 in a work by Johannes Tinctoris in which he claimed that the instrument was "invented by the Catalans," the inhabitants of what is now north-east Spain.

In common with lutes of this period, the guitar was fitted with a rose over the sound hole. This was an ornately carved piece of wood. The frets were made of gut, which would be tied around the neck. The number of frets the guitar possessed would vary depending on the type of music to be played upon it. Simple strumming required no more than a handful of frets, whereas more complex music called for a greater number.

The five-course guitar appeared during the sixteenth century, and was essentially the same instrument with the addition of an extra course in the bass register. Again, it seems that the instrument originated in Spain and is likely to have been produced to satisfy the demands of the slightly more ambitious pieces being composed at that time.

STAUFFER "LEGNANI" ▲
c.1820

The most noted of the Viennese school of nineteenth century luthiers, Johann Georg Stauffer (1778–1853) also trained other notable guitar makers such as Schertzer and C F Martin.

Stauffer's best-known instrument is the "Legnani" model, based on a collaboration with the Italian guitar virtuoso Luigi Legnani. Incorporating a number of innovative and influential features, the most immediately visible is the "Persian slipper" headstock, with all six machine heads positioned along one side.

The body was built from maple or rosewood with a spruce top and the shape has rather more exaggerated upper and lower bouts than other guitars of the time. The neck was particularly unusual in that it was adjustable: using a clock-key mechanism, the player was able to raise and lower the height of the fingerboard to set the action. (Altering the action on other "classical" guitars of the period required surgery to sand down the nut or bridge piece.)

Stauffer's influence was widespread. A century after his death, the "single-sided" headstock design was widely adopted by electric guitar makers.

TORRES ▸
c.1855

Antonio de Torres Jurado is the single most important figure in the evolution of what we now call the "classical" guitar.

Born in Almeria, Spain in 1817, the son of a tax collector, Torres began his working life as a carpenter. Moving to Granada in 1850, he learned his trade under the tuition of the luthier,

Jose Pernas. Although little information exists about his time with Pernas, by all accounts even his earliest efforts produced excellent results. A meeting with concert performer Julian Arcus evidently convinced Torres to dedicate his efforts exclusively to the guitar.

There are two definable "periods" of Torres' career as a luthier. The first phase begins in his workshop at Calle Cerregeria 32 in Seville in 1852 and ends in 1869. It was during this period that nearly all of his pioneering work took place.

Among his most celebrated instruments was La Leona, built in 1856. In 1858 he won a bronze medal in the Seville Exhibition for an extraordinarily decorated instrument in bird's eye maple.

Torres' most visibly dramatic development was in altering the proportions of the guitar, in particular elongating the body and "doming" the lower bout. He also experimented with materials. He firmly believed that the key to a guitar's sound was in its top, so he tried lighter and thinner woods. To give the instrument greater strength, he created a system of strutting on the underside of the top. Although other earlier luthiers had used this approach, the seven "fan" struts developed by Torres gave the instrument greater strength and bass response.

The first guitarist to benefit from these new developments was the nineteenth century's greatest virtuoso, Francisco Tárrega. Performing widely in the concert halls of Europe, Tárrega evolved new playing techniques that resulted directly from Torres' work. Another notable client of the time was Miguel Llobert.

In spite of Tárrega's patronage, Torres was unable to make a good living as a luthier, and in 1870 he moved back to his native Almeria, where he opened a china shop. After 1875, he resumed guitar making, but on a part-time basis. Until his death in 1892 he produced around twelve guitars every year. Indeed, according to the biography written by José L. Romanillos, *Antonio de Torres, Guitar Maker: His Life and Work* – a scholarly work from which most our knowledge of the man is derived – Torres manufactured only around 320 guitars during his lifetime, 66 of which are known to remain.

Numerous inventions connected to the guitar have been attributed to Torres over the years, but his real genius was less as an innovator than in his effectiveness at improving the most important developments of the day, and in doing so creating an instrument which has remained a template for the modern classical guitar.

MARTIN O-45 ▼
1904

The famous Martin O-45 was introduced in 1904. The body is made of rosewood with a spruce soundboard. Martin guitars are categorized by their styles and body shapes.

BODY SHAPES

O	Concert size
OO	Grand concert size
OOO	Auditorium size
D	Dreadnought size
DS	Dreadnought with 12-frets to the body
M	Grand auditorium size
MC	Grand auditorium with cutaway body
OM	Orchestra model
C	Classical
N	Classical (European)
F	F-hole model

MAJOR STYLES

16-	Spruce top, quarter-sawn mahogany back and sides, slotted headstock, wide rosewood fingerboard, no fret markers or fingerplate.
18-	14-frets to the body, solid headstock, white dot position markers, "belly" bridge, dark edgings and fingerplate.
28-	Rosewood back and sides, spruce top, and white edging.
45-	Spruce soundboard, rosewood back and side, ebony fingerboard, and abalone pearl inlays.

GIBSON L-5 ▲
1922

Although it was C F Martin and his ancestors who established the US as the home of most of the important post-Torres innovations, it was Orville Gibson who founded the company that would not only provide an alternative tradition to the flat-top acoustic guitar, but would later play a crucial role during the transition to the electric era.

The son of a British immigrant, during the 1880s Gibson began producing a range of beautifully carved mandolins using methods of construction more usually applied to violins. The principal difference was in the intricately curved tops with the bridge and saddles positioned across the apex. During the following decade, Gibson applied the same ideas to his guitars, which became known as "archtops."

Surprisingly, perhaps, after Orville Gibson's death in 1918, the company began to flourish, and was responsible for a number of developments that would have a major impact on the future of the guitar.

Steered by the innovative research of Lloyd Loar, in 1922, Gibson launched the first in a succession of historically important production archtop guitars – the Gibson L-5.

Among this instrument's unusual features was the replacement of the conventional circular soundhole with two violin-style tuned "f-holes." This, along with the "Virzitone" sound producer built into the body, helped to create a strong, full, warm sound which was able to project chord work through the brass-dominated dance

bands of the period. It could even be said to have influenced the very course of American popular music – with the capability of producing greater volume, the L-5 was so successful that by the end of the decade it had all but replaced the banjo and ukulele in dance bands. Indeed, many of the early pioneers of jazz guitar used a Gibson L-5.

RO-PAT-IN "FRYING PAN" ▶
1931

No single figure can be credited with "inventing" the electric guitar. Instead, we find ourselves with a disparate group of far-sighted individuals, all of whom made their own important contributions to what eventually become the most influential musical instrument of the twentieth century.

In 1919, Gibson hired Lloyd Loar to head their Kalamazoo engineering and research departments. During his five years with the company he made a huge impact on those around him. Not content with overseeing the creation of the revolutionary L-5 guitar, he was perhaps the first person to experiment with the idea of using a magnetic pickup to amplify stringed instruments. His first designs were for an electric double bass – there have even been claims that he produced a crude electric guitar during this period. Sadly, it soon became evident that Loar's ideas were too futuristic for the notoriously conservative Gibson, and he went his own way. During the 1930s, Loar's own Vivi-Tone company would produced some of the first true electrified guitars.

The second significant character in the story was a charismatic Texan named George Beauchamp. Initially a partner of the

Dopyera brothers, and one of the creators of the "Dobro" resonator guitar, in 1931, he teamed up with designer Paul Barth and toolmaker Adolph Rickenbacker to form the Ro-Pat-In Company. Together they produced an electrified lap-steel "Hawaiian" guitar. Because of its distinctive shape, it quickly became known as the "Frying Pan." The instrument first went into production under the Ro-Pat-In brand name, but was soon replaced by the Rickenbacker brand.

The Frying Pan was powered by a pair of large horse-shoe magnets that passed under the strings. The body and neck of the prototype models were made from a single piece of maple, however by the time they became publicly available cast aluminum was used instead. This was not entirely successful, since the use of aluminum evidently resulted in problems keeping the instrument in tune. Later in the decade Rickenbacker produced lap-steels made from strong bakelite plastic which proved to be more successful. Variations on the "Frying Pan" design remained available until well into the 1950s.

Although not guitars in the conventional sense, these were the first commercially produced electric instruments. (However, the Dopyera brothers – from whom George Beauchamp had earlier parted company with some acrimony – would later claim that they produced an electrified National earlier than the Frying Pan.)

For many modern guitarists, the idea that their electrified instruments owe their heritage to such a "minority" instrument, may seem strange. The reason is simply that Hawaiian music was extremely popular in the US during this time, and, for a brief period, the lap steel was more popular than the "Spanish" guitar.

SELMER MACCAFERRI ▶
1932

One of the most fascinating figures in the development of the twentieth century guitar, Mario Maccaferri was not only an innovative luthier but a celebrated guitarist.

Maccaferri was born in Bologna, Italy in 1900, and at the age of eleven he became apprenticed to the Italian master luthier and musician, Luigi Mozzani, where he concurrently pursued the study of guitar making and playing. Graduating with the highest honours from the Sienna Conservatory, he embarked upon a successful concert career. In 1929, Maccaferri settled in London where, in between touring and teaching, he began to conceive of an instrument that combined a smooth tone with a high volume. By 1932 Selmer of Paris was producing his design.

The most striking visual feature of the Selmer Maccaferri is the perpendicular cutaway in the upper bout that allows easy access to the upper register. The guitar's distinctive tone and high volume was created by a revolutionary internal sound chamber built into the body. However, following a dispute with Henri Selmer, production ceased within a year.

Fewer than three hundred of these guitars were originally made. Popularized by the great European jazz guitarist Django Reinhardt, the Maccaferri is now highly prized by guitar collectors.

DOBRO "RESONATOR" ▼
1934

As the guitar became more widely used for ensemble playing, the most significant trend among luthiers of the 1920s was to produce instruments capable of generating a higher volume. One of the most innovative solutions was developed by the Dopyera Brothers, a family of four Slovakian immigrants living in California – it was the so-called "Resonator" guitar.

The acoustic principle on which it worked was similar to an audio loudspeaker. The Dopyeras fitted a floating aluminium cone into the top of a regular guitar, and attached it to the bridge. Whenever a string was struck the vibrations were passed through the bridge saddles and transferred to the cone, which "resonated" back and forth. The sound it created was a rather harsh, distinctive metallic jangle, but it was nonetheless much louder than any other acoustic guitar of the time.

The earliest resonator guitars were built in 1926 for the National Guitar Company, in which one of the Dopyera brothers – Louis – had invested. The following year, however, the other three brothers – John, Rudy and Ed – broke away to build guitars for their own Dobro company. The main difference between the instruments produced by the two companies was that Nationals not only featured aluminium resonators, but aluminum bodies; whereas Dobros had the aluminum cone fitted into regular flat-top acoustic guitars.

LES PAUL "LOG" ▶
1941

The Gibson ES-150 was a milestone in the story of the guitar. Not only were jazz musicians such as Charlie Christian turned on to the potential of the electric guitar, but also emerging country stars such as Chet Atkins and Merle Travis, and bluesmen like Muddy Waters and Elmore James.

A fundamental problem of the early electric guitars – which were, after all, little more than acoustic guitars with pickups fitted – was that if the amplifier volume was too great, sound from the loudspeaker could easily cause the body of the guitar and strings to vibrate on their own. This created a howling noise referred to as "feedback."

Whilst rock players in the 1960s began to harness this sound as a part of their playing technique, to the early electric players it was merely a nuisance. The logical solution to this problem was to increase the body mass of the instrument – without a working soundbox the guitar's capacity for vibration would be greatly reduced. From the beginning of the 1940s, a number of generally unrelated parties set about designing and building a solid-body electric guitar that would achieve this end.

No-one can truly say who produced the first purpose-built solid-body electric guitar but there are a number of candidates whose research work was unquestionably important. Designer-engineers Lloyd Loar and O W Appleton are known to have at least experimented with solid bodies while developing magnetic pickups.

One clear candidate is country-jazz guitarist Les Paul. Born Lester William Polfus, as a musician he is best-remembered for easy listening hits of the late 1940s accompanying his wife, Mary Ford. However, it is his signature on one of the most famous guitars ever made that will guarantee his immortality. A keen inventor from an early age, Paul was given full access to the Epiphone workshop by owner and friend Epi Stathopoulo. Here he created his own "Log" guitar using a Gibson neck attached to a solid piece of pine on which the pickups and bridge were mounted – the bouts from an Epiphone hollow-body archtop were added to the side to give the guitar a broadly normal appearance.

In 1949 he took his prototype to Maurice Berlin, the president of Gibson's parent company, CMI. As Paul remembers: "He said 'Forget it.' He called it a broomstick." Within two years he was called back.

BIGSBY MERLE TRAVIS ▲
1947

In 1947, engineer Paul Bigsby produced a solid-body instrument designed in conjunction with country guitarist Merle Travis. Bigsby and Travis had first collaborated three years earlier when the guitarist had requested some improvements be made to the vibrola on his Gibson guitar. Bigsby came up with a completely new design for a vibrato arm, which would be widely used over the next twenty years. This Bigsby-Travis guitar represented an important development for a number of reasons. The shape of the body and headstock was clearly influential – some of the lines are clearly echoed in the early Fender and Gibson guitars that followed over the next decade. So, too, was the thinline "bird's-eye" maple body and the fact that it featured a "straight-through" neck.

Since at least a dozen of these instruments were produced, the Bigsby Merle Travis could lay a reasonable claim to having been the first "production" solid-body electric guitar.

GIBSON ES-175 ▼
1949

By the start of the 1940s, Gibson had assumed pole position as far as the electric guitar market was concerned. By far the biggest-selling electric guitar of the 1930s, the ES-150 had been a down-the-line, gimmick-free instrument. However, for all of its success, essentially it was merely a high-quality acoustic guitar with an attached pickup.

In 1944, Gibson was taken over by the Chicago Musical Instrument Company (CMI). Foreseeing an unprecedented demand for guitars after the end of the Second World War, a new young president, Ted McCarty, was brought in, with a brief to concentrate on a new line of electric models. In 1949, Gibson unleashed the ES-175 – a guitar specifically designed as an electric instrument, rather than an acoustic with a pickup.

Although launched as a economy instrument, construction of the ES-175 remained typical of the Gibson tradition. The hollow body features a "Florentine" cutaway and two "f-holes"; the front and back are cut from pressed maple plywood, with solid maples sides. The neck was made from mahogany with a pressed rosewood fingerboard.

The original ES-175 featured a single P90 pickup with individually adjustable polepieces – this effectively allows the volume of each string to be tweaked in relation to the overall volume. Other pickup options have become available over the years.

The ES-175 has stayed in production ever since, becoming one of Gibson's biggest selling guitars. Its rich tone continues to find favor, particularly among jazz players.

FENDER BROADCASTER ▶
1950

It's difficult to overestimate the significance of the launch of the Fender Broadcaster in 1950, not only to the evolution of the electric guitar, but to the music that would emerge over the decades that followed.

The Broadcaster was by no means a work of startling originality: the pioneering efforts to create a solid-body electric guitar had been worked out a decade earlier by the likes of Les Paul, Merle Travis and Paul Bigsby. The genius of Leo Fender and his engineer George Fullerton was to conceive a production-line approach to electric guitar manufacture. In the past, guitar makers had been master craftsmen; Fender sought to demystify the process.

The Broadcaster dispensed with the complex contours associated with traditional archtop guitars, its body a simple slab of solid ash that – as Fender's early critics decried – could be cut out and fashioned by anyone who owned a buzz-saw. But this was precisely the point: everything about the Broadcaster was basic, from its minimalistic body shape to the simple bridge pickup construction. The maple neck was not precision-glued to the body, but was bolted on using four self-tapping screws. The electronic circuitry was mounted on the inside of a chrome plate, which was itself secured to the body with a pair of screws. Such simplicity was well-suited to the production line, and also meant that any part of the guitar could be easily replaced in the event of damage. Fender's aim was to mass-produce an electric guitar at an affordable price. As such, the Fender Broadcaster was a critical landmark.

Early in 1951, Leo Fender was advised that his use of the name Broadcaster had infringed a copyright – the New York Gretsch instrument company had long been producing a range of drums using the name "Broadkaster." To avoid litigation, from February 1951, the Broadcaster transfers on the headstock of unsold guitars were scratched off, leaving just the Fender logo. (These so-called "No-casters" are now highly prized collectibles.) It was Fender employee, Don Randall, who came up with a new name. Post-war America having rapidly fallen under the spell of television, he sought a word that would make a clear connection: the Fender Telecaster was born – a modern instrument for the modern world.

Most early sales of the Broadcaster/Telecaster were made at bandstands or direct from the factory, but word soon spread. Initially favoured by country musicians, the "Tele" would quickly find a home in every possible future musical genre.

Although Telecasters are most often seen in their traditional "blond" or natural finishes, a number of alternatives have appeared over the years. In the late 1960s, Fender paid homage to the psychedelic era with a limited run in "Paisley Red" – this effect was achieved by pasting wallpaper to the body before varnishing. The Telecaster has also appeared in a number of variations, among them the lighter, hollow-body Thinline, and the souped-up Elite, featuring humbucking pickups and active circuitry.

The first production-line solid-body electric guitar, the Telecaster has been in production ever since, and remains an undisputed classic instrument.

GIBSON LES PAUL MODEL ▲ ("GOLDTOP") 1952

By the early 1950s, it became clear that Gibson was in danger of losing its coveted position as the world's most significant guitar manufacturer. Only a few years earlier, country player Les Paul had brought his prototype "Log" guitar to the company headquarters in Kalamazoo. As certain as he was that the next stage of the instrument's development would be the use of a high-density body crafted from solid wood, Gibson's decision makers were unimpressed. At the time they laughed at "the kid with the broomstick guitar," but the success of Leo Fender's first production-line solid-body models now gave his prophesy some credibility.

In 1951, Les Paul was invited to collaborate on the design for a solid-body instrument. The brief was simple: the guitar would combine innovative design with the high production values for which Gibson was famed. Above all, it would provide serious competition to Fender's upstart designs. A year later, the first Gibson Les Paul Model rolled off the assembly line. With its brightly-coloured finish, it soon became known as the "Goldtop."

Although guitar folklore may suggest otherwise, Les Paul's role in the design process was ultimately limited to the electronics and the tailpiece mechanism. The body and headstock design were evidently closely modelled on the smooth curves of Gibson's ES295 electric acoustic.

It's odd to think that an instrument now imbued with such iconic status should initially have been so unsuccessful. One reason was cost: compared to the no-frills pragmatism of Fender guitars, the Les Paul was more obviously a work of fine craftsmanship, but that came at a price. The body was cut from natural mahogany with a carved maple top. The neck was fixed to the body with glue, providing (in theory, at least) greater sustain than Fender's less fancy bolt-on jobs. A 22-fret rosewood fingerboard featured ornate mother-of-pearl fingerboard inlays. This was without doubt a luxury instrument.

FENDER STRATOCASTER ▶ 1954

There could be little argument that the Fender Stratocaster is the most popular – not to mention most copied – guitar ever made. Indeed, such is its iconic status that the mere silhouette of its body outline would be immediately recognisable, even to many outside guitar-playing circles.

The Telecaster had been an immediate success, even if it was conceived and produced as a basic, functional instrument. However, Leo Fender wanted to consolidate his business with a more sophisticated, upmarket model. However, the changes that he and fellow designer Freddie Tavares had in mind were more than cosmetic.

To begin with, the sharp edges of the Telecaster body – a deliberate design feature for ease of mass production – were uncomfortable for many players. So, the team began to experiment with smoother body contours. In doing so they developed the first solid-body electric guitar with twin cutaways. This gave the player unprecedented access to the highest notes on the fingerboard, as well as creating both a balanced look and feel.

In terms of functionality, there was even greater ambition. The Telecaster bridge unit had featured three independent string saddles, each one controlling the height and length of a pair of strings; Fender began to investigate the idea of using six, fully adjustable saddles, making it possible for each string to be adjusted independently. Furthermore, although the twin pickups of the Telecaster were capable of creating very different sounds, a third, middle pickup would surely provide even greater versatility. Some Telecaster players had also complained about the ease at which their connecting leads became detached from their guitars, so Fender gave the new model a jack-plug socket recessed in the front of the body. Finally, a vibrato arm was provided as a standard feature.

Whereas the Telecaster derived its name from the popularity of the new TV medium, Fender's new guitar played on a fast-growing national obsession with space exploration. With the Stratocaster a true star was born.

After a long association with Gibson guitars, Eric Clapton acquired his first Stratocaster in 1967. The model shown here – dubbed "Brownie" – was used on the 1970 rock classic "Layla" by Derek and the Dominos. He also played a composite Strat which he constructed himself. This was famously known as "Blackie."

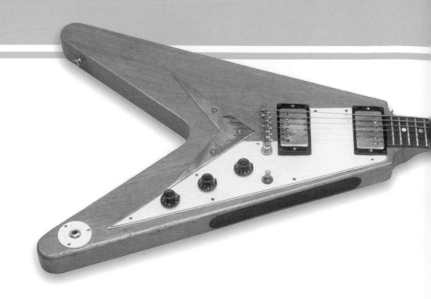

GRETSCH 6120 CHET ATKINS ▼
1954

The guitars produced during the 1950s by the Fred Gretsch company are the very embodiment of the art of the guitar. Whilst Fender aimed for production-line simplicity, and Gibson upheld their traditional high production values, the Gretsch boast was that their guitars were prettier than the rest!

Launched in 1954, the Gretsch 6120 was a collaboration with Country's greatest picker, Chet Atkins. A hollow-body model, the 6120 was styled in a glowing orange "Amber Red." As a testament to its Country roots, the original models featured a "G" branded on the body, a longhorn motif at the top of the headstock and a variety of cactus images on the fingerboard inlays.

As with other Gretsch guitars, the 6120 was a delicate creature – extremely light, with a body made from thin laminated maple. Nor was it a masterpiece of practical design: the bridge was not attached to the body, but held in place by string tension, making it easy to knock out of position if light strings were used; furthermore, it was only possible to alter the overall height of the bridge, not the individual strings. The guitar also featured the famously chunky Bigsby Patent vibrato arm, which, if over-used, could send the instrument out of tune. It was the

DeArmond pickups that gave the 6120 its fabulously distinctive sound – one that would make it a favourite among 1950s rockabilly players like Eddie Cochran and Duane Eddy. Later 6120s used the improved Filtertron humbucking pickup (as shown on this 1958 model).

A frequent criticism of Gretsches was that no two examples of the same model ever sounded the same. But when a guitar looks as good as this, who could really care less?

GIBSON FLYING V ▲
1958

By the middle of the 1950s, a pattern of dominance had emerged in the market for solid-body electric guitars. The two major rivals vying for supremacy were Gibson and Fender. It was a battle of the old established giant versus the young upstart; less than a decade old and already a world-beater. As Gibson's president of the time, Ted McCarty, remembered: "Leo [Fender] was going around telling people that Gibson was stodgy and never had a new idea…and that Fender were the guitar company of the future."

Struggling to match Fender's success, in 1957 McCarty set a new goal: "To prove that Gibson was more modern than the rest." He looked at developments in other areas of American life, and in particular the angular shapes being used by the car designers of the era. In 1958, the first of Gibson's "new" instruments appeared: the Flying V. Previously, designs for solid-body electric guitars had been based largely around the curves of the traditional acoustic guitar; the Flying V, however, took its cue from the lines of the triangular tailfins that featured on many of the mighty American automobiles of the decade.

The Flying V wasn't the most practical instrument: since the body made no reference to the standard figure-of-eight guitar shape, there was no way it could be played in a sitting position. No, it was aimed squarely at the stage performer, and since, by comparison, it rendered every other instrument conservative in the extreme, we can assume that Gibson had the more extrovert musician in mind.

It may have been a revolutionary instrument, but the Flying V bombed spectacularly. Only about eighty originals were produced, and the line was dropped in 1959. Like the Les Paul, it later found favor among a number of rock players, prompting Gibson to produce a modified version in 1966. Authenticated originals now change hands for hefty sums of money.

GIBSON SG ▶
1961

The early 1960s saw Gibson still struggling with the phenomenal growth of the solid-body electric guitar market. The Les Paul Standard in its original form had been taken off the production line to be replaced, in 1961, by the new Les Paul Standard – a modern-looking instrument that Gibson hoped would capture the imagination of young, image-conscious players.

Although the two instruments were similar in most respects, the body shape represented something of a departure. Whereas the "old" Les Paul featured a small upper bout with a single cutaway, the new version styled both upper and lower bouts in broadly similar proportions, creating an almost traditional figure-of-eight effect. The heavily bevelled twin cutaways were designed to give the player unprecedented access to the top of the fingerboard.

Despite the fact that the instrument was initially launched as the next incarnation of the Standard, Les Paul himself didn't like the new body shape and requested that his famed signature be removed from the headstock. So, from 1962, the guitar became known as the Gibson SG – "Solid Guitar."

Like the many reissues of the Les Paul over the fifty years following its launch, a number of variations on the original SG design have appeared. The version shown here is an early-1960s SG custom featuring three humbucking pickups.

FENDER JAGUAR ▼
1962

Based on the styling of the Jazzmaster, the Jaguar became Fender's flagship model from 1962 until its discontinuation in 1975. In terms of playability, the main difference was the use of a stunted neck. This was available in four alternative widths, to accommodate different preferences and fingerspans.

The Jazzmaster had faced criticism for being noisy and prone to electrical interference. The Jag confronted these problems with metal shielding on the pickups and sophisticated electronics that incorporated a variety of tone switches. The Jaguar also arrived with a spring-loaded string mute fitted across the bridge. This allowed players to mute the strings evenly by pressing down the palm of the picking hand. They were usually quickly discarded.

Like many of Fender's earlier instruments, reissues were launched during the 1990s. Although the Jaguar was not a massive success at the time, it remains popular with guitarists who have a penchant for things retro.

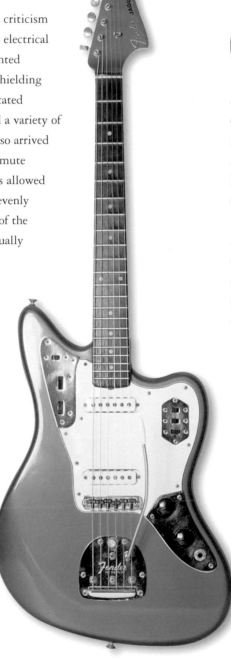

RICKENBACKER 360-12 ▲
1964

As one of the most significant pioneering names in the story of the electric guitar, the Rickenbacker company enjoyed a surprisingly low profile during the 1940s. In 1953 the company was sold to American businessman, Charles C Hall. Under his guidance, the Rickenbacker name enjoyed a considerable revival, producing some of the most fashionable instruments of the 1960s.

From their inception in 1958, the sweeping lines of the Rickenbacker hollow-body six-string electrics were more than capable of turning heads. There were certainly no other electric acoustic instruments quite like them, the distinctive "slash" soundhole a dramatic contrast to the usual double "f" holes more commonly found.

Rickenbacker guitars became massively popular in 1963 when John Lennon and George Harrison were seen playing short-scale 325 guitars on stage. During the Beatles' 1964 US tour, George Harrison was presented with one of the first 360-12s: one of its first uses can be heard on the opening E seventh suspended chord that heralds the opening of the classic single, "A Hard Days Night." Patronage followed by the revered US country-rock band the Byrds, whose sound all but revolved around the jangling 360-12.

A unique features of the 360-12 were the headstock designs and machine head mechanisms. Whereas other 12-string makers produced ugly elongated headstocks large enough to accommodate the additional six machine heads, Rickenbacker devised a cunning system, mounting the extra six heads in classical-style slots between and perpendicular to the others. Although they could be fiddly

to use they nonetheless gave an overall sense of balance to the guitar.

Although by no means the original twelve-string electric guitar, the Rickenbacker 360-12 was certainly the first to become fashionable. Its importance to the sound of some of the most enduring mid-1960s pop music ensures its place in guitar history.

OVATION BALLADEER ▶
1970

The American Ovation company is the most significant manufacturer of acoustic guitars to have emerged since the war. The company was founded in 1966 as a division of Kaman Aerospace, a company owned by a wealthy industrialist called Charles Kaman, who had made his fortune in designing and manufacturing helicopter blades. A keen musician, Kaman used his extensive engineering expertise to produce a design that would revolutionize the world of the steel-string acoustic and electro-acoustic guitars.

The fundamental design principle saw a complete overhaul of the traditional acoustic guitar body. The back and sides were replaced with a single, one-piece bowl, crafted using a newly developed fibreglass called Lyrachord. With no joins or body strutting needed to support the top of the guitar, the sound could no longer be trapped in the corners of the soundbox. This duly created a purer tone and greater volume.

The Balladeer was the first Ovation guitar to be launched. The early models,

produced in 1966, featured a top made from sitka spruce with a cross-bracing system on the underside. The neck construction was also unique. It was built from mahogany with a maple fingerboard, and a steel truss rod was set inside an aluminium channel passing the full length of the fingerboard.

In 1970, the Balladeer was made available as an electro-acoustic instrument. It was here that Ovation found their greatest success. A traditional problem for live performers is that the miking-up of an acoustic guitar poses all kinds of logistical difficulties for the sound engineer – variations in tone and volume, depending on the position of the guitar in relation to the microphone, feedback and sound spillage from other instruments. One attempted solution had been to fit pick-ups which clamped on the inside of the sound hole. However, this meant only the string vibrations were picked up, creating a sound more like a semi-acoustic electric guitar.

Ovation's solution was to create a unique electro-acoustic instrument which had six individual piezo-electric transducer pick-ups on the underside of the bridge saddle. Crystals in each piezo unit generated electrical energy when placed under mechanical strain, such as the vibrations of the strings from the bridge above, as well as the sound from within the "bowl" coming from below. The overall effect was to create a far more natural acoustic guitar sound when the instrument was plugged into an amplifier. It also guaranteed the player a consistency of sound irrespective of venue.

Since the development of the Balladeer, Ovation has largely dominated the professional electro-acoustic market, and by the beginning of the 1980s Ovations had become as common a feature on the wish-lists of aspiring players as Stratocasters or Les Pauls. They remained out of the price range of many non-professional users until Ovation launched the Matrix budget range, and then expanded into the Applause diffusion line.

YAMAHA SG2000 ▼
1976

From time to time, a single product comes along which completely revolutionizes an entire industry. Until 1976, Japanese-built guitars were simply not rated. The prevailing thinking was that these cheap, mass-produced instruments were fine for beginners or impoverished amateurs, but you'd never see a professional playing one. It's no exaggeration to say that the Yamaha SG2000 turned this notion upside down. For the first time it was shown that in terms of quality a Japanese-built production model could not only compete, but could wipe the floor with the traditional US competition.

Yamaha was founded in 1887, and began making acoustic guitars after the end of the war. The first Yamaha production electric guitar emerged in 1966. Like other Japanese makers of the time, it looked to Mosrite for inspiration. During the following years, Yamaha gained a reputation for producing slightly eccentric – if reasonable quality – takes on the Gibson Les Paul shape.

Perhaps the most surprising aspect of the SG2000's design is that it looks so "normal," eschewing the needless gimmickry often previously found on Japanese guitars. What we have here is essentially a Les Paul Standard, with a double cutaway – not a

million miles removed from Gibson double-necks of the late 1950s – but carefully redesigned and assembled using state-of-the-art construction techniques of the day: a fine blend of old and new.

Like the Les Paul, the SG2000 featured carved maple on a mahogany body. But unlike the flat back of the original, the Yamaha was contoured in a way that made it extremely comfortable to wear. A brass block was set into the maple beneath the bridge to improve sustain. Particularly unusual for a six-string guitar, the SG2000 featured a multi-laminate "through" neck built from a central strip of maple surrounded by mahogany.

Popular wisdom of the period was that genuine Gibson guitars were no longer being built to the exacting standards of yore. When former Gibson endorsee Carlos Santana made the SG2000 his main instrument, the battle was won. The SG2000 has remained in production ever since, making it that rarest of creatures, a genuine "modern classic."

JACKSON SOLOIST ▲
1981

Californian Grover Jackson is widely credited with inventing the concept of the so-called Superstrat. However, he owes some of this success to a man named Wayne Charvel, who during the mid-1970s established a bold new venture, providing spare parts that would enable players to soup-up their production-line guitars. In 1978, with business not quite booming, Charvel sold out to guitar maker Jackson. The company took off in 1980 when Randy Rhoads – Ozzy Osbourne's brilliant young guitarist – approached Jackson to build him a custom guitar. This evolved into the Soloist, the first production Superstrat.

The body of the Soloist is clearly derived from the classic Stratocaster shape, albeit with extended horns on the upper bout. However, rather than using a bolt-on neck *a la* Fender, the neck and body centre are machined from a single piece of maple; the "wings" are made from softer poplar. This rather more costly approach to construction was used for a while at Gibson on mid-1960s guitars such as the Firebird. The Soloist, like pretty well all Superstrats that have followed, pioneered the idea of a two-octave fingerboard – three more frets than are found on a standard Stratocaster.

Although the Soloist is clearly derivative in design, Jackson came up with what has effectively become his own visual trademark – the angular, pointed headstock. Yet even that has a clear antecedent in the ill-fated Gibson Explorer, produced briefly in 1958.

Jackson made the Soloist available in a wide variety of pickup combinations, and in 1990 added a range of exotic finishes, among them the "California Sunset" shown here.

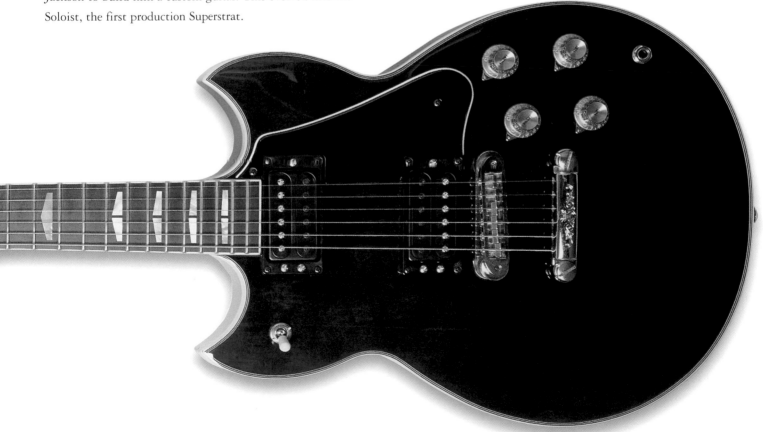

IBANEZ JEM ▼
1987

Despite having produced some distinctive, high-quality models, by the mid-1980s the Ibanez name was still associated with derivative guitars. In an attempt to alter this perception, parent company Hoshino set up a US wing, aimed at recruiting star talent. The first player targeted was Steve Vai. Their approach was simple: they researched Vai's tastes in guitars, produced a one-off of what they thought would be his perfect guitar, wrapped it up and sent it to him as a Christmas present! Vai's response was so positive that he spent the next three months refining the design. The result was the 1987 Jem, a high-performance Superstrat with a locking tremolo, three custom-designed DiMarzio pickups, and a two-octave scalloped fingerboard. A magnificent versatile instrument, the Jem is arguably one of the finest production-line guitars ever made.

One unusual aspect of the Jem's design is the "monkeygrip" carrying handle. However, what made the Jem so distinctive was the variety of outlandish finishes along with intricate matching fretboard inlays.

PARKER FLY ▲
1993

One of the most significant guitars of the late twentieth century, the Parker Fly proves that it's possible to come up with a radical contemporary take on the design and construction of the solid-body electric guitar. Designed in 1991 by Ken Parker and Larry Fishman, as futuristic as the Fly may appear visually, at its core are ideas that return to the guitar's early origins. Ken Parker explains: "I think of this guitar as harking back to things like Renaissance lutes, which would have soft woods veneered in ebony. We're doing the same thing, with modern materials."

From the earliest solid-body experimenters in the 1940s to Ned Steinberger's revolutionary "graphite" guitars, the conventional wisdom was to construct instruments whose bodies were as dense and free from natural resonance as possible: hence, hardwoods such as alder, ash and mahogany have always been most commonly used. Parker turns this idea on its head by building the

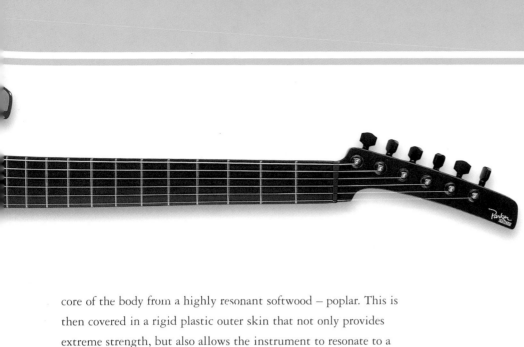

core of the body from a highly resonant softwood – poplar. This is then covered in a rigid plastic outer skin that not only provides extreme strength, but also allows the instrument to resonate to a far greater degree than other solid-body guitars – a fact that is evident when the guitar is played "unplugged." A similar neck construction makes the Fly a fabulously lightweight guitar.

As well as featuring two humbucking pickups, the Fly also has Piezo pickups built into the bridge. This takes full advantage of the guitar's resonance, producing a natural acoustic sound.

PAUL REED SMITH DRAGON 2000 ▶
1999

With its richly ornate body, the Paul Reed Smith Dragon series is without doubt a design classic. It's also the most collectible of modern guitars: the series are made in extremely small numbers (between fifty and a hundred of each one) and retail at a hefty price – you're unlikely to see too much change from $20,000. The first Dragon appeared in 1992. Periodically, new models – with differing dragon motifs – are introduced. The model shown here is a prototype for the Dragon 2000.

The PRS Dragon is part of an ongoing dream fulfilment for Smith, who recalls: "I knew I wanted to make guitars when I was 16. I even had a poster on my wall that said 'Les Paul Custom Dragon.' Someday, I was going to build Dragon guitars."

Of course, the idea of decorating musical instruments is not a new one – tacky airbrushed images have been adorning guitars since the 1960s. But good taste aside, the difference here is that the Dragon's appearance is created using inlays of such amazing intricacy that each guitar really is a work of art. Indeed, the PRS Dragon has been given the ultimate recognition of a place in the Smithsonian Institute.

PART 2

FIFTY GREAT GUITARISTS

If we were to sit a dozen guitarists down and ask them to discuss their nominations for the ten most important guitarists ever to have lived, then the chances are that before long the sparks would start to fly. At the very least we'd get some highly divergent lists.

What follows makes no claims to be the definitive list of the fifty best guitarists of all time. It's just one person's view taken at one moment in time. This list is entirely subjective and your own opinion on who should or shouldn't be on it is just as valid, if not more so, as that of the author.

DUANE ALLMAN
1946–1971

Even today, many still mourn the tragic passing of Duane Allman, a man whose death at the age of 24 in a motorcycle accident left the music world scratching its head, wondering what might have been.

Allman first made his mark in the late 1960s as a session player on the Muscle Shoals scene. Here he worked with many of Atlantic's top stars like Clarence Carter, Wilson Pickett and Aretha Franklin. His reputation soared, some finding it hard to believe that his electrifying fusion of soul and blues could be the work of a young white musician.

With the formation of the Allman Brothers Band (with Greg Allman and Dickey Betts) in 1969, Duane Allman was at once elevated to rock's premier division. The three albums released while he was alive provided a showcase for some of the finest bottleneck slide guitar playing ever heard. Also remarkable was that two such outstanding guitarists could co-exist within one band, Betts' country leanings complementing Allman's fiery passion to the full. In spite of his band's rapidly growing reputation, Allman still found time to pursue a session career – it's strange to think he is probably best remembered for his solo on an Eric Clapton record (Derek and the Dominoes' "Layla"), rather than for cutting some of the definitive solos in rock history.

CHET ATKINS
1924–

Country music's greatest virtuoso guitarist, Chet Atkins is one of the architects of the Nashville Sound. At the heart of his playing style lies an awesome fingerpicking technique and sophisticated syncopation of muted bass strings. This has been a major influence on every notable country player of the past 40 years – little wonder, then, that he is so widely known as "Mr Guitar," or more recently "Chet Atkins CGP – Certified Guitar Picker."

Born in 1924 in the Appalachian hamlet of Luttrell, Tennessee, Chet Atkins was surrounded by music from an early age, both his parents and grandfather having been musicians. His first great influence was his half-brother James (his elder by 12 years) who was already a well-established country performer having played with another of Chet's heroes, Les Paul.

DUANE ALLMAN: PERHAPS THE GREATEST ROCK GUITARIST TO DON A BOTTLENECK.

A prodigious talent, at the age of 18 Atkins successfully auditioned to join the house band on Knoxville's WNOX radio station. Within months he was given his own daily solo spot. By his early twenties he had worked on dozens of similar country radio stations, although his style of playing, which introduced elements of jazz to his country picking, was sometimes viewed as too arty for the down-the-line barn dance music he was paid to play.

In 1947 he began his long association with the RCA label. Although his first few records were not as successful as had been hoped, the label felt he had the potential to be a new Merle Travis. Six years later they were rewarded with his first solo instrumental hit, "Gallopin' Guitars." That same year, Atkins' career shifted up a gear when he joined Mother Maybelle and the Carter Sisters. They were invited to play at Nashville's Grand Ole Opry.

Although Atkins has been a successful hit artist in his own right, much of his finest work has been heard accompanying others. In fact, it's no exaggeration to say that every major Nashville artist of the period – Hank Williams, Faron Young, Porter Wagoner, Waylon Jennings, to name but a few – enjoyed some level of involvement with the Chet Atkins sound. Such was the strength of his public association with the guitar that manufacturer Gretsch gave him his own signature models, one of which was the legendary "Country Gentleman" – named from one of Atkins' instrumental hits. He stayed linked to Gretsch until 1977, when he switched to Gibson, who also gave him his own signature model.

Much of Atkins' long-standing influence has come not only from the fact that he is country's greatest ever guitarist, but from his role in the music business as well. During the mid-1950s he began managing RCA's studios in Nashville's Music Row, and acted as a freelance talent-spotter for the label. It was this period that saw him steer country music towards a newly sophisticated sound – it was christened the Nashville Sound.

Atkins was soon promoted to RCA's Head Of Operations for Nashville, making him country's most important record executive – in time, Music Row would become as much a shrine for country fans as Chess Studios or Sun Studios are to fans of blues or rock 'n' roll. His significance to the development of modern country music was ratified in 1973 when, at the age of 49, he was indicted into the Country Music Hall of Fame. He is still the youngest person to receive such an honour.

Having long since become bored with the business side of music, in 1981 Atkins resigned from his executive position at RCA to concentrate on the thing he loved the most – playing the guitar. He still records and performs widely and has also produced a number of best-selling tutorial videos that illustrate the sheer complexity of his picking technique. Too often in the past, simple song formats have led to country players being overlooked by listeners of more "serious" types of music. Chet Atkins' pursuit of musical excellence stands alongside virtuosos in any genre.

CHET ATKINS, CGP (CERTIFIED GUITAR PICKER).

JEFF BECK
1944–

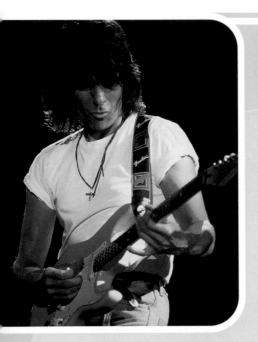

JEFF BECK, AN UNCOMPROMISING MUSICIAN.

More than any other contemporary guitar legend, Jeff Beck is perhaps the very essence of the cliché "the guitarist's guitarist." Much to the chagrin of those who have tried to impose their will on his direction, Beck has shown time and time again that he will do what he wants to do, and commercial considerations don't necessarily get a look-in.

An art school student, Beck's professional career leapt out of the starting gate in 1965 when he joined the Yardbirds, Britain's premier blues band. He was given the thankless task of replacing Eric Clapton, a blues purist uncomfortable with the band's new-found pop success. Undaunted, Beck steered the Yardbirds through a transitional phase as they became one of the most original rock bands of the mid-1960s. Classic cuts such as "Evil Hearted You," "Shapes Of Things" and "Heart Full Of Soul" capture Beck in all his youthful glory – a technical wizard whose playing seemed to based firmly on pure instinct.

Not the most conformist of characters, Beck parted company with the Yardbirds while touring America in 1966, the addition of session man Jimmy Page to the line-up having affected the band's chemistry. While the Yardbirds came apart (to re-emerge two years later as Led Zeppelin), Beck engaged on a solo career that over the next thirty years would be glorious, difficult and bizarre in broadly equal measures.

Signed up by pop impresario Mickey Most for his new RAK label, Beck cut a series of extraordinary singles which brought him brief pop stardom. Hits included an instrumental version of "Love Is Blue" and the party perennial "Hi Ho Silver Lining," which revealed his vocal talents to be less advanced than his guitar work. Sensibly retreating, he formed his own Jeff Beck Group in 1968, with vocalist Rod Stewart and guitarist Ronnie Wood (who switched to bass for the gig). Playing extensively throughout

Britain and the US over the next year they showed themselves to be the only real competition for Led Zeppelin in the blues-based heavy rock stakes. But it didn't last long – Beck's unpredictable behaviour affected their success in reaching the audience they deserved. Stewart and Wood teamed up with ex-members of the Small Faces to form the Faces – they would become perhaps the greatest live band of the 1970s.

Beck devoted much of the 1970s to session work and jazz-rock fusion. Among those benefiting from his tasteful contributions were Stevie Wonder – indeed, Beck's spine-tingling solo on "Lookin' For Another Pure Love" from the *Talking Book* album is surely one of the finest ever consigned to tape.

Those who favour Beck in his "guitar hero" mode usually cite *Blow By Blow*, produced by George Martin, or *Wired*, on which he shared the limelight with synthesist Jan Hammer. Both albums showcased a growing interest in jazz, even if his fusion take on Charles Mingus' "Goodbye Pork Pie Hat" would not have amused too many purists. Although he has continued to play as a hired hand since the 1980s, sessioning with Mick Jagger, Buddy Guy and Kate Bush, to name but a small sample, his own releases have become more sporadic, if not downright mercurial – 1993 saw the release of *Crazy Legs*, a bizarrely out-of-character tribute to little-known 1950s rockabilly guitarist Cliff Gallup.

The rollercoaster ride that has been Jeff Beck's career has undoubtedly been compounded by a genuine compulsion to follow his own muse rather than satisfying managers, record labels or fans. Although admirably uncompromising, he continues to enjoy a smaller scale of commercial success than many of his considerably less capable peers.

GEORGE BENSON
1943–

George Benson is largely known to mainstream audiences as the silky-smooth voice behind such million-selling soul hits as "Give Me The Night." A much smaller number are aware of his considerable contributions to jazz and his total mastery of the guitar.

Singing and playing the ukulele from an early age, Benson was a prodigious talent who cut his first record at the age of 11. While still in his teens he recorded sessions with the Hammond players Jimmy Smith and Brother Jack McDuff for top jazz labels Blue

Note and Prestige. In 1965 he formed his own quartet and shortly afterwards recorded a series of highly rated (if not commercially successful) albums for Columbia.

The 1970s saw Benson increasingly drawn to the jazz-crossover market. It was in 1976 that he hit paydirt with the easy-listening classic *Breezin'* – the biggest-selling jazz album of all time.

GEORGE BENSON: THE BIGGEST-SELLING JAZZ GUITARIST BY SOME DISTANCE.

Although the title track was a Top 10 hit in its own right – an unusual feat for an instrumental – it was the follow-up, Leon Russell's "'This Masquerade," that introduced his voice to pop audiences. Displaying hints of both Stevie Wonder and Nat King Cole (another great musician whose vocal success overshadowed his influential playing), this set the pattern for future releases well into the 1980s – Benson's playing took a back seat role.

Strongly influenced by Wes Montgomery and to a lesser extent by Tal Farlow, Benson remains among the greatest of jazz soloists: even his most commercial releases have often featured superbly executed instrumental flourishes, sometimes played in unison with scat-style vocals.

CHUCK BERRY
1926–

There is a good case for citing Chuck Berry as one of the most influential guitarists of all time, and few could argue with the view that he is the most significant musician in the early development of rock 'n' roll.

Berry arrived on the music scene relatively late in life. Although he had taught himself a few chords at high school, he didn't take the guitar seriously until he was in his mid-twenties. While playing in his own trio, a meeting with Muddy Waters put Berry in contact with Leonard Chess, the owner of the famous Chicago-based blues label, Chess Records. Initially following a blues path, Chess was impressed with his own up-tempo material. Berry's first single at the end of 1955, "Maybellene," was the first R&B record to make a really big impact on white audiences.

Over the next decade Berry wrote numerous rock 'n' roll classics, many of which feature some of the most immediately recognizable guitar riffs ever recorded. A style of playing that simultaneously mixed rhythm and lead elements was a major influence of the next generation of young guitarists, among them Keith Richards of the Rolling Stones.

Berry was also a pioneering lyricist. His songs were full-blooded mini-soaps at a time when pop lyrics at best skirted around "real" issues. In fact, Berry put the case for the American teenage lifestyle of the 1950s better than just·about anyone – mildly ironic in that he was already well into his thirties when he wrote such classics as "Route 66" and "Johnny B. Goode."

In spite of his indisputable importance in the history and development of popular music, Berry seems to have been unimpressed with precious accolades. He has always seen himself more as an entertainer going about making his living, rather than one of the great "artists" of the post-war era.

CHUCK BERRY ALMOST SINGLE-HANDEDLY WROTE THE ROCK 'N' ROLL GUITAR BOOK.

GLENN BRANCA
1948–

It is Glenn Branca's innovative approach to composition that is noteworthy in taking the guitar into new and exciting territories. His style takes an orchestral approach that crosses the idea of a classical symphony with something approaching New York indie thrash. In fact, Branca's early work featured Sonic Youth's Thurston Moore and Lee Renaldo and was released on US thrash labels.

GLENN BRANCA – A NEW FORM OF CLASSICAL GUITAR?

Although Branca's "orchestras" are not restricted only to the guitar, they form the primary components. The most interesting aspect is that conventional tuning is abandoned. Each string of the guitar is tuned to the same note, although not all of the instruments are tuned to the same note. This creates a monumentally powerful impact, especially in an auditorium where the volume can be overwhelming.

JULIAN BREAM
1933–

Although there remains one pre-eminent name in the world of the classical guitar – the great Andrés Segovia – if one musician can be said to have carried on in the master's tradition it is Julian Bream.

Born in London in 1933, Bream was first taught to play guitar by his father, an amateur musician. However, it was exposure to records by Segovia that fired his passion for the instrument. His first formal lessons were taken with exiled Russian guitarist Boris Perrot. He took a major step forward in 1947 when Segovia first played in London. Bream not only attended the recital but received some personal tuition from the master himself. That same year he gave his first solo performance.

Bream's formal music education consisted of studying the piano and cello at London's principal music establishment, the Royal College of Music. It seems strange to imagine that, in spite of the work of Segovia, even then the guitar was not on the curriculum in music schools (see The Torres Revolution and the Classical Guitar). In fact, there was no professor of the guitar at the Royal College until 1960, when Bream's friend and collaborator John Williams (the other great post-Segovia guitarist) was offered the position.

On leaving music school Bream was obliged to do a period of National Service in the army. He chose to join the Royal Artillery, primarily so he could join the regiment's dance band. It was here he had his first experience of the electric guitar, but it was not one that he would repeat too often during this career. His first classical recital was in 1951 at London's Wigmore Hall. Like Segovia's previously, Bream's early concert career drew a large part of its repertoire from the player's own transcriptions of music written for other instruments, a fine example being his 1957 recording of works by J S Bach, most of which were originally written for the organ.

BREAM IS PERHAPS THE MOST SIGNIFICANT CLASSICAL GUITARIST SINCE SEGOVIA.

By the end of the 1950s, Bream had established a worldwide reputation for his playing. During the following decade his public fame and the respect held for him within the music world enabled him to make perhaps his greatest, lasting contributions to the classical guitar. Throughout the 1960s Bream commissioned some of the finest post-war composers to produce pieces for the guitar. In fact, many of the works written specifically for Bream are standard parts of the modern classical repertoire. Lennox Berkeley wrote *Sonatina* in 1958, Benjamin Britten wrote *Nocturnal* in 1964 – other composers adding their weight to the growing canon have included Richard Rodney Bennett and Hans Werner Henze.

As he began his career, Bream also took up the lute, primarily to offer him a second source of income when guitar work dried up. In fact, Bream has brought the same scholarly approach to this instrument, to point where he is now widely considered to be the finest lutenist working in the world.

While Bream and John Williams are widely spoken of in the same breath – there are many who rate Williams every bit Bream's equal as a player – it is Bream's work in broadening the classical repertoire, either as a commissioner, transcriber, or archaeologist of obscure works from the past, that makes him the most valuable classical guitarist of the post-war era.

ROY BUCHANAN, ONE OF THE FINEST PLAYERS TO STRAP ON A TELECASTER.

ROY BUCHANAN
1939–1988

In the 1970s, Roy Buchanan was known as one of the finest players working between the fringes of blues and rock – a master craftsman more appreciated by his fellow players than the public at large. And he seemed happy with that, more concerned with the important business of making music than being famous. Yet a decade after his death – he hanged himself in a police cell – Roy Buchanan stands on the brink of being sadly forgotten.

Starting out as a sideman with rocker Dale Hawkins in the late 1950s, Buchanan put in ten years of relatively anonymous session work before beginning a solo career in 1972. His playing style was strongly centred on the blues tradition – Albert King being a particular favourite. However, his breakneck solo flourishes were more akin to jazz players in the Charlie Christian mould.

Buchanan's reputation was forged with albums like *That's What I'm Here For* and *A Street Called Straight*, on which his ever-present Telecaster invariably burned a hole through largely undistinguished material. And this seems to have been his problem – apart from the awesome guitar technique his music had little widespread appeal. His legacy is having influenced some of the finest guitar craftsmen, among them Jeff Beck. This alone must make him worthy of the title "The Guitarists' Guitarist's Guitarist."

MARTIN CARTHY
1941–

A pivotal figure of the English folk movement, Martin Carthy has over the past thirty years played with every major name associated with the scene, from the Watersons to Steeleye Span.

Like many British teenagers growing up during the 1950s, Carthy found the impetus to learn guitar with skiffle and the music of Lonnie Donegan. When skiffle fell from fashion, many of the musicians who hadn't drifted towards R&B explored traditional folk forms. It was here that Carthy found his true direction. Developing a fingerpicking style which combined American folk idioms with the phrasing of indigenous Celtic music, he recorded a succession of albums, many with violinist Dave Swarbrick (Fairport Convention), all of which successfully used the traditional English folk song as a point of development.

Carthy was an early member of the successful folk-rock group Steeleye Span, who took traditional songs and gave them rock arrangements. But Carthy never seemed entirely at ease playing electric guitar, and left the band before their most commercial period. He continued to work intermittently in the folk-rock sphere with the Albion Band.

Although Carthy's music is quintessentially English, he is now among the most respected folk guitarists in the world.

CHARLIE CHRISTIAN
1916–1942

Whilst Django Reinhardt had pioneered and mastered the use of the acoustic guitar as a solo instrument during the 1930s, it was Charlie Christian who made a similar leap forward for the newly developed amplified guitar. Part of the mystique surrounding Christian is the unbelievable impact he made during such a brief career. The entire body of his recorded works were produced within a period of barely three years before his tragic death in 1942 at the age of 25.

Charlie Christian was born into a musical family. His father had been a professional singer and guitarist, and all four of his brothers were also musicians. He became adept on the trumpet, double bass and piano before realizing that the guitar was his forte, although it was as a bassist that he first found paid work, in 1934.

It was seeing Eddie Durham playing an amplified arch-top guitar in the Jimmie Lunceford band in 1937 that first aroused Christian to the possibilities offered by the instrument. Spotted by jazz entrepreneur John Hammond, he was recommended to Benny Goodman, who showed little interest in auditioning him. According to jazz mythology, Hammond organized Christian to gatecrash one of Goodman's shows – enraged at first, then hearing the audience response to Christian's playing, Goodman gave him the job. Within a year he was widely recognized as the finest jazz

CHARLIE CHRISTIAN PLAYING A GIBSON ES-150.

guitarist working in America. (Belgian-born Django Reinhardt's reputation had reached epic proportions, but it would be another six years before he was to cross the Atlantic.) Barely four years later – after redefining the meaning of jazz guitar – he was dead, having contracted pneumonia while convalescing from tuberculosis. It was said that Christian was a victim of the pace of the Big City life, to which this Oklahoma farm-boy never happily adapted.

Although Christian remained with Goodman until his death, it was his extra-curricular activity during his final year that cemented his position as one of the most influential figures of his time. He became a key player in the regular after-hours jam sessions at Minton's Playhouse in Harlem, New York, which brought together a new generation of gifted, technically brilliant young musicians like Charlie Parker, Dizzy Gillespie and Thelonious Monk. It was the birthplace of bebop – a movement that would permanently change the face of jazz.

Considering his influence in the development of jazz guitar and new musical directions, Charlie Christian remains a slightly controversial figure. Whilst his sweeping, high-speed flurries and complex use of harmony redefined the electric guitar as a solo instrument, some critics of the past have claimed that he simply adapted the style of saxophone genius Lester Young to another instrument. For the guitarists who followed in his footsteps, however, he was viewed as nothing less than a genius. It was not until the arrival of Wes Montgomery in the late 1960s that a similar influence on jazz guitar would emerge.

As with other great bebop players of the period, through the legacy of his recordings, the power and emotion of Charlie Christian's playing continues to thrill each successive generation of guitarists.

ERIC CLAPTON
1945–

1963 was the year that the British R&B scene really took off. The Rolling Stones had already carved out a reputation based on their Sunday night residency at Richmond's Crawdaddy Club. The Stones were followed by the Yardbirds, featuring 18-year-old Eric Clapton on lead guitar.

Clapton had grown up listening to Chicago bluesmen, in particular Big Bill Broonzy and Muddy Waters. To him the Yardbirds were an extension of this tradition, but when a pop

ERIC CLAPTON. HE TRADED THE LICKS FOR WORLDWIDE AOR SUCCESS.

song – Graham Gouldman's "For Your Love" – was chosen for their debut single, he decided to leave the band.

Clapton next found himself working alongside British blues veteran John Mayall in the Bluesbreakers. With them he established himself as one of Britain's greatest home-grown talents. Essentially applying a refined technique to Muddy Waters' emotive playing style, Clapton's effortless performances earned him the ironic nickname "slowhand." Worldwide fame came in 1966 when he formed Cream – the first rock power trio. The idea of duplicating guitar riffs on the bass provided the template for most of the heavy rock bands that followed in their wake.

Thereafter, Clapton began to show errors of judgement that would continue to dog his career. The first was the formation of "supergroup" Blind Faith with Steve Winwood, which barely stumbled out of the starting gate. He next chose to step back, working as backing player for Delaney and Bonnie. In 1970 he put together his first band, Derek and the Dominoes. Although their only album produced the rock classic "Layla," it was Duane Allman who took credit for the guitar heroics.

During the first half of the 1970s, Clapton was inactive, fighting a battle against heroin addiction. Since then his solo career has increased momentum to the point where he is once again among the most successful guitarists in any genre. Despite the recent tendency towards adult-oriented rock, Clapton's instrumental greatness and the appeal of his voice continue to guarantee him popularity.

RY COODER
1947–

In trying to evaluate the music of Ry Cooder one is faced with the problem of the sheer diversity of his expertise. That he is one of the finest guitarists of his generation is beyond dispute. However, the fact that he has managed to assimilate the widest variety of jazz, country, blues and rock styles with such brilliance is little short of miraculous.

A largely self-taught player, Ryland Peter Cooder first picked up the guitar at the age of three. In his teens, he developed an interest in traditional blues forms while listening to old recordings of Josh White. Living in Los Angeles, as a teenager he gravitated towards the Ash Grove – the home of the LA blues scene. It was here that he met ragtime blues legend Reverend Gary Davis, an association that led him to investigate bottleneck guitar and other traditional instruments such as the mandolin and banjo.

It was also at the Grove that the 17-year-old Cooder met another guitarist, Taj Mahal. The pair, both naturally curious to experiment with new musical forms, began a brief but rewarding collaboration under the name the Rising Sons. Although Taj Mahal vanished from LA before they could complete their intended recording debut, the mysterious bluesman remained a significant influence on the young Cooder.

By the time he was 20 Cooder was a well known figure on the West Coast blues scene, and had already established himself as an in-demand session player. One of his first freelance jobs was as a hired hand on Captain Beefheart's 1967 debut *Safe As Milk*. Although the recording process was said to be chaotic, and the Captain was not the easiest person to get along with, the end result was an impressive one, paving the way for the ground-breaking *Trout Mask Replica*. For the next two years Cooder seemed to work

THE TERM ECLECTIC DOESN'T DO JUSTICE TO THE BREADTH OF RY COODER'S MUSIC INTERESTS.

with just about every West Coast artist from popsters Paul Revere and the Raiders to the eminent Randy Newman.

Cooder first came to the attention of a wider public in 1969 when he was brought to London by producer Jack Nitzsche to work on the Rolling Stones' *Let It Bleed* album. So successful was the association that he was even rumoured to be first choice as replacement for the Stones' late guitarist, Brian Jones. But it was the other paid work he undertook while in England that would have a greater impact on his future. Working with Nitzsche, he recorded the soundtrack to the film *Candy*. It was first of many soundtracks he would compose and record over the next three decades.

With his stock as a session man running so high, the Reprise label offered Cooder the chance to record his own solo album. His 1970 debut, *Ry Cooder*, provided a showcase for his blues and folk inclinations, covering a wide selection of twentieth-century American songs. Although less successful in some other ways, it showed the attention to the smallest detail that would characterize his future recordings, and that would earn him a reputation as something of an academic of historical American musical forms.

Cooder's debut also hinted at the eclectic choice of styles and materials that was to follow. Future albums would see him tackle classical guitar (*Boomer's Story*, 1973), gospel (*Paradise And Lunch*, 1974), Hawaiian music (*Chicken Skin Music*, 1976), old-time jazz (*Jazz*, 1978), and rock 'n' roll (*Bop Till You Drop*, 1979), each one

masterfully researched, performed and recorded. These albums saw Cooder amass an unexpected and substantial following in Europe, peaking with *The Slide Area*, which hit the British Top 20. Impressive as all of these works undoubtedly are, however, his thirst for experimentation has confounded those critics who have been unable to make the necessary mental leap from, say, a Bix Beiderbecke tune to The Drifters' "Money Honey" on successive albums.

It is, however, in his parallel career composing music for cinema soundtracks that Cooder has perhaps been most consistently successful. In fact, since the early 1980s Cooder's slide bottleneck playing has become almost obligatory for certain types of road movie, such as the widely admired *Paris, Texas*, on which he uses the simplest of slide devices to echo the barren landscapes seen throughout the film. But perhaps his greatest success came in the late 1990s with the release of the Cooder-produced *Buena Vista Social Club* album and film, which were made in collaboration with some of Cuba's finest (and oldest) musicians.

ROBERT CRAY
1953–

The most commercially successful of the latest generation of blues musicians, Cray is unusual in that he came to the blues via the rock, soul and funk he listened to as a teenager. It was a chance meeting with Albert Collins' bass player that took Cray straight from playing in his school band to second guitar with arguably the greatest post-war blues musician.

In 1975 Cray left Collins to form his own band. A solid-gigging outfit, by the middle of the 1980s they had recorded a series of Grammy-winning albums which transformed Cray into the biggest-selling blues artist of the period. He also began to attract attention in the rock world, his profile rising as a result of regular appearances with Eric Clapton.

The key to Cray's success has been in redefining the traditional blues of Collins and Muddy Waters and infusing it with a feel that comes close to the great house bands of 1960s soul. While his period with Albert Collins clearly made an impact on him – Cray, too, has often used the open minor tuning – the influence of guitarists from other genres, such as Steve Cropper or Jimi Hendrix can also be heard.

ROBERT CRAY UPDATED THE CLASSICAL ELECTRIC BLUES SOUND.

STEVE CROPPER
1942–

During the 1960s the guitar solo was the measure by which a guitarist was usually judged. Often it was a case of the faster and flashier the technique the better. In the more enlightened 1990s we came to accept that space and taste can tell us far more about a player's worth. Steve Cropper might not have topped many guitarists polls at the peak of his career in the mid-1960s. And yet three decades on he is widely rated as one of the masters of his instrument.

It was while still at university that Steve Cropper enjoyed his first flush of success. When his old high-school band the Royal Spades – renamed the Mar-Keys – produced the instrumental hit "Last Night," Cropper quit his engineering course to concentrate on music. Playing around the Memphis area, the Mar-Keys became the original house band for the Stax and Volt labels, not only recording under their own name, but acting as backing band for the label's burgeoning vocal talent.

The Mar-Keys' formula was simple but effective: stabbing horns played over Cropper's crisp rhythm phrasing and Donald "Duck" Dunn's loping bass lines. It was a unique sound that helped to define what became known as Southern Soul. Indeed, for many years – given the musical company he kept – many listeners assumed that he must have been a black musician, rather than a clean-cut, middle-class American.

Leaving the Mar-Keys, Cropper moved towards studio work, writing and producing hits for the Stax label. At the same time,

STEVE CROPPER – THE FINEST RHYTHM
PLAYER OF THEM ALL.

he put together a new studio band featuring Dunn and the prodigious keyboard talents of 16-year-old Booker T Jones. They called themselves the MGs. The legend was created one hot summer afternoon in 1962. A session had been scheduled to record a singer named Billy Lee Riley. When Riley failed to turn up, the MGs whiled away the time jamming around a simple blues progression. Startled by what he was hearing, Stax owner and session engineer Jim Stewart switched on a tape machine and recorded the jam. He was impressed and thought the results were releasable. He encouraged the band to play on. This time they fooled around with a riff Jones had been working on – within a few hours one of the all-time classic R&B instrumentals, "Green Onions," had been born.

A chart hit the world over, Booker T and the MGs (as Stax christened them) followed up with a succession of hip grooves that appealed to black and white audiences alike – a rare achievement in the pre-integrated Deep South of 1962. Hits like "Soul Dressing," "Boot-Leg," "My Sweet Potato," "Groovin'," "Soul Limbo" and "Time Is Tight" made the MGs the most successful instrumental R&B band of all time.

And yet there is so much more to Steve Cropper's story than this. Functioning as the Stax house band, the same line-up backed up virtually every soul artist who recorded for the label right through to the late 1960s. The Stax and Volt roster at this time reads like an A to Z of soul and R&B – names like Otis Redding, Sam and Dave, Rufus Thomas, Carla Thomas, Eddie Floyd, William Bell and Johnnie Taylor, to name but a few.

Many of the biggest Stax hits were written and produced by Cropper, and featured his sparse, measured rhythm work. Some of his most successful compositions include timeless soul classics like "Dock Of The Bay," "Midnight Hour" and "Knock On Wood." Examples of his work can be heard on the awesome nine-CD box detailing singles released on the Stax and Volt labels between 1959 and 1968.

In the late 1970s Cropper and Dunn joined forces with Levon Helm (of the Band) to play in the RCO All-Stars – a kind of 1960s R&B soul review. This led to their recruitment as members of the Blues Brothers Band, lending a rare authenticity to the film starring John Belushi and Dan Aykroyd. The film, *The Blues Brothers*, and its soundtrack were a massive success, which spawned some live tours and a further two albums before Belushi's death.

In 1988 the three surviving MGs (drummer Al Jackson was murdered in 1975) reunited for a series of shows, and in 1992 they received the ultimate music industry accolade as they were inducted into the Rock and Roll Hall of Fame.

That same year they acted as the house band for the Bob Dylan tribute concert held at New York's Madison Square Garden. Here they were given the task of backing everyone from Eric Clapton, Stevie Wonder and George Harrison to Lou Reed, Johnny Cash and Neil Young. Suitably impressed by their virtuosity, Young then asked the group to accompany him as his backing band on his 1993 tours of Europe and North America.

Throughout his career, Cropper has always seemed happy to let others grab the limelight, and yet his unique ability for writing and playing simple, yet immediately recognizable, licks is second to none.

DICK DALE
1937–

In the early 1960s, before the Beach Boys had gripped America, Dick Dale was the undisputed king of surf guitar. The technique and sound of the left-hander epitomized the surf instrumental. By alternating pick strokes at a lightning speed Dale was able to produce a unique staccato sound on his Stratocaster. When smothered in a heavy spring reverb its overall effect simulated the rhythm of riding the surf. His playing had many imitators – not least Carl Wilson of the Beach Boys.

In spite of his heroic status in California, Dale was overshadowed by the Beach Boys as they became one of the few bands in America capable of rivalling the Beatles during the 1960s. By the time he retired from the music world in 1969, in favour of a life of farming and surfing, he was largely a forgotten figure.

Nonetheless, independent reissues of Dale's records have enthralled successive generations and by the 1980s he had become something of a cult figure for many young guitarists. He finally hit the big time in 1995 when Quentin Tarantino used his recording of "Miserlou" as the main theme for the film *Pulp Fiction*. The track became one of the most heavily played instrumentals of the 1990s and Dale was lured out of retirement, whereupon he showed the world that at 60 his left hand was still firing as fast as ever.

BO DIDDLEY
1928–

A stablemate of Chuck Berry at Chess
Records, Bo Diddley's contribution to
the guitar is based on a unique approach
to rhythm.

Although he was a Chicago blues
player, he rarely used the traditional
12-bar structure, his songs often appearing
as a series of lengthy verses punctuated by
the odd break. Many of his best-known
songs were played on a single chord.
His formula was a simple one: his own
chugging guitar melded with the bass,
drums, piano and maracas to produce a
unified rhythmic front that he called his
"jungle" sound.

Although Diddley never really hit the big
time himself, his approach to rhythm seeped
into the mainstream through the young
white blues bands of the early 1960s. The
early Rolling Stones did note-for-note covers
of some of his songs, and the trademark
jerky rhythm can be heard on pop hits like
"Not Fade Away." Later, Diddley's "Cops
And Robbers" provided inspiration for
David Bowie's "Jean Genie."

JOHN FAHEY
1939–

A singular musician, John Fahey is a
guitarist like no other. He is a superlative
solo performer and his steel-string
instruments traverse the boundaries of
country, blues and folk. In spite of a
succession of album and song titles that
seem unhealthily obsessed with the darker
side of life – such as the marvellously titled
Death Chants, Breakdowns and Military

BO DIDDLEY – "500 PER CENT MORE MAN," AS HE CLAIMED.

Waltzes – his music is without exception passionate, exhilarating and uplifting.

Fahey built up a considerable following on the 1960s folk circuit, and his unusually avant-garde approach to what has tended to be – almost by definition – a form aimed at preserving tradition has attracted many admirers, and influenced a great many other guitarists, among them one of his few collaborators, Leo Kottke.

Through a remarkably consistent 40-year career, Fahey has pursued his path with single-minded zeal. Truly an uncompromising artist.

ROBERT FRIPP
1946–

It's not unusual for experimental protagonists to find themselves sidelined, their impact on the mainstream restricted to the occasional subtle dose. Although Robert Fripp has had more mainstream successes than most in his field, they are in no way in line with the influence he has exerted on several generations of guitarists and experimental soundmakers.

King Crimson were one of the most interesting of the progressive rock bands. It was largely the carefully balanced playing of Robert Fripp that set them apart from others in

JOHN FAHEY IS ONE OF THE MOST UNUSUAL GUITARISTS OF THE PAST FORTY YEARS.

the field. Quite simply, there always seemed to be a good reason for what Fripp was playing. In the early 1970s he hooked up with Brian Eno, with whom he made the ground-breaking "Frippertronics" albums – a technique he developed that involved passing tape across the heads of two linked Revox tape recorders, enabling lengthy loops of sound to be layered into lush soundscapes over which Fripp could then play solo parts.

One of the few prog-rock musicians whose reputation increased throughout the new wave era, Fripp resuscitated King Crimson in 1980 in a line-up featuring Adrian Below. The two guitarists interlocked brilliantly on their "debut" album *Discipline*.

In recent years Fripp has concentrated on his Guitar Craft schools, teaching an alternative philosophy of the instrument that includes altered standard tunings, and recording with Guitar Craft students or his wife – former new wave star Toyah Willcox.

ROBERT FRIPP, ONE OF THE INTELLECTUALS OF ROCK GUITAR.

PETER GREEN
1946–

The saga of Peter Greenbaum is one of the strangest in rock history. Another high-profile graduate of John Mayall's Bluesbreakers, he first appeared on the 1966 album *A Hard Road*, given the fearsome job of filling the slot vacated by Mayall's previous discovery, Eric Clapton. Green was easily up to it, impressing with a more measured, economical style.

Green left Mayall the following year to form Fleetwood Mac. Combining self-penned hits, such as the classic instrumental "Albatross" and a smattering of covers like Willie John's "Need Your Love So Bad," Fleetwood Mac became one of the biggest-selling British bands of the late 1960s.

With a rare luxury of being loved by blues purists, music critics and the mainstream record buyer, Green seemed to have the world at his feet. But all was not well. In 1970, with the band at its peak, he quit and retired from the music world. Since then he is rumoured to have given away all of his guitars and to have variously been a tramp, gravedigger and hospital orderly. But such tales have boosted his reputation as one of rock's great enigmas and the late 1990s saw his most concerted period of activity since his heyday.

BUDDY GUY
1936–

The original young gun of the Chicago blues scene, even though he's more than 60 years old, and at an age when most bluesmen have already become venerated senior statesmen, Buddy Guy still plays and performs with a life-loving zeal that most players half his age would be hard pressed to match.

Guy was born and raised in Lettsworth, Louisiana. He learned to play guitar at the age of 13 on a home-built instrument. His earliest influence was John Lee Hooker. Unlike many of his peers,

PETER GREEN WITH HIS LES PAUL STANDARD.

who struggled for years before gaining recognition, Guy was something of a prodigious blues talent. By the time he was 17 he was already performing with such notables as Slim Harpo, Lazy Lester and Lightnin' Slim.

It was when he decided to move to Chicago at the age of 21 that his career shifted into the next gear. Initially finding it a struggle to live, under the guidance of Muddy Waters he honed his raw fret work so successfully that in 1958 he was able to beat Otis Rush, Junior Wells and Magic Sam in a Battle of the Blues contest at the Blue Flame Club. As a result of this success he was signed up to the Cobra label, where he worked as a back-up player and was given the chance to cut some sides of his own.

In 1960, having impressed no lesser name than Willie Dixon, Guy joined the legendary Chess label, where he recorded with the likes of Muddy Waters and Howlin' Wolf. His association with Chess only lasted for five years, but it was during this period that he recorded some of his best work. In 1965 he moved to Sam Charters' Vanguard label, probably hitting his peak with fine albums like *A Man And His Blues* and *This Is Buddy Guy*. 1965 was also the year he formed a particularly fertile association with singer and harmonica player Junior Wells. The pair would record and perform together intermittently over the next 25 years.

The 1970s were a difficult time for some blues artists. Often overshadowed by the growth of rock and the developing soul scene, the heyday of Chicago blues was well and truly a thing of the past. Whilst Guy continued to record and perform increasingly in Europe, where his regular performances at the Montreux jazz festival invariably stole the show, back in Chicago things were tougher. He chose to open up his own club, the Checkerboard Lounge, where he busied himself performing on a small stage most nights – and sometimes behind the bar. A small venue, the club attracted packed houses, including numerous visiting rock musicians, eager to see one of the greatest blues players working in a small club setting.

 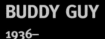

The 1980s saw Buddy Guy re-emerge with a new-found confidence. Blues was gradually gaining a new audience, aided by the emergence of new stars like Robert Cray, who infused elements of rock and soul and championed modern production values. The decade ended with the dazzling reinvention of John Lee Hooker, who at the age of 69 leapt back into the spotlight with *The Healer*, the biggest-selling blues album of all time.

Joining Hooker's British-based Silvertone label, Guy recorded his own "comeback" album in 1991. *Damn Right, I've Got The Blues* gave Guy his biggest-selling single album and established him as, arguably, the greatest living Chicago bluesman. He continues to perform all over the world.

BUDDY GUY, THE GREATEST LIVING CHICAGO BLUESMAN.

GEORGE HARRISON
1943–2001

When discussing the development of the modern guitar, the name George Harrison is all too frequently overlooked. And yet his influence, even if you view him as "merely" the lead guitarist in the most popular group of all time, is extremely significant.

It is beyond doubt that a number of interesting developments in the use of the guitar were first popularized – sometimes even initiated – by the Beatles. "I Feel Fine" features feedback, the first time such a sound had hit the pop charts. The driving guitar sound of "Paperback Writer" led John Lennon to dub it "the first heavy metal record." There was the studio trickery heard on the pioneering psychedelic classic "Tomorrow Never Knows," the fuzz box heard throughout "Revolution" – and would the exotic sound of the sitar (and such widespread fascination with all things Indian, for that matter) have been so characteristic of the era without Harrison's pioneering interest shown on album tracks like "Within You Without You"?

But what of George Harrison's playing? Throughout most of the Beatles' career he showed extreme restraint as a lead player, offering crucial licks rather than taking a rip-roaring solo. Their final recording, the *Abbey Road* album (recorded after *Let It Be*, but released before it), signalled Harrison's stepping out. For the first time, his own compositions could seriously be viewed as among the strongest on the record. A new self-assurance could be heard in his playing – aided, no doubt, by his close friendship with Eric Clapton – most notably on the beautifully executed solo on "Something."

THE MUCH UNDERRATED
GEORGE HARRISON.

JIMI HENDRIX
1942–1970

As far as the electric era is concerned, one single name towers above all other guitarists – James Marshall Hendrix.

Hendrix was given his first electric guitar in 1954. He learned to play by listening to the first wave of great Chicago blues players such as B B King, Muddy Waters and Elmore James. While he was in the US Army he formed his first band, King Kasuals, with fellow soldier Billy Cox, who would later play with Hendrix again in the Band Of Gypsies.

On leaving the army, he found work as a back-up player for touring rock 'n' roll artists. Among Hendrix's numerous credits were performances with Little Richard, Ike and Tina Turner, B B King and Jackie Wilson. In 1965 he moved to New York where he became a member of the Isley Brothers band. At this stage he was using the pseudonym Jimmy James.

In 1966 Hendrix decided to strike out on his own, forming the band Jimmy James and the Blue Flames. It was while performing at a club in Greenwich Village that he was spotted by Chas Chandler, former bassist with the Animals who was looking to start a career in management. Chandler convinced him that London would be a more suitable environment from which to launch himself. In October 1966, he formed the Jimi Hendrix Experience with drummer Mitch Mitchell and guitarist Noel Redding, who switched over to bass just to get the gig. Chandler immediately found the band a record deal and by the end of the year their debut single "Hey Joe" was a Top 10 hit. Hendrix followed up this immediate success with a sequence of three peerless albums which redefined the electric guitar for every player who followed.

In 1967 Hendrix returned to his home country, where he still remained relatively unknown. The situation changed overnight following his performance at the Monterey Pop Festival. One of the lesser known names on the

bill, he gave a performance that defied the eyes and ears of a massive outdoor crowd, ending a high-octane set by setting fire to his guitar.

Like many inspirational players, Hendrix would continue to be heard at his best in concert. Indeed, the lessons learned while he served his apprenticeship with rock 'n' roll showmen like Little Richard became an unexpectedly valuable asset to his live show, his party pieces including playing the guitar behind his neck or with his teeth, as well as other moves of a more sexual nature.

With US military activity getting out of hand in Vietnam, the rock world would begin to take a vocal stand against the war. By the end of 1968 his shows would climax with his own version of the "Star Spangled Banner," the US national anthem. Starting out as a simple unaccompanied solo, the piece ended with an effective recreation of the noises of warfare – exploding bombs, gunfire – all of them performed on a heavily overdriven guitar. This was captured for eternity at the Woodstock Festival in August 1969 – even if the rest of his set showed that he seemed then to be tiring of the rock 'n' roll treadmill.

This spectacle was widely perceived as a political gesture, although Hendrix himself was less than forthcoming about his views. Whatever he felt about the war in Vietnam was tempered by his respect as a former paratrooper for the military professional. Nonetheless his "protest" brought further unwanted pressure from black radical groups.

Towards the end of his life a never-ending search for new ways to develop took Hendrix into less popular areas. Disbanding the Experience, he formed the Band Of Gypsies with Buddy Miles and Billy Cox. Three virtuoso musicians they may have been, but the results were not widely viewed as the greatest listening experience. However, during the same period he seemed to spend most of his waking hours in recording studios, improvising alone or with anyone (literally) who happened to walk in. In a career which saw the release of only five albums during his lifetime, these recordings (and endless live tapes) have resulted in nearly 500 releases since his drug-related death in 1970.

In the space of just four years, Jimi Hendrix took the electric guitar into uncharted territory, setting new standards for rock and blues improvisation and influencing a generation of musicians like no one before or since.

JAMES MARSHALL HENDRIX TAKING THE GUITAR
INTO UNCHARTED TERRITORY.

JOHN LEE HOOKER
1920–2001

When John Lee Hooker's *The Healer* was released in 1989 few imagined that it would create much of an impression outside the blues scene. Fewer still would have predicted that a 69-year-old man with over 100 albums to his name would suddenly become the hippest thing around, and produce not only the biggest-selling album of his career, but the biggest-selling blues album of all time.

Born in the Mississippi Delta region, Hooker moved on to Detroit in his twenties. In 1948 he made his first recording, "Boogie Chillen." It was as if an alien had arrived from another planet, heard the blues and tried it out – it was that different. But this was no gimmick: fifty years later Hooker still sounds much the same.

The elements that make Hooker's sound so unique are difficult to pinpoint. The guitar and his deep groan of a voice are interwoven so tightly that it is pointless discussing one without the other. But the overriding effect of his style is one of structural freedom – Hooker has never felt the need to adhere to a simple 12-bar formula, moving from bar to bar as he feels fit, extending vocals as the mood takes him.

Throughout his long career, Hooker saw his popularity wax and wane with some regularity, but he remains one of the most influential figures in modern music, who continued to inspire new generations of players right up until his death in 2001.

BLIND LEMON JEFFERSON
(1897–1929)

The first star of the blues, between 1925 and his death Blind Lemon Jefferson was the biggest-selling black artist. He was the first blues guitar player to sell records in any great quantity. And, with a tragic predictability given the time and place he lived, Jefferson saw almost no financial reward and was buried in a pauper's grave.

Born in Couchman, Texas, Jefferson was blind from birth. In his teen years he made his keep begging and performing on the streets of Dallas and Houston. He was later discovered playing at rent parties in Chicago, which led to him cutting the 78s for the Paramount label which brought him fame.

JOHN LEE HOOKER, TOP OF THE BLUES PREMIER LEAGUE.

Jefferson's recordings are now readily available, some of his songs having been passed down to new generations. However, it is his guitar technique that astounds to this day. His peers found it impossible to copy and developed their own takes on the Jefferson style. These players – Leadbelly, Lightnin' Hopkins, Robert Johnson and T-Bone Walker – provided the blueprints from which most R&B and rock guitar styles have evolved. Whilst it's possible (if demanding) to learn one of Jefferson's pieces like "Easy Rider Blues" or "See That My Grave Is Kept Clean," one can never understand *why* he played what he did. And this is the mystery. Rather than accompanying his singing with any conventional structure, much of what he did seemed to be improvising around the theme. As such, analysis fails to come up with any useful conclusion – Jefferson was just doing what came naturally, and he probably didn't give it a great deal of thought himself.

In 1967, blues enthusiasts discovered his unmarked grave at the Negro Cemetery in Wortham, Texas and belatedly added their own fitting tribute – "One Of America's Outstanding Original Musicians."

STANLEY JORDAN
1959–

Stanley Jordan created something of a stir when he performed at the 1984 Kool Festival in New York with what seemed to be a revolutionary approach to playing the guitar. Positioning the instrument on his lap, as if it were a piano keyboard. he presses his fingers down on the fretboard rather than holding notes with his left hand and picking the strings with his right. This gives him the ability to play melodies by hammering on with his right hand, and chords and bass lines by hammering on with his left hand.

Awesomely spectacular though this technique is, it seems a little sad that Jordan – a Princeton music graduate – has so far tended largely to have been marketed as a gimmick. Indeed, his Blue Note debut, on which he played unaccompanied, proudly declared on the jacket that no overdubs had been used in making the record, as if that were particularly important to the quality of the music.

Jordan's music has not advanced as quickly as some might have hoped – his playing style a restrictive variation on jazz piano. He remains, however, in a league of his own, and his progress will continue to be viewed with great interest.

MICHAEL KAROLI
1948–

The genre known as "Krautrock" was one of the oddest to find widespread popularity in the early 1970s, not least because the music, which crossed "hippy" rock improvisation with elements of modern classical, had little obvious commercial appeal. Of the bands that emerged, such as Tangerine Dream, Kraftwerk and Faust, Can were probably the most fascinating – not least because two of its members – Irmin Schmidt and Holger Czukay – had studied under noted avant-garde composer Karlheinz Stockhausen.

Although they could hardly be described as a "guitar band," Michael Karoli's playing in Can showed an admirable understanding of space and dynamic restraint that fitted neatly and precisely into their long hypnotic improvisations.

Can have been a major influence on a lot of experimental music that has come since, perhaps the closest in spirit being Public Image Limited's *Metal Box* set.

STANLEY JORDAN, THE MAN WITH TWO LEFT HANDS.

BARNEY KESSEL
1923–

Noted for the rich precision of his chord work, Barney Kessel is one of the finest exponents of solo and small group jazz.

Although for much of his long career he has played anonymous sessions for television and films, from the late 1940s he became a well-known jazz player in his own right, having recorded with both Charlie Parker and Oscar Peterson, and featured in the Jazz at the Philharmonic tours.

Kessel is also well known for some notable non-jazz work, such as the fabulous *Cry Me A River* sessions for Julie London, as well as dates with the Beach Boys and Phil Spector. This lack of perceived "jazz purity" has led him to be undervalued by some jazz critics.

B B KING
1925–

Not only one of the greatest blues guitarists of all time, B B King, whose career has lasted over half a century, is perhaps the most famous blues artist in the world. His legacy to the pantheon of modern guitar techniques is the extensive use he makes of string-bending, either as a playing device or as an alternative vibrato technique.

B B King was born in 1925 in Itta Bena, a small area outside Indianola, Mississippi. His parents parted when he was three and he moved with his mother to the nearby town of Kilmichael. Throughout much of his early life he was raised by a white family who employed him as a farmhand. It was here that he first picked up the guitar. His first influences were Charlie Christian and T-Bone Walker.

In 1946 King moved to Memphis to try to make a living as a musician. Before arriving at the blues he spent a good deal of time playing gospel music. His first break came in 1949 when Sonny Boy Williamson II gave him an unpaid 10-minute slot on his KWEM radio show. Shortly afterwards King had his own show on WDIA in Memphis billed as "Riley King, The Blues Boy From Beale Street." Following sponsorship he became known as the "Pepticon Blues Boy," a name which was soon shortened to "blues boy," and finally just "B B."

It was Ike Turner, then a session player, who brought King to the attention of RPM. His first single for the label, "Three O'Clock Blues," sold over a million copies and topped the R&B chart for almost four months. King made over 200 recordings over the next 10 years with RPM, among them such classic electric blues compositions as "Woke Up This Morning" and "You Upset Me, Baby."

By 1961, King was sufficiently famous nationally to sign for ABC, a mainstream pop label. Although this period failed to produce outstanding results in the studio,

King did establish himself as a truly exceptional live performer, as can be heard on *Live At The Regal*, which is simply one of the finest concert albums ever made.

Until the early 1960s, the audience for blues music had largely been restricted to black America, or the hipper young urban whites. However, this situation changed when King and fellow blues players like Muddy Waters were surprised to find themselves the subject of veneration by a new young generation of white blues musicians. In Britain, Eric Clapton, John Mayall, Brian Jones and Keith Richards had been inspired to produce their own takes on the works of the veterans. Thus, the electric Chicago blues of the 1950s found itself a principal influence on the rock music of the mid-1960s.

Not slow to see that King had a potentially new young audience, manager Sydney Seidenberg successfully began to steer him towards the crossover market. This approach has typified King's career ever since. With his music and playing always firmly rooted in the blues tradition, he has been able to adapt himself to changes in fashion. During the 1980s he even tried his hand at country and jazz crossovers, although neither are generally thought of as living up to his best work. Nonetheless, King remains one of the greatest living concert performers and continues to find himself a figurehead for successive generations of new musicians, particularly those in search of that elusive "authenticity."

THE BLUES BOY WITH THE
EVER-FAITHFUL LUCILLE.

MIKKO LANKINEN
1961–

If you thought the surf guitar instrumental genre died out 40 years ago, then you may be surprised to learn that a thriving underground independent scene has existed for the past two decades. More surprising, perhaps, is that the coolest of the new bunch – Laika and the Cosmonauts – hail not from the beaches of California, but sun-kissed Finland.

Laika and the Cosmonauts were founded in 1987 by guitarist Mikka Lankinen. A year later they released their debut album *C'mon Do The Laika*. Unusually, their following in Europe only began to take off after such albums as *Absurdistan* and *The Amazing Colossal Band* had been adopted by the US surf/garage/punk scene. Touring extensively in the US, Lankinen's superb playing received the thumbs-up from none other than the "King of Surf Guitar" himself, Mr Dick Dale.

The Laika formula is quite a simple one, their set comprising a mixture of originals and well-known tunes (among them a very groovy version of the theme to Hitchcock's *Psycho*). However, beneath this simplicity, clever arrangements and neat instrumental interplay lifts them into a different league from others of their ilk. To hear the band at its best, seek out their fantastic 2000 live album, *Laika Sex Machine*.

PACO DE LUCIA
1947–

One of the foremost virtuoso guitarists of any genre, Paco de Lucia has done more than anyone to popularize flamenco, the music of the Andalucian region of southern Spain. He has given widely acclaimed solo performances on most of the notable concert platforms throughout Europe and America.

De Lucia was first noticed in the early 1970s accompanying Camaron de la Isla, one of Spain's greatest singers. The duo recorded together extensively – the album *Arte Y Majestad* is a particularly vibrant offering. Although they are considered to be among the best flamenco performances ever captured, sadly little of this collaboration is widely obtainable outside Spanish-speaking countries.

De Lucia has also delved into the world of jazz, having recorded the successful *Passion, Grace And Fire* album with fellow guitarists John McLaughlin and Al DiMeola.

JOHN MCLAUGHLIN
1942–

A much maligned musical form, jazz-rock fusion has too often been characterized by the pursuit of technical skill for its own sake. John McLaughlin is a shining exception to this excess.

McLaughlin began playing the guitar at the age of 11. His earliest interests were in traditional American bluesmen like Leadbelly and Big Bill Broonzy. In the early 1960s he moved to London to be a part of the blues scene. Under the influence of eccentric band leader Graham Bond he began to develop an interest in Eastern philosophies, religions and cultures which would shape his direction in the future.

An increasing interest in free jazz led him to record his debut solo album in 1969. A ground-breaking piece of work, *Extrapolations*, with its high-technique jazz-style rock soloing, anticipated the whole fusion movement and created a sizeable buzz on the international jazz scene. This led to him being drafted into the Miles Davis band, with whom he recorded *In A Silent Way* and *Bitches Brew*, a double-album set that for many established fusion as the next leap forward in the development of jazz.

In 1971 McLaughlin formed his own band, the Mahavishnu Orchestra, mixing jazz and rock electronics even further. Their albums achieved wide crossover success and also became mainstream chart hits, heavily influencing the jazz-rock bands that were about to emerge.

Much of McLaughlin's subsequent work has been on the acoustic guitar, often featuring Indian, classical and flamenco musicians. (In the mid-1970s, he abandoned electricity for a while and formed an all-acoustic trio, Shakti, with Indian musicians.) He remains widely respected by musicians of all genres, and is one of the most influential guitarists of the past 30 years, having anticipated not only fusion, but also much of the "ambient" jazz music produced in the past decade.

BRIAN MAY
1947–

Queen were unique. A mixture of Brian May's heavy Zeppelinesque riffs and the vaudeville and cod-operatic proclivities of singer Freddie Mercury may not have seemed like a winning formula,

took control of his life. Whilst individually Queen were all highly accomplished musicians, it was May's guitar work that stood out. Always happy to make use of technology, the most dramatic device in May's armoury is the sound of his hallmark harmonized guitar "orchestras," built up one track at a time in the studio. This impressive effect can be heard on every one of a dozen or more Queen albums, but with greatest impact on *Sheer Heart Attack*'s "Brighton Rock." This sound is so strongly identifiable that any guitarist who plays harmonized solos is now likely to be compared to Brian May.

JOHN MAYALL
1933–

Although John Mayall is a fine blues guitarist in his own right, his real significance in guitar history is as a catalyst of the British blues scene. Indeed, Mayall could be said to have had a sizeable impact on rock music since the mid-1960s. From 1963, his band, the Bluesbreakers, provided the launching ground for some of the finest guitarists in rock.

and yet from the mid-1970s Queen sold truckloads of records and were one of the biggest live draws the world over.

Like the other members of his band, May was unusually well educated for a pop star, having studied astronomy at London's Imperial College, and completed much of his PhD before music

Eric Clapton (1965), Peter Green (1966) and Mick Taylor (1967) were all teenage stars discovered by Mayall. Listening to Bluesbreakers albums from this period therefore provides a fascinating glimpse of some of the greatest young raw talents that were coming into bloom.

PAT METHENY
1954–

Of all the jazz guitarists to emerge since Wes Montgomery's death in 1968, Pat Metheny is one of a select group who can truly be said to have found his own unique voice.

Metheny's first instrument was the French horn, which he continued to play throughout his school life. However, from the age of 13 the guitar has been his overriding interest. The term prodigious doesn't really do justice to the progress Metheny made as a guitarist – by the end of his teens he had *taught* at both the Berklee School of Music and the University of Miami.

He burst onto the jazz scene at the age of 19 when he joined vibes star Gary Burton, but it was the formation of the Pat Metheny Group in 1977 which indicated that a major new talent had arrived on the scene. His albums for the German ECM label stand out as examples of the state-of-the-art jazz, featuring accessible compositions and a melodic style of soloing a million miles away from the speed-over-content merchants who too often find homes in the jazz world.

Metheny is now consistently among the biggest-selling jazz artists around, many of his albums having sold well in excess of 100,000 copies – a figure beyond the wildest dreams of most jazz musicians. That he has been able to do this without even the slightest hint of compromise is a remarkable feat.

WES MONTGOMERY
1925–1968

Wes Montgomery was the indisputable master of post-war jazz guitar. Alongside Django Reinhardt and Charlie Christian he remains one the three most influential guitarists in jazz history. A list of successors in whose playing he can be heard includes George Benson, Pat Metheny, Herb Ellis, John Scofield – indeed, pretty well every noteworthy jazz guitarist of the past 30 years.

Montgomery taught himself to play the guitar during his teenage years, inspired (and which post-war jazz guitarist wasn't?) by the single-string soloing of Charlie Christian. After a brief period of playing locally in his native Indianapolis, Montgomery left to tour with vibes legend Lionel Hampton's band in 1948. In spite of two years solid gigging on the professional jazz circuit, he returned home in 1950, unable to sustain a professional career. Throughout the 1950s Montgomery worked by day as labourer and by night played in jazz clubs with his two brothers Monk and Buddy.

In spite of having won widespread admiration with his brothers, Montgomery's career looked to be going nowhere fast until 1959 when, at the suggestion of Cannonball Adderley, producer Orrin Keepnews signed him up for the Riverside label. A succession of genre-defining performances were captured on recordings such as *The Wes Montgomery Trio* (1959) and the befittingly titled *The Incredible Guitar Of Wes Montgomery* (1960), which transformed him almost overnight into the most widely imitated jazz guitarist of

WES MONTGOMERY – AFTER CHARLIE CHRISTIAN, THE MOST SIGNIFICANT GUITARIST IN JAZZ HISTORY.

the period. He suddenly found himself working with major league stars like John Coltrane and Wynton Kelly, and later organ legend Jimmy Smith, Milt Jackson and George Shearing.

The most unusual aspect of Montgomery's style was his use of the thumb to pick the strings. With the "attack" characterized by the absence of the traditional plectrum, Montgomery produced a mellower sound than had been heard before in jazz. At the same time he perfected Django Reinhardt's unison octave playing – a technique which adds a second note an octave above during soloing – and use of swiftly executed parallel chording. The unaccompanied track "While We're Young" shows Montgomery's playing at its finest – sumptuous and rich with a seemingly endless capacity for reworking the most traditional of blues-styled sequences without ever resorting to cliché.

Hopes ran high when Montgomery signed to the Verve label – home to so many jazz masters. For many of his most fervent followers these were soon dashed as he found himself in lush orchestral surroundings producing an easy-listening style of jazz. Although Montgomery's mellow tone fitted neatly above the syrupy strings his playing lacked the sheer vitality of his Riverside recordings. It's not that his Verve work was bad, simply that stripped of the challenge of the small group situation Montgomery lacked the impetus to fire on all cylinders. However, his orchestral recordings were staggeringly successful in the commercial sense, and television appearances with Herb Alpert in 1967 – a year before Montgomery's death from a heart attack – allowed him to reach an audience that other jazz musicians could only dream about.

His early death left a gaping hole in the world of jazz guitar, which only the likes of George Benson and Pat Metheny – two of Montgomery's many young acolytes – have come close to filling. His influence has, if anything, grown in the years since his death – a fact illustrated by the Kool Festival all-star tribute concert held in his honor at New York's Carnegie Hall in 1985.

SCOTTY MOORE
1931–

As guitarist with the "King" of rock 'n' roll, Elvis Presley, during his peak years, Scotty Moore can be said to have had a considerable impact on the development of the guitar as a "rock" instrument.

It was label owner Sam Phillips who brought Elvis Presley, Scotty Moore and bassist Bill Black together for the first time in 1954. Although it was his RCA work (starting two years later) that made Presley the biggest music star the world has ever seen, the sessions that the band recorded for Phillips' Sun label have become part of music folklore. Classics like "Mystery Train" and "That's All Right, Mama" set a pattern for much of what directly followed. Although the sound is obviously dominated by Presley's extraordinary voice, Moore pretty well defined rockabilly guitar by crossing R&B with country picking.

Presley's Sun recordings represent a genuine turning-point in the history of popular music, and still sound as fresh and vibrant to this day. They remain an essential purchase for any true music fan.

SCOTTY MOORE DEFINED THE FUSION OF COUNTRY AND R&B GUITAR.

TOM MORELLO
1964–

Rage Against The Machine were one of the more interesting new bands to emerge during the first half of the 1990s. Avowed socialists, their direct-action politics brought them into conflict with several conservative US national institutions. They were banned from TV's *Saturday Night Live* for making a political gesture with the US flag, and once performed an all-feedback set, naked with taped-up mouths, in protest against Tipper Gore's music censorship organization.

The RATM sound was a powerful hybrid of heavy rock and rap, which revolved around Tom Morello's radical guitar work. His credentials for working in such a politicized band are impeccable: his father was a member of the Mau Mau guerrilla army which freed Kenya from British colonial rule; his mother is a well-known anti-censorship organizer. Morello himself graduated in political science from Harvard University.

Morello's first band, the Los Angeles-based Lock Up, released a major-label album in the late 1980s, but it was the birth of RATM in 1991 which brought him worldwide success. Although clearly

a formidable technician, Morello's style is strongly influenced by the sampled sounds of rap and hip hop. Using a variety of custom-built guitars and effects, he has created his own hyper-modern rhythmic style, which gives the impression of triggered digital samples but in fact is performed live.

It all adds up to a cutting-edge guitar sound that makes the Vais and Satrianis of this world sound as if they come from a bygone age.

JIMMY PAGE
1944–

Of the many British guitar heroes who emerged out of the blues boom, such as Eric Clapton, Jeff Beck and Peter Green, it is ultimately Jimmy Page whose work has displayed the most variety and enduring appeal. And the influence of his band, Led Zeppelin, can be heard in the new wave of rock bands that emerged during the 1990s.

Page joined his first band, Neil Christian and the Crusaders, in 1960, when he was 16 years old. Even at that age his playing was already remarkably developed and it wasn't long before he began to find regular work playing on the London session scene. During the early 1960s he gained a reputation for being one of the most versatile and hard-working guitarists around, often playing three or four sessions a day. Among the earliest beneficiaries of his playing were the Who's "Can't Explain," Them's "Baby Please Don't Go" and Tom Jones' "It's Not Unusual."

In 1964, when Clapton left the Yardbirds, Page was offered the job of replacing him as guitarist, but he turned it down in favour of continuing his lucrative session career. Two years later, however, he had a change of heart and joined when bass guitarist Paul Samwell-Smith left. The Yardbirds now starred Jeff Beck in

TOM MORELLO OF RAGE AGAINST THE MACHINE WITH HIS CUSTOMIZED GUITAR.

The band completed the Scandinavian
tour as the New Yardbirds, but then
began playing in England under a new
identity: Led Zeppelin. Their debut
album was recorded in the space of
30 hours and was released in early 1969.
The sound was an awesome "heavy" blues,
each musician giving virtuoso performances.
The album was an immediate hit on both
sides of the Atlantic, launching what
would become the most successful rock
group of all time.

At the heart of the Zeppelin sound lay
the intricate guitar work and production
skills of Jimmy Page. His brilliance on the
acoustic can be heard on his altered-tuning
version of the folky "Black Mountain Side."
On this track Page uses what is known as
the "D-A-D-G-A-D" tuning system (these
are the notes the guitar is tuned to from
bottom to top) – a notoriously tricky
tuning. However, it is his electric playing
that has influenced so many, not least the
gently picked arpeggios of Zeppelin's
"theme tune," "Stairway To Heaven."

The band broke up following the
death of John Bonham in 1980, but
Page has continued to work at a pace ever
since. After a false start in 1985 with Paul
Rodgers' band the Firm, Zeppelin fans the
world over were thrilled to hear of Page and
Plant's new partnership in the early 1990s.

the leading role, but the new combination didn't work and when
Beck finally left in early 1968, the Yardbirds disintegrated, leaving
Page on his own with rights to the name of the band and a
contracted tour of Sweden to fulfil. With Peter Grant as a manager,
Page went about forming a New Yardbirds band for the tour. The
musicians they found were session veteran John Paul Jones,
drummer John Bonham and singer Robert Plant.

However, it is with the eleven Led Zeppelin albums that
Page's reputation will always rest. This is an extraordinary
body of work – Led Zeppelin set a new benchmark for technical
excellence in rock without ever seeming to be dull, self-important
or over-indulgent. It is a benchmark that no other band has really
come close to meeting.

JOE PASS
1929–1994

A prodigious talent, Joe Pass had already performed with a number of well-known artists on the New York jazz scene by the time he left high school. In spite of this, however, he spent most of his twenties in unspectacular surroundings, first playing in Las Vegas backing bands and then serving time for narcotics offences. On release from prison his career suddenly took off. He immediately secured a solo record deal and began playing actively on the West Coast scene. By 1963 he was named Best New Instrumentalist by *Downbeat* magazine.

In 1972 Pass was signed up by Norman Grantz, manager of pianist Oscar Peterson and owner of the Pablo label, with whom he stayed for the rest of his life. During the next 20 years he performed and recorded with just about every notable jazz legend, from Ella Fitzgerald, Duke Ellington and Count Basie to Dizzy Gillespie and Stéphane Grappelli.

Pass was less an innovator than a technical master who consolidated different jazz idioms to produce something new. Perhaps his greatest legacy is in his unaccompanied work in which his playing was able to encompass the role of the traditional jazz bass, and integrate lead lines within his considerable chord vocabulary. For this alone he is arguably the most influential jazz guitarist since Wes Montgomery.

JOE PASS – PERHAPS THE FINEST EXPONENT OF UNACCOMPANIED JAZZ GUITAR.

DJANGO REINHARDT
1910–1953

Jean Baptiste "Django" Reinhardt was not only the first great virtuoso jazz guitar soloist, he was also the first non-American musician to make a notable impact on the world jazz scene.

Born in 1910 to a nomadic caravan-dwelling gypsy family, Django Reinhardt was the son of an entertainer who worked in a traveling show between Belgium and France. As a child he learned to play violin and banjo before moving on to the guitar. However, it was at the age of 18 that a fire in his caravan famously disabled his left hand, leaving only the thumb and first two fingers functioning. Although most young musicians would have given up under the same circumstances, Reinhardt used his limitations to develop a unique technique which enabled him to performing lightning-fast single note runs the likes of which had rarely been heard before.

Influenced by early jazz pioneers like Louis Armstrong, Duke Ellington and guitarist Eddie Lang, Reinhardt began his professional career playing in the coffee houses of Montmartre in Paris. It was here that he was introduced to the popular young French crooner Jean Sablon in 1933. Reinhardt spent a fruitful year as Sablon's solo accompanist until he joined up with violinist Stéphane Grappelli in the Quintet du Hot Club de France.

Within a year, the Quintet – which also featured Louis Vola on bass and Roger Chaput and Reinhardt's younger brother, Joseph, on rhythm guitars – had built up an international reputation based largely on the interplay between the soloing violin and guitar. It was a unique sound that matched Grappelli's elegantly flowing lines with Reinhardt's high-speed, single-string runs and swift chord work. The Hot Club played widely throughout Europe, regularly topping the bill over visiting American stars. During the five years in which the Quintet were active they cut over 200 sides, most of which are now viewed as being among the high points of pre-war jazz.

When war broke out in Europe in 1939, Grappelli based himself in London. Reinhardt chose to return to his former gypsy life, traveling through France and Belgium. During this period he seemed to lose some of his passion for the guitar, taking an interest in other musical forms, and devoting much of his time to painting and fishing.

In 1946 Reinhardt received a cable from Duke Ellington, inviting him to perform in the US. Through a mixture of Hot

Club recordings and word-of-mouth reports from American jazzmen returning from Europe, Reinhardt's arrival in New York was preceded by a reputation that was impossible to follow. Partly because he was playing electrified guitar for the first time, the concerts were not entirely successful and, disappointed by the reaction, he cut short his visit and returned to Europe.

In truth, Reinhardt's visit to the home of jazz had been an underwhelming experience for everyone. Whilst he had towered above his peers for much of the 1930s, the end of the decade had already seen the emergence of the next generation: the electric guitar was now an instrument in its own right and in a fleeting career, over almost as quickly as it had begun, Charlie Christian had already redefined the role of the guitar in jazz.

In later years Reinhardt struggled to keep up with the changing face of jazz. Whilst his leaning shifted towards bebop, its style and intellectualism was suited to neither his playing nor personality. By all accounts, Reinhardt had also found it difficult to adjust to life away from his gypsy roots, and was ill-equipped to deal with the by-products of success. The many apocryphal stories of his struggles with the modern world – he was once reputed to have permanently discarded a new car on the roadside after it had run out of petrol – have only served to reinforce his image as an "other-wordly" stranger. But although he could neither read nor write, his classic recordings of the mid-1930s reveal a latent musical literacy that was way ahead of its time.

DJANGO REINHARDT, THE FIRST GREAT JAZZ GUITAR SOLOIST.

RANDY RHOADS
1956–1982

Born in Santa Monica, the son of two music
teachers, Rhoads started taking guitar lessons at the
age of seven. By all accounts a precocious learner, at
the age of 12 his guitar teacher is reputed to have
visited his mother telling her there was no more he
could teach him. Having played in several school
bands, in 1976 he formed Quiet Riot. In spite of
building a following on the West Coast college
scene, they failed to interest any record labels, and
Rhoads was forced to supplement his income as a
guitar teacher. The band's fortunes changed when
in 1978 they were signed to CBS/Sony in Japan,
who released two albums to considerable acclaim.
Sadly, sales failed to match the enthusiasm of the
press, and Rhoads quit the band.

Rhoads's career shifted up a gear at the end of
1979 when he auditioned as guitarist in ex-Black
Sabbath frontman (and latter day cultural icon)
Ozzy Osbourne's new band, Blizzard of Ozz.
Having tried out the cream of LA's players with no
success, Osbourne was about to give up and return
to England when he encountered Rhodes. As one
of several apocryphal tales goes, Rhodes visited the
singer in his hotel room, plugged his guitar into
a practice amp and started playing a few warm-up
exercises, and was offered the job on the spot.

The band's first two albums, *Blizzard of Ozz* and
Diary of a Madman, were massive hits, with critics
singling out Rhoads's guitar work for special praise.
He also garnered awards in guitar and music
magazines on both sides of the Atlantic. During
the same period he hooked up with guitar maker
Grover Jackson – then working for Charvel –
and the two of them created his famous white
"Flying V"-style custom model that a few years
later would help to make Jackson the premier
marque of rock players.

The Randy Rhoads story ended in tragedy
when, during Blizzard of Ozz's 1982 US tour,

KEITH RICHARDS, STILL GRINDING OUT THE RIFFS AFTER 35 YEARS.

he was killed when a plane stunt went horrifically wrong. His name lives on, both in a handful of recordings, a famous guitar, which later went into production, and the memory of a major talent that was never able to reach full bloom.

KEITH RICHARDS
1943–

In the realm of rock 'n' roll rhythm guitar, Keith Richards has few rivals. Taking his cue from Chuck Berry – his greatest idol – he has spent the last 35 years pumping out Telecaster riffs in the engine room of the mighty Rolling Stones. With a tenacious instinct for survival, even during his darkest periods in the 1970s, "Keef" managed not only to retain an almost child-like enthusiasm for rock 'n' roll, but sought to bring new influences, such as reggae and country, to his beloved band.

Although his lead work can be heard on rare occasions, Richards has always been more of a team player, viewing himself simply as a component of the rhythm section, allowing the likes of Brian Jones, Mick Taylor and Ronnie Wood to take the bows for their soloing. As he says, "The whole secret, if there is any secret behind the sound of the Rolling Stones, is the way we work two guitars together." In fact, few twin-guitar rock bands have ever come close to matching the interaction of the Stones at their best.

Although not a virtuoso guitarist in the conventional sense, many of the top session men who have worked with the Stones over the years have testified that Richards' rhythm work and natural sense of timing are second to none. More than that, however, he is one of the great riff composers, having written any number of simple, and yet immediately recognizable opening lines – just listen to tracks like "(I Can't Get No) Satisfaction," "Brown Sugar" and "Honky Tonk Woman" for the evidence.

CARLOS SANTANA
1947–

It was an appearance at the Woodstock festival in 1969 that introduced Mexican-born Carlos Santana to a wide audience. Merging blues-based rock with Latin-American rhythms, Santana created a genuinely new sound. Similarly, as a guitarist, he is one

of a rare breed whose tone – with its pure sustain and overdriven valves – is recognizable at once.

He scored a 12-million selling hit with the release of the *Supernatural* album, which went on to win nine Grammy awards and was voted US album of the year in 2000.

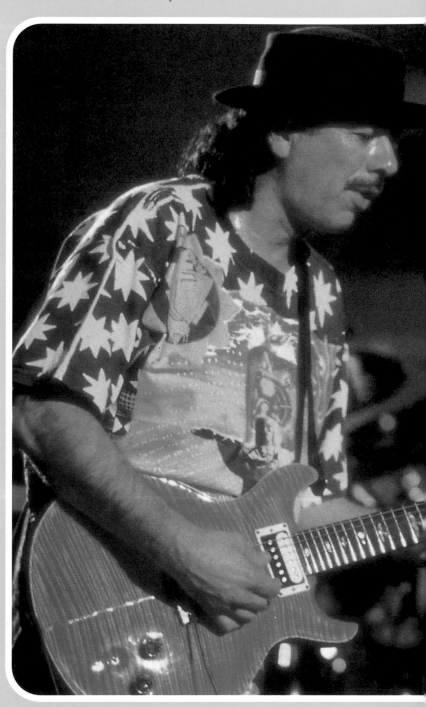

FEW GUITARISTS HAVE SUCH A RECOGNIZABLE SOUND AS CARLOS SANTANA.

ANDRÉS SEGOVIA
1893–1987

More than anyone before or since, it was Andrés Segovia who brought widespread respectability to the guitar and helped the instrument gain acceptance in the elite world of classical music. Until then, despite the works of composers and musicians from Sor to Tárrega (see chapter on the Torres revolution and the classical guitar), the guitar was still considered a rather crude and limited "boudoir" instrument. All the more remarkable, then, is the fact that Segovia was a self-taught maestro – indeed he was always proud to declare that he had always been his own master and pupil.

Born in 1893, Segovia studied music in Granada against the wishes of his family, but abandoned all other instruments in favor of the guitar. Under his own extraordinary tuition, he refined many of the revolutionary developments in playing that had been made by Tárrega during the previous century, most notably the relaxation of Tárrega's rigid right-hand technique. He also developed the range of possible guitar tones in his playing by striking the strings either with the nails or with nails and fingertips.

Remarkably, by the age of only 16 Segovia had already made his first professional recital in Granada, which he followed up with performances throughout Spain. In 1916 he made his first tour of South America, where his concerts were met with sensational acclaim.

In 1924 Segovia made his debut in Paris. Among the audience were Manuel de Falla and Albert Roussel, both of whom would compose seminal works for the guitar. Segovia's debuts in Moscow (1926) and New York (1928) were met with similar enthusiasm. Thereafter he toured widely throughout world, astounding audiences with an unprecedented virtuosity on an instrument which was still largely unfamiliar to the masses. Although Segovia never actively sought widespread popularity – indeed he spoke out against artists who pandered to mass appeal – he was one of the most popular soloists performing in the classical field.

ANDRÉS SEGOVIA – A SELF-TAUGHT MASTER.

It was Segovia's visits to South America that had wider implications for the development of the classical repertoire. It was here that he encountered some of the greatest composers of the period, such as the Brazilian Heitor Villa-Lobos. His 1929 piece *Douze Etudes* is widely thought to be the first composition for the instrument by a non-guitarist. The lack of knowledge of the instrument's limitations paved the way for the development of future composition that would place increasing technical demands on the musician. Another notable composer to benefit from meeting Segovia was the Mexican Manuel Ponce, who produced works such as *Twelve Preludes*, *Chanson* and *Concierto del Sur*, all of which were given their concert debuts by Segovia.

The importance of Segovia's role as the instrument's greatest ambassador during the first half of the twentieth century cannot be overestimated. Not only the greatest maestro the instrument has yet seen, he was responsible for making the guitar a truly international instrument. Also, in bringing a new repertoire to the classical stage, he could be viewed as being responsible for widening the twentieth-century tradition for guitar composition. Without his influence it is doubtful that such fine composers as Castelnuovo-Tedesco (*Cavatina*) and Rodrigo (*Concierto de Aranjuez*) would enjoy such widespread popularity throughout the world. His own transcriptions of works for other instruments (such as the vihuela and lute) and of works by composers of the stature of Bach, Mozart and Chopin also greatly increased the guitar's classical repertoire.

Also significant is Andrés Segovia's role in encouraging many young musicians such as John Williams, amongst others, in masterclass courses at music academies in Italy and Spain.

Even though Segovia's greatest work was done over 40 years ago, he remains the single most important figure in the history of the classical guitar, and whilst a number of outstanding players have succeeded him, his own recordings of the standard classical repertoire are still held up as the benchmarks against which all newcomers are measured.

FRANCISCO TÁRREGA
1852–1909

The revolutionary work by Torres in reinventing the guitar (see earlier chapter) brought about new possibilities in playing the instrument. The first man to build on those new beginnings was Francisco de Asis Tárrega y Eixea, the man who laid the foundations for the modern classical technique and first suggested that the guitar could be taken seriously as a classical instrument to rival any of its more noble rivals.

Francisco Tárrega was born in Villareal, Valencia in 1852. Although at the age of 10 he studied classical guitar with Julian Arcas, at the wish of his father he studied piano at Madrid's prestigious Conservatorio. A brilliant student, he was awarded first prize for harmony and composition. However, he soon returned to the guitar, the instrument on which he would become the dominant figure of the nineteenth century.

In 1869, Tárrega was fortunate enough to acquire a guitar built by Antonio de Torres, a luthier based in Seville. By 1877 Tárrega was making a living as a music teacher and concert guitarist. At his first performances in London and Paris during 1880 he was hailed as "the Sarasate of the guitar," — Sarasate being the most eminent violinist of the period. At the end of the century Tárrega traveled widely throughout Europe, his virtuoso performances allowing the guitar to be viewed in a much more serious light.

He also composed many original pieces for the instrument, although they are by no means viewed as the most interesting new works of the period. On the other hand, his transcriptions of Beethoven (the *Addagio* and *Allegretto* from the *"Moonlight" Sonatas*) and Chopin's *Preludes* were valuable additions to the instrument's repertoire.

It was as a teacher and innovator that Tárrega won his reputation as a legend of the guitar. Many of the standard techniques used right up to the modern day originated from him. The most dramatic development was the positioning of the guitar on the left leg, a move which came about as a result of the increase in the size of its body. This position had been previously identified as preferable, but the narrow waists and overall smaller size of the older instruments had made it impossible to adopt with any comfort.

Tárrega also revolutionized right-hand techniques, bringing about the widespread use of the *apoyando* stroke, with which the finger pushes through the string and comes to rest on the next one.

Previously, although this had been standard for the thumb, finger strokes had more usually been played *tirando*, the tips rising after the string had been struck. Whichever stroke was used, however, Tárrega was the principal voice to suggest that the little finger should not rest on the guitar body, but that the entire right hand should be poised free above the strings. This approach also came about through Torres' new designs which saw the height of the fingerboard raised so that it was no longer flush with the surface of the guitar body. This in turn required the bridge saddle to be heightened, which made the technique of the little-finger support extremely uncomfortable to use successfully.

Among the many guitarists who received personal tuition from Tárrega were fellow Spaniards Miguel Llobert, Maria Rita Brondi and Emilio Pujol, all of whom were among the most eminent practitioners of the instrument during the first half of the twentieth century.

In 1906, at the peak of his fame, Tárrega was struck down with paralysis of his right side. Although he continued to appear in public, he never fully recovered. He died in Barcelona in 1909.

THE REVOLUTIONARY TÁRREGA OPENED UP NEW POSSIBILITIES IN GUITAR-PLAYING.

STEVE VAI
1960–

One of the modern guitar's great pyrotechnicians, New York-born Steve Vai took up the instrument at the age of 13, his earliest influences including John Lee Hooker, Jimmy Page, Jimi Hendrix and Roy Buchanan. Following a spell at Boston's prestigious Berklee School of Music, Vai first made an impact when he was offered the daunting role of second guitar in Frank Zappa's band in 1979. The ideal home for a rigorous disciplinarian, Vai had previously initiated his own austere ten-hours-a-day practice regime. Vai then moved into the conventional rock mainstream, first replacing Yngwie Malmsteem in Alcatrazz, then in ex-Van Halen frontman Dave Lee Roth's band, before settling briefly with Whitesnake in 1989.

His ascension to guitar-god status arrived with 1990's award-winning solo album, *Passion And Warfare*, a rare kaleidoscope of guitar wizardry featuring some of the most awesome high-speed soloing to be heard anywhere. 1993's *Sex And Religion* cemented his reputation as top dog in a select league alongside the likes of Eddie

STEVE VAI PLAYS THE IBANEZ JEM, WHICH HE HELPED TO DESIGN.

Van Halen and Joe Satriani. However, unlike Van Halen, whose band produced some of the most appealing rock albums of the 1980s, Vai's music is bought primarily by those in awe of his technical prowess rather than the quality of the music itself.

Vai has also involved himself in the development of new instruments, having worked with Japanese guitar makers Ibanez to produce the highly rated Jem and seven-string Universe models.

EDDIE VAN HALEN
1957–

Throughout most of the 1990s the likes of Joe Satriani and Steve Vai have taken the plaudits for their awesome displays of sheer technique. However, a decade earlier it was a young Eddie Van Halen who helped drag rock music out of the realms of *Spinal Tap*-style parody and made the high-performance guitar solo respectable once again.

Born in the Dutch town of Nijmegen in 1957, Van Halen moved to California with his family in the middle of the 1960s. Initially starting life as a drummer, Eddie and his brother Alex formed the band the Broken Combs in 1973 while they were still at school. Changing their name to Van Halen, they found fame with their 1978 debut album, *Van Halen*. It became something of a rock classic, selling well over two million copies and giving heart to a generation of young musicians who felt marginalized by the "anti-muso" stance of the new wave.

Perhaps more than any other single track, it was Van Halen's finger-tapping extravaganza on Michael Jackson's million-selling 1983 hit "Beat It" that had analysts of the guitar solo scratching their heads. Since then, finger-tapping (or fret-tapping as it is also known) has become a standard part of the modern guitarist's armoury.

STEVIE RAY VAUGHAN
1954–1990

When Stevie Ray Vaughan lost his life in a helicopter crash in 1990, the music world, and blues in particular, was stripped of one of its star guitarists. It left a hole that no one has yet come near to filling.

Born in Dallas, Stevie Ray Vaughan was taught to play guitar by his elder brother Jimmie. His earliest playing influences were Otis Rush, Howlin' Wolf, Albert King and Jimi Hendrix. In his late teens Stevie Ray followed his brother to Austin where in 1978 he formed the band Double Trouble. Although his talent was quickly recognized on the blues scene, his big break came in 1982 when he created a sensation at the Montreux Jazz Festival. This resulted in numerous session offers, most notably David Bowie's *Let's Dance* album. When Vaughan made his first solo album that year he immediately found a rock crossover audience for his playing. Recorded by veteran producer John Hammond, *Texas Flood* was a big seller and Grammy award-winner.

On later albums Vaughan followed a rockier path. 1985's *Soul To Soul* featured the crucial addition of a keyboard player, and a title track indicating that Jimi Hendrix may have been a bigger influence than some might have thought (or hoped). His career

STEVIE RAY VAUGHAN COULD HAVE TAKEN BLUES GUITAR INTO THIS CENTURY.

during the second half of the 1980s was interrupted sporadically by drug problems and a resultant lapse in the quality of his work. However, his final two studio albums – *In Step* and *Family Style* (recorded with his brother Jimmie) – saw him fully restored and in peak form.

Vaughan's recordings are now viewed as templates for aspiring blues players. In 1992 Fender paid the ultimate posthumous complement – the introduction of a signature model Stratocaster. But perhaps a greater measure of the respect for him held by his fellow musicians can be seen in the names who happily agreed to be a part of a 1996 tribute album in his honour, including Eric Clapton, B B King, Robert Cray and Bonnie Raitt.

MUDDY WATERS
1915–1983

Muddy Waters brought the music of the Mississippi Delta into the modern world, becoming the first great electric blues guitarist in the process. He was largely responsible for introducing R&B to white audiences, and in so doing laid the foundations for much of the rock music of the 1960s and beyond.

Growing up in Clarksdale, Mississippi, McKinley Morganfield learned to play the guitar and harmonica at the age of 17. His

earliest influences were Son House and Robert Johnson. Working on a local plantation, Muddy Waters (as Morganfield was known by then) made a name for himself locally both as a musician and as a moonshine bootlegger.

Waters' first records were cut during the war years for blues archivist Alan Lomax – a man responsible for rediscovering many of the great blues artists of the 1920s and 1930s who, at that time, had been almost entirely unknown to white audiences. Lomax had been scouring the state with his Library Of Congress team looking for the legendary Robert Johnson. Before discovering that Johnson had died three years earlier, Lomax was told that there was a local man who played like him, and was directed towards the Stovall Plantation where Waters was employed. Over the space of two years Waters cut 13 sides for Lomax, mostly accompanying himself. Songs like "You Got To Take Sick And Die Some Of These Days" and "I Be's Trouble," revealed a raw, as yet undeveloped talent, both in his powerful, even menacing, vocals and the intensity of his slide-playing.

Taken under the wing of blues ambassador Big Bill Broonzy, in 1943 Waters moved to Chicago, where he got his first electric guitar. In 1948 he cut some unsuccessful records for the Aristocrat label, which was run by, among others, the brothers Leonard and Phil Chess. Two years later when they formed their own Chess label, Waters was one of their first signings. His debut recording for Chess was made with harmonica soloist Little Walter Jacobs. The combination of heavily amplified harmonica and guitar, and Waters' close-miked bass growl made "Louisiana Blues" a national R&B hit.

Like many greats in other areas of music (Duke Ellington and Miles Davis to name but two), Waters was notable for surrounding himself with up-and-coming young players eager to learn from the master – and many notable names from the next generation of the blues passed through his ranks. Continuing to work with Little Walter, Waters formed an expanded line-up which included second guitarist Jimmy Rogers, drummer Elga Edmonds and pianist Otis Spann. Muddy Waters' ensemble recordings made between 1952 and 1960 provided the single most succinct blueprint for the next phase of development in R&B as a musical form. A succession of timeless anthems such as "I'm Your Hoochie Coochie Man" and "Got My Mojo Working" can truly be said to have dragged the blues into the modern age.

Waters' influence cut further afield, though, as his classic Chess recordings were plundered by the second-generation rock 'n' rollers

MUDDY WATERS – A TRULY ELECTRIC PERFORMER.

of the early 1960s. Indeed, Waters' "Rollin' Stone" even inspired the very name of one young English group. But if there existed a great divide between the two, it was the difference between man and boy. Through the lips of Mick Jagger, "I Just Wanna Make Love To You" sounded more like a teenage fantasy. When Waters first boomed out the same song a decade earlier it was nothing less than a declaration of intent. This was a 40-year-old man of the world who knew what he wanted. And he knew that no woman in her right mind would refuse him: Muddy Waters was the *real thing*.

Throughout the 1960s and beyond, few would dispute that Waters was the greatest living bluesman. He continued to record fine albums, often collaborating with the younger musicians such as Paul Butterfield, Mike Bloomfield, Johnny Winter and Buddy Guy. Waters remained an active performer until his death in 1983. A venerated figure in his later years, even when he was well into his sixties, he could still blow any performer off stage with the sheer force of his personality.

Any list of American cultural pioneers would include names like Woody Guthrie, Duke Ellington, George Gershwin and Bob Dylan: the name of Muddy Waters stands tall in such exalted company.

FRANK ZAPPA
1940–1993

"Uncompromising" may be the best single word to describe the prodigious output of Frank Zappa.

Appearing on the San Francisco scene in the mid-1960s, he formed the Mothers of Invention, a satirical fusion of rock, pop, modern jazz, modern classical, doo-wop and just about any other kind of music imaginable. The targets included politicians, the mores of the middle classes, and even the hippy movement that (in part) had embraced the band. The Mothers peaked with 1967's *We're Only In It For The Money*. Thereafter, Zappa followed his own path, often working in an area that could just about be described as jazz-rock, although sometimes adding elements of dubious humor. Throughout, however, his bands were run with an orchestral discipline, calling on the talents of the likes of Lowell George and Steve Vai.

Zappa not only invariably made high quality recordings of most of his live concerts, he also recorded guitar solos endlessly at home,

some of which have been made available for public consumption. Although not exactly easy listening, they represent a fascinating glimpse into the creative process of one of the most creative musicians to have worked in the rock *oeuvre*.

FRANK ZAPPA, WHOSE CREATIVITY SEEMINGLY KNEW NO BOUNDS.

PART 3

PLAYING THE GUITAR

Now it's time to get down to the serious business of making a noise.

This part of the book is separated into a series of small sections that you could think of as lessons. The suggested way forward here is to take each lesson slowly and methodically, and avoid the temptation to leap forward until you have completely mastered each one.

As with any learning process, you will only get to be good by **PRACTISE.** The finest musicians combine a mental facility – an understanding of **WHAT** they are trying to play – with the motor skills necessary to carry out these commands. The acquisition of the latter will only come about by repetition. I'm sorry to have to tell you that there really is no short-cut to having your fingers "learn" how to move automatically to the right places to play chord shapes or scales.

Here is one final thought for you. Think of the guitarist you most admire. Be it Andrés Segovia, Wes Montgomery, Eric Clapton, Eddie Van Halen or the guy with the funny rubber mask in Slipknot, every one of them had to pass through the same learning process on which you are about to embark. So you're in good company.

CHOOSING YOUR EQUIPMENT

The absolute basics that you will need to use this book are just an acoustic guitar and a pick. If you're going to play an electric guitar, of course, you will also need an amplifier – and a lead to connect the guitar would be handy. And if you intend to play standing up, then a strap will be essential.

For the beginner, just choosing a guitar can be a complicated process, and it's a good idea to take advice from someone familiar with guitars before making a purchase – especially if you are looking at second-hand instruments. In fact, buying a used guitar can allow you to start out with a good quality model you might otherwise not be able to afford, although some of the really "classic" vintage instruments can go up in value. Follow this simple check list of ten essential things that you should look out for when you are thinking of buying a guitar or amplifier.

TEN CHECKPOINTS TO LOOK OUT FOR

CHECKPOINT 1 – QUALITY

As with many things, it can often be a false economy to buy cheaply for the sake of it. Reliabilty and ease-of-use comes with a quality instrument, so buy the best you can afford; an inferior instrument can make playing harder from the start.

CHECKPOINT 2 – WARPING

A warped or curved fingerboard will affect the sound and render the guitar more difficult to use. The neck of the guitar should look perfectly even, the best way to test this being to look down the top surface of the neck while holding the guitar as if aiming a rifle. The golden rule is that if there is the slightest hint of a twist, don't buy it – the intonation will be impaired, and subsequent repair work expensive. On examination you will, however, be likely to observe a slight curving when looking down the side of the neck, somewhere between the 7th and 9th frets. This is nothing unusual, and can be adjusted with the truss rod.

CHECKPOINT 3 – INTONATION

When you play a note on the 12th fret, it always has to be an exact octave higher than when the string is played open. Alternatively, the note has to match the harmonic on the 12th fret. The more the notes are "out" with each other, the more out of tune the guitar will be as you play further along the neck. This is easy enough to put right, but if you are new to the guitar it would be a good idea to get a shop assistant to do it for you.

CHECKPOINT 4 – THE ACTION

The "action", which refers to the height of the strings from the frets, can be guaged by the distance between a string and the top of the 12th fret. The "action" is so-called beacause a "low" action, with the frets close to the strings, means the fingers don't have to press so hard to achieve a note, an important factor in playing fast solos. You also need to check that all the frets are the same height, by playing every note on the fingerboard, to avoid a "buzzing" effect when certain notes are played.

CHECKPOINT 5 – MACHINE HEADS

Machine heads are the little "machines" which control the tension of the strings from the top of the neck (the headstock). The strings will slip, with the guitar going out of tune, if they turn too easily – though this is less critical in a guitar with a locking tremolo unit.

CHECKPOINT 6 – SUSTAIN

Sustain is the time a note carries on ringing before it fades completely, and depends largely on the shape and structure of the guitar. It's advisable to try every note to make sure that they all sustain in equal measure. Acoustic guitars which produce "dead" notes – often resulting from an instrument's natural frequencies – are to be avoided.

CHECKPOINT 7 – PICKUPS

After plugging an electric guitar into an amplifier, listen to the relative volume string-by-string. If it varies noticably, it means adjusting the height of the pickups. This can be done simply if each pickup pole (a node beneath each string) can be adjusted individually. If not, it may be necessary to replace the entire pickup.

CHECKPOINT 8 – NOISE

Stand close to the amp, with the guitar still switched on, and just listen. If you can hear any trace of whistling feedback, it could mean that the pickups are not isolated correctly, leading to real problems when you want to play at high volume.

CHECKPOINT 9 – EFFECTS

You need to satisfy yourself that the sounds coming out of the amplifier in the store are not a result of special effects in the amp itself – make sure they are switched off so you just hear the guitar.

CHECKPOINT 10 – SATISFACTION

All guitars have an individual character. Just as you get on with certain people from the outset so, with luck, you will come across an instrument that you immediately identify with. You have to feel happy with a guitar from the start to have a meaningful relationship – a bond that will be a major factor in achieving the satisfaction of coming to terms with the instrument.

HOLDING THE GUITAR

As with any musical instrument, it's essential that you feel confortable and relaxed just holding the guitar. The actual stance you adopt will, to some degree, be defined by the type of music you are playing. Very generally, it's reasonable to say that classical, folk and flamenco players (for instance) perform seated, whereas most rock and country players play standing up. But before you start actually playing the guitar, you also need to learn the basics of fretting notes with the left hand and actually tuning the instrument.

SITTING

There are two quite separate modes of playing the guitar in a seated position, one almost exclusively associated with classical players. The "classical" method, strongly infuenced by the 19th century guitar maker Antonio de Torres and musician Francesco Tarrega, has the "waist" of the guitar placed between the legs to rest on the left thigh. The neck of the guitar has to be held at an approximate angle of 45°, and an adjustable footstool is often used – or a simple 6 in (150mm) box – to accomodate people of different heights. This angling of the neck means that the left hand is in the optimum postion for its movement up and down the fingerboard, and the right hand in its position over the strings.

This particular playing posture can, of course, be spotted being utilized in various forms of guitar music, but is in the main a style that has been adopted by classical musicians. The more usual sitting position is where the player rests the guitar on the right thigh, the neck being held at a horizontal angle with the left hand, and the body of the instrument stabilized by the inside of the right arm. This seems the

STANDARD
SITTING POSITION.

"CLASSICAL"
POSITION.

ALSO WORTH REMEMBERING...

You need to consider the clothes you are wearing when playing the guitar. Clothes that are too big and bulky are liable to restrict your movement, while hanging sleeves on loose-fitting items can get in the way of the strings, dulling the actual sound. And you have to watch out for jewellery, metal buttons and zips, that can scratch the instrument as well as making an unwelcome noise. And don't forget not every form of seating is suitable for playing the guitar. A solid sturdy base is essential, and if you're using a foot stool that needs to be on a rigid surface as well. Chairs with arms that get in the way have to be avoided, as do soft seats or couches; practising in your bedroom is fine, but sitting on the bed while playing will just lead to an incorrect posture and very quickly acquired bad habits.

most comfortable and natural position to adopt when playing an acoustic guitar.

The sitting position can be a little more problematic, however, when playing a solid-bodied electric guitar. Designed basically to be played standing up, the balance of the weight between the neck and body can make the instrument tilt when sitting down, in which case a shoulder strap should be worn.

Left-handed players can come up against additional problems. Although most good guitars are available in a left-handed version, most players find it easier and cheaper to simply re-string the guitar "upside-down". This works perfectly adequately as far as the fingerboard itself is concerned, but your hand movements can be affected by the shape of the body and, with electric models, the postion of the controls. Shifting one's posture can alleviate this, but ideally purchasing a left-handed model is more satisfactory, even though famous left-handed musicians like Jimi Hendrix have managed perfectly well on a right-handed instrument.

STANDING

The first essential when playing a guitar standing up is a shoulder strap. Most straps on the market are perfectly adequate for the job, although a cheap one without reinforced strap holes will be more liable to snap mid-performance. Investing a bit more cash for a quality

STANDING
POSITION.

leather strap is usually money well spent, with a strap that should never need replacing.

Hanging from its shoulder strap, with the guitar leaning against your body, both your arms should be in a natural position, free to move unhindered. The strap should be adjusted for the guitar to hang at the right height – a useful guide for the starter is for the bridge to be at around the same height as your waist, though this will vary from person to person. And the neck of the guitar should be held at an angle of between 30° and 45°.

Once you are playing regularly, you will gradually adjust the straps and guitar to a height and neck angle that suits your own needs. But be careful: we've all seen rock musicians performing with extremely low-slung guitars, but because it involves the left hand stretching further and adopting a more pronounced angle, this "cool" pose will make learning more difficult and – it has to be said – often physically uncomfortable.

Even playing in a standard position brings into action various muscles in the wrist which have hitherto had little or no exercise – so starting out is not without its aches and pains.

THE LEFT HAND

Playing a note requires the fingers of the left hand to press down the strings between particular frets on the fingerboard. It is vital that you adopt the correct left-hand posture, particularly in technically demanding playing. The biggest danger for the beginner is acquiring bad habits which are difficult to shake off later on.

BASICS

Guitar players of all styles use one of two distnct left-hand techniques, the classical technique and what we might call the "alternative". The classical discipline calls for the thumb to be held against the back of the neck at all times, the tension produced allowing the neck to be clasped firmly, and creating extra pressure when fretting notes along the fingerboard. The strictly correct classical posture has the thumb kept absolutely straight.

A lot of self-taught musicians, however, slide the left-hand thumb around the neck, letting it rest along the edge of the fingerboard. An easy habit to get into when learning, the practice is severly discouraged by classical guitar teachers. Having said that, it's not necessarily a bad habit. It's more comfortable in many ways, and players with a wide fingerspan can use the thumb to fret the 5th and 6th strings, useful for playing particular chords. But if it is relied on too much, this technique can certainly hamper a player's speed and agility. On balance, there are adavantages to be found in both techniques.

FRETTING

Establishing a good fretting technique is likewise an important element in developing the left hand. The secret is to make sure the tip of the finger falls just behind the fret. If it's too far back, the

THE STRING IS HELD DOWN AGAINST THE FRET BY THE PAD ON THE TIP OF THE FINGER.

string will buzz against the fret; if it's right on top of the fret, the string will produce a muted sound.

All the fingers should be held as vertical as possible against the fretboard, in order to avoid the accidental muting of other strings. For this reason, the classical technique has a real advantage over the "alternative", where it's harder to keep the fingers properly vertical when the thumb is resting on the edge of the fingerboard .

CLASSICAL LEFT-HAND TECHNIQUE REQUIRES THE THUMB TO BE HELD AGAINST THE BACK OF THE NECK.

WHEN FRETTING A NOTE, ENSURE THAT REDUNDANT FINGERS ARE HELD CLEAR OF THE STRINGS.

THE "ALTERNATIVE" NON-CLASSICAL STYLE, WITH THE THUMB HELD
OVER THE SIDE OF THE FINGERBOARD.

THE THUMB BEING USED TO FRET NOTES.

EXERCISING THE LEFT HAND

The aim of the two exercises below is purely to get the learner
used to the idea of using different fingers of the left hand to fret
notes. It should be remembered that that the notes in
each of these exercises are the same ones played on different
strings, so exercise 1 shows different ways of playing the note C,
exercise 2, the note G.

Each time you must depress the string with the finger and
pluck the string with the right hand – it doesn't matter if you are
using your fingers or a plectrum at this stage. Make sure you apply
just the right amount of pressure on the fingerboard for the note to
be heard clearly. Too little pressure will produce a muted sound,
too much and your fingers will get tired – not to mention the
danger of developing some painful blisters!

Take a rest from playing once your fingers start to feel tired or
painful. It will take a while for the tips of your fingers to become
hardened to the continual pressure on metal or nylon strings, when
previously they have probably done nothing more demanding than
holding a pen or pencil.

WATCH THOSE NAILS

It will be quite impossible to achieve a satisfactory
fretting technique if your fingernails are too long. A
simple test is to put them down vertically on a
smooth horizontal surface; if the tip of the nail
hits the surface before the pad of the finger, then
your nails need cutting. On the other hand
guitarists such as
classical players
who don't use a
pick sometimes grow
the nails of their right hand
long enough for them to
pluck or strike the strings. If
you see a person with short
nails on one hand and long
on the other, no prizes for
guessing the reason why!

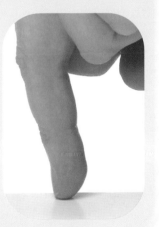

EXERCISE 1	STRING	FRET	FINGER
	1	8	1st
	2	1	1st
	3	5	2nd
	4	10	3rd
	5	3	4th
	6	8	4th

EXERCISE 2	STRING	FRET	FINGER
	1	3	1st
	2	8	1st
	3	12	2nd
	4	5	3rd
	5	10	4th
	6	3	4th

UNDERSTANDING
WRITTEN MUSIC

For anyone completely unfamiliar with the notion of written music, this spread presents a very brief overview of basic principles. Although it can seem rather mysterious to the novice, music is an extremely logical discipline – in fact Pythagoras saw music as part of the same system as mathematics and philosophy. In this book several different devices are used to get across musical ideas. The majority of the exercises use standard music notation (the five-line treble staff) and the alternative, guitar tablature. Diagrams looking down onto the fingerboard are a convenient visual tool to illustrate chord positions, and photographs are also used to show some examples.

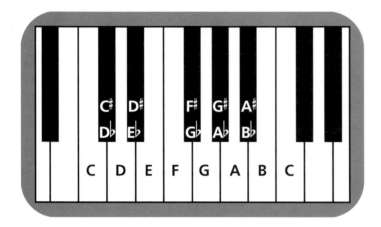

THE NOTES

Western musical systems are characterized by having 12 fixed pitches, or notes, the interval between each known as a "half-step" (or "semitone" in Europe). We can think of them most easily as they appear on a piano keyboard, the white notes being named from A to G. Each black note can have two possible names, depending on musical context. They can be thought of as a "sharpened" version of the note to their immediate left, taking the name of that note followed by a "sharp" symbol (♯), or as a "flattened" version of the note to the immediate right, taking the name of that note followed by a "flat" symbol (♭). These dual-identity notes are known as "enharmonic". The sequence of lettered

names repeats itself after 12 notes, so the note C on a piano keyboard can be found again 12 half-steps to either side, but pitched in a different register. The complete interval of 12 of these half-steps is called an "octave".

STANDARD NOTATION

The traditional way music is written is on a five-line grid known as a "staff", or "staves" in the plural. Various symbols that are written on and between the lines of the staff are used to indicate both the pitch of a note, and how long it should be held – its duration.

Some musical instruments, such as the piano, have a very wide range of notes. For instance, the notes of a concert grand piano can cover over seven octaves. All of these notes, therefore, cannot be accomodated within a single staff, so a staff can be alloted its own range of notes by inserting a symbol at the start of the music.

In this way, notes that are predominantly above "middle C" on the piano are written on a "treble" staff, which is indicated by a treble clef (𝄞); while the notes appearing mainly below middle C are to be found on a staff prefixed by a bass clef (𝄢). This is why piano music is written over two parallel staves, with the treble notes usually being played by the right hand and the bass notes played by the left.

The range of the guitar, on the other hand, is limited to a maximum of four octaves, and although if annotated correctly the

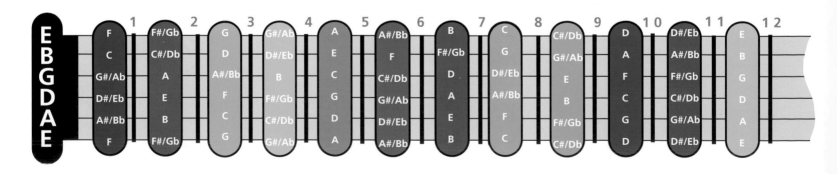

A MEMORY AID

The names of the notes as they appear in order on the staves can be easily remembered with little phrases where the initial letter of each word stands for the individual note names.

THE TREBLE STAFF

In this way we can easily recall the notes that pass through each line of a treble staff, with the phrases **E**at **G**ood **B**read **D**ear **F**ather or **E**very **G**ood **B**oy **D**eserves **F**avours, and with the notes in between the lines spelling the word **FACE**.

THE BASS STAFF

As a guitar player you won't have a lot to do with the notes that appear on the bass clef, but it won't do you any harm to remember them – it might be useful in future if, for instance, you are transcribing a part from the bass notes on some piano music. The phrases that can be used in this respect are **G**ood **B**oys **D**eserve **F**un **A**lways for the notes on the line, and **A C**ow **E**ats **G**rass for the four notes that occur in between.

written music would be split over two registers, for convenience it is written an octave higher that the real pitch, allowing it to be accomodated on a single treble staff.

The notes on and between each line on the staff are defined by the clef. With a treble clef, the notes written on the lines are E, G, B, D, and F, while the notes between the lines are F, A, C, and E. If a note is out of the range of a staff, extra "ledger" lines can be added above or below for each such note. Enharmonic notes are written on the appropriate line of their name, with the indicative "flat" or "sharp" symbol alongside.

THE TABLATURE SYSTEM

Another widely-used form of written music is the tablature system, often applied to the guitar and other fretted instruments. Tablature (TAB for short) takes the form of a simple six-line grid with each line representing a string, from top to bottom. The specific fret to be played is indicated by a number written on a line. The main advantage of this over standard notation is that it represents very precise playing instructions. The example below illustrates how the note E, positioned on the top space of the staff, can be played in the same register on every string of a 24-fret guitar.

The diagram running along the bottom of these pages shows the full range of notes along the fingerboard of a guitar .

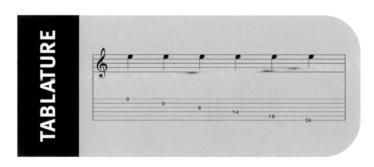

THE TREBLE STAFF

E G B D F

F A C E

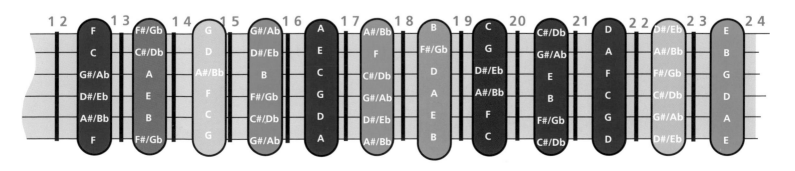

TUNING

It might be stating the obvious, but the most fundamental rule in playing the guitar – as with any instrument – is to ensure it's in tune. A less-than-obvious aspect of this, when learning to play an instrument, is developing an "ear" that recognizes tiny variations in pitch and knows when the intonation is correct. Not everyone has a natural "musical ear" of course, but like most skills it's something that can be learned and improved upon – the learner shouldn't be concerned if it doesn't come naturally at first.

BASICS

Regardless of the instrument that has produced it, the pitch of any note is governed by the frequency of sound waves moving through the air, measured in hertz or cycles per second. This frequency, when measuring a note played by striking a guitar string, is detemined by three elements – the length, thickness and tension of the string. And although guitar strings are the same length as each other, each open string is of a different thickness – known as the gauge. The thinnest strings produce the highest notes and the thickest the lowest notes. The pitch of a particular string is adjusted by turning one of the machine heads located at the top of the neck on the headstock, which increases or reduces the tension, allowing the player to control the pitch.

TURNING A MACHINE HEAD.

GUITAR STRING NOTES

The six strings on a guitar are tuned to specific musical intervals. From top to bottom, these notes are E, B, G, D, A, and E. The same intervals apply to 12-string guitars, but while the top two pairs of strings are tuned in unison, the bottom four pairs are usually tuned at octave intervals. The diagram below illustrates the relationship between the strings of the guitar and the corresponding notes on a keyboard.

Tuning a guitar can involve one of several different techniques, although just making sure all the strings are in relative tune with each other will suffice for you to play on your own. But once you want to play with other instruments, then the guitar needs to be tuned to what we call "standard concert pitch". This is a tone of reference for all instruments, fixing the value of the note of A above middle C on a piano keyboard with a frequency of 440 hertz. Consequently the only certain way of tuning your guitar with absolute accuracy is to use an independent reference tone, such as that produced by a guitar tuner, tuning fork, or pitch pipes. You can also use a well-tuned piano or electronic keyboard.

TUNING TECHNIQUES

The various techniques that are to be found on the next four pages represent the systems for tuning the guitar that are most commonly employed. They all, in one way or another, tune one string as a reference point for the other five strings. But as will be realized working through this book, or when you try things out for yourself, the standard E-A-D-G-B-E tuning is certainly not the only way to tune a guitar. We look at this in greater depth on pages 182–185.

REFERENCE POINT TUNING

To start with, we look at a technique that begins with tuning the top (1st) string to a reference point, such as a keyboard or electric guitar tuner, then tuning the other five strings relative to that note. This system can also be applied in reverse, first tuning the 6th string to a reference tone and working back up to the top string. This is done by simply tuning the bottom string and working backwards.

1ST STRING – OPEN E

Play your E reference note, playing the top string at the same time. Then turn the machine head until the notes coincide, repeating the process until you're satisfied that the string is properly in tune.

2ND STRING – OPEN B

Placing your index finger on the 5th fret of the 2nd string, play the note following it with the open 1st. Turn the machine head of the 2nd string until the top two

strings are in tune, comparing your open B to a fixed reference tone if possible.

3RD STRING – OPEN G

Sound the 4th fret of the 3rd string with the open 2nd string, adjusting the 3rd string machine head until it's in tune. Again, you should try to compare your open G to a reference tone.

4TH STRING – OPEN D

Play the 5th fret of the 4th string at the same time as the open 3rd. Turn the machine head on the 4th string until it is in tune. Compare the open D with a fixed reference tone if you can.

5TH STRING – OPEN A

Play the 5th fret of the 5th string (D) along with the open D on the 4th string. Then adjust the machine head that controls the 5th string until it is in tune. Tuning the bass strings can sometimes have the effect of putting the treble strings out of tune, so it's recommended that you keep checking them.

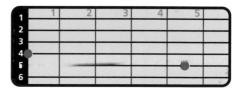

6TH STRING – OPEN E

Play the 5th fret of the 6th string simultaneously with the open 5th string, turning the machine head on the 6th until it sounds in tune. Then give all the strings a final check.

TUNING TIPS

- A good habit from the start is to check that your guitar is properly in tune every time you are about to play.
- Avoid plucking the strings too vigorously with your right hand when you are tuning, as it can cause the sound produced to distort, making accurate tuning that more difficult.
- If you're trying to tune two strings together, but you can hear a slight pulsing noise even though the notes are almost identical, it's a sign that the tuning isn't quite spot-on yet.
- Be careful to avoid fretting the notes too hard with your left hand, particularly when using low-gauge strings, as the string is quite liable to go out of tune when you take your hand off the fingerboard.
- When fitting a new set of strings on your guitar, make sure you "stretch" them right away, to avoid the guitar going out of tune. Further information on strings can be found on pages 208–209.

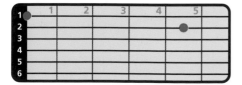

OCTAVE AND HARMONIC TUNING

Individual guitar players have their own favourite methods of tuning. One widely used alternative to the tuning systems outlined on the previous pages is to compare octave intervals or harmonics. As soon as a reference note has been established, many guitarists prefer to hold down a chord with the left hand, tuning the other five strings accordingly.

OCTAVE INTERVALS

This technique compares the same notes played on different strings at octave intervals. Start by tuning the 5th string – open A – to a reference tone.

- Play the 7th fret of the 5th string (E), using this to tune the 1st and 6th strings.
- Play the 7th fret of the 1st string (B), tuning the open 2nd string to that note.
- Play the 8th fret of the 2nd string (G), tuning the open 3rd string to that note.
- Play the 7th fret of the 3rd string (D), tuning the open 4th string to that note.

MIXED TUNING

It's also possible to tune the guitar using the top string and the lower frets, starting by tuning the 1st string to a reference tone.

- Play the 7th fret of the 1st string (B), using this to tune the 2nd string.
- Play the 3rd fret of the 1st string (G), tuning the open 3rd string to that note.
- Play the 3rd fret of the 2nd string (D), tuning the open 4th string to that note.
- Play the 2nd fret of the 3rd string (A), tuning the open 5th string to that note.
- Play the 2nd fret of the 4th string (E), tuning the open 6th string.

TONES OF REFERENCE

The traditional method of tuning to concert pitch, especially among classical guitarists, has always been to use a a piano keyboard for reference tones. It's still a popular method – the keys you need to locate are illustrated in the diagram on page 114.

In the absence of a piano or electronic keyboard, other sources can be used, a simple one being the tuning fork. This provides one single tone – usually the A below middle C.

After striking the fork, hold it against the body of the guitar and it will produce a clear tone. Likewise, tones for all six strings can be produced by pitch pipes.

These days, electronic tuners are used more often than not, with many inexpensive and reliable models appearing on the market over the last twenty years or so. On these devices, the pitch is monitored on a VU meter after the guitar is plugged into the unit. More sophisticated units allow the guitar to be remotely connected to the tuner, so the guitarist can re-tune on stage without having to be disconnected. Also, built-in tuning facilities are now often provided in various multi-effects units. Acoustic guitar players need to remember, before buying a unit, that in order for an electronic tuner to work for them it has to have a built-in microphone.

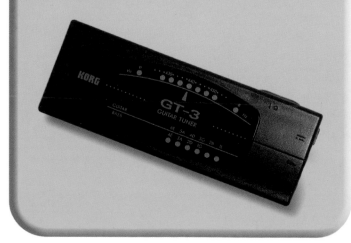

HARMONIC TUNING

The sound produced when you strike a guitar string is the result of a complicated set of elements known as the "harmonic series", with the dominant sound being known as a "fundamental". Placing your finger lightly on any of the strings directly over the 12th fret, you will hear a bell-like tone instead of a fretted note. This sound is what we call a harmonic, and can also be produced by playing above other frets on the fingerboard. Harmonics are covered in

greater depth later in the book (see pages 170–171), but at this stage we are just dealing with them in relation to the actual tuning of the guitar .

Start by tuning the 6th string to concert pitch, after which the other five strings can be tuned by matching the harmonics as outlined below.

- Play the harmonic on the 5th fret of the 6th string, followed by the harmonic on the 7th fret of the 5th. Turn the 5th string machine head until it is in tune.
- Tune the 4th string by matching harmonics on the 5th fret of the 5th string to the 7th fret of the 4th .
- Tune the 3rd string by matching harmonics on the 5th fret of the 4th string to the 7th fret of the 3rd.
- Tune the 2nd string by matching the harmonic on the 7th fret of the 6th to with the open 2nd.
- Tune the 1st string by matching harmonics on the 5th fret of the 2nd string to the 7th fret of the 1st.

BEWARE THE TREMOLO

Tremolo units have long been considered hazardous when it comes to tuning. Developed in the 1950s, the old Fender and Bigsby systems were well-known for going out of tune while the guitar was being played, and even while the guitarist was tuning up. The answer to many of these problems came with the advent of the Floyd Rose locking nut system in the 1980s, versions of which are now standard on most guitars. But, although they might make your instrument seem indestructible, they can still create various problems for initial tuning. Start by unlocking the nut with an Allen key, then tune the guitar in the usual fashion, turning the machine heads to alter the tension of the strings. When each string is roughly in tune, lock the nut. The strings can now be fine-tuned utilizing the hand-adjustable screws on the bridge.

◀ Unlock the nut unit by turning the Allen key in an anticlockwise direction.

▶ Using the screws on the hand-adjustable locking unit, fine-tune the strings.

PICKING THE STRINGS

As we know, in order to make a sound the guitar string has to be struck by the right hand, and this can be achieved in various ways. Classical and flamenco players, and other musicians who play nylon-string guitars, usually pluck the strings with their fingers – or fingernails – but most guitarists in other areas of music utilize a pick held between the first finger and the thumb of the right hand. Although usually made from plastic or tortoiseshell and triangular in shape, the picks or plectra – also known as "plectrums" or "flatpicks" – are to be found in many different materials, shapes and sizes.

THE BASICS

Although the size and thickness of the pick you select is a question of personal taste, it needs to be remembered that the type you select can have a big influence on the tone of your playing. For simple strumming, a thin and flexible pick is recommended, whereas a smaller, heavier pick is better suited to fast solo work. Another style, common with folk and country musicians are picks that slide over each finger of the right hand like extensions of the fingernails. The best plan for a beginner is to try out as many different types of pick as possible, you'll soon settle on the one you feel is right for you.

HOLDING THE PICK

The way you hold the pick is all-important. Grip the pick between the thumb and the top joint of the 1st finger, at an approximate angle of 90° to the body of the guitar and parallel to the strings. You should grip the pick in a reasonably relaxed way, but not so loosely that it moves around while you are playing. It's important that striking the string should be a seamless, smooth, flowing movement – swivelling the wrist and forearm, moving the joints of the fingers and thumb.

DIRECTIONAL PICKING

Self-explanatory, the two basic ways to strike a string with a pick are are commonly referred to as "downstrokes" and "upstrokes". Taking the tip of the pick above the string and pushing down constitutes a downstroke, while the upstroke is the reverse – placing the tip below the string and pulling up. Each type of stroke has its own symbol, which means that it can be indicated in written music, the notation usually being found above the notes on the staff.

DOWNSTROKE ⊓

UPSTROKE V

In order to master this type of playing technique (with each sroke making its own unique sound) you need to become adept at mixing the strokes. The most effective way of playing is making an upstoke after a downstroke in one smooth movement, and is the only way for the guitarist to play fast lead parts.

FINGERPICKING

Fingerpicking is a technique common to classical and flamenco music, as well as a wide variety of folk styles. Within these various genres there are a multiplicity of variations, but the most commonly adopted technique is the standard one taught in classical playing. Often known as "PIMA" , the technique uses particular fingers of the right hand to play specific strings. The thumb plays the bass strings (strings 4 to 6) while the 1st, 2nd, and 3rd fingers play each of the treble strings respectively (1 to 3). Sometimes this fingering is indicated on manuscripts of printed guitar music, in which case the fingers are referred to by the initials of their Spanish names. Therefore the thumb is "P" (*pulgar*),

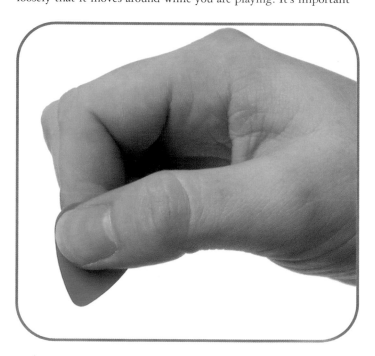

CLASSICAL HAND STYLE.

CLAWHAMMER STYLE.

the 1st finger is "I" (*indice*), the 2nd finger "M" (*medio*), and the 3rd is "A" (*anular*). The 4th finger is rarely utilized in this way, but it is it is often referred to as "C" (*meñique*), or sometimes as "X" or "E."

THE RIGHT-HAND POSITION

In classical guitar-playing, the musician is taught to strike the strings with the fingernails rather than the pads of the fingers, although there have been some famous exceptions to this rule. This technique, however, is not generally to be found in other areas of music, the "clawhammer" style associated with steel-string players being the most used alternative. The pictures above show how the position of the right hand differs greatly, the "classical" position resting the inside of the forearm at the upper edge of the guitar's body; the "clawhammer" resting the palm on the bridge.

PICKS OR FINGERS?

To a degree, the choice of whether you use a pick or your fingers can be dictated by the type of music you play, insofar as in classical or flamenco music picks are seldomly used. In other less specific areas of music, however, where styles cross over and the boundaries between them become less distinct, options are more flexible. While it's broadly accepted that the direct contact of fingers and strings, without any plastic coming between, allows a player more dynamic control, rapid passages on an electric guitar with low-gauge strings would be difficult to play in this way. In country music and jazz, the best players are invariably masters of both styles, but in rock music we find mostly pick-oriented players – not least because in the area of rock, reliance on volume-heavy electronic effects like compression and distortion rules out any

subtle dynamics. Having said that, in the largely self-taught field of rock music, where techniques are frequently acquired via all sorts of short-cut solutions, many musicians have realised by trial-and-error that it's actually easier to pick out the notes of a chord (called an arpeggio) with their fingers than with a pick.

HYBRID PLAYING

Found mainly in the realm of country players, a unique hybrid technique integrates fingerpicking and using a pick. This unorthodox – and partcularly demanding – method uses the little finger to play the top strings. In order to try out this technique you need to hold the plectrum in the standard way between index finger and thumb, leaving the remaining three fingers free to play each of the treble strings respectively.

Perhaps the trickiest part of this type of playing is disciplining the 3rd and 4th fingers of the right hand to move independently of each other. As will be found with the left hand when more demanding chords are attempted, there are certain muscles in the fingers that got virtually no exercise before you started playing the guitar.

At this stage there's no need to worry too much about this technique. Difficult even for more seasoned players who are adept at playing with both pick and fingers, it does serve to illustrate one of the things that will become more apparent as you progress – that hard-and-fast rules for playing the guitar are relatively few and far between.

OPEN-STRING CHORDS

Chords are a central part of all guitar-based music, whether we're talking about pop, rock, country, classical, jazz, or flamenco. Basically the effect of three or more notes being played simultaneously, guitar chords are formed by pressing the fingers of the left hand onto specific positions on the fingerboard. Soon after you get started, the basic chord fingering will become increasingly familiar to you, as will how the chords actually sound in relation to each other. There are nine examples over the next four pages of the simplest and most commonly used chords. In fact, once you are able to play these chords with a reasonable degree of confidence, you'll probably be in a position to have a go at some of your favorite songs.

THE CHORD DIAGRAMS

All the chord diagrams you will see in the book are easy to understand. Just think of each one as the fretboard of a guitar, with the dots marked between the frets on the strings representing the positions where your fingers should be placed. Which finger to use is indicated by the number on each dot, 1 to 4 representing the index finger to the little finger.

Where there is no number, it means fretting the note is optional. Beside the chord chart you will find the note names of each string. Any note marked "X" means that the the string should not be played, and a note appearing in brackets also indicates that the note is optional.

TRIADS

This section features chords that are known as "triads", so-called because they are made up of three different notes – although, because the chords are being played on six-strings on the guitar, some notes are repeated in other registers. The open E major chord shown on the right, for instance, includes the note E played over three different octaves.

You can also achieve the effect of a chord by playing just two different notes, although this is regarded technically as an "interval" rather than a chord. The intervals of notes we find in every triad are identical in relation to the chord's "root", i.e. the note by which we identify the key of the chord. In a major triad, the sequence of intervals are called root, major 3rd and perfect 5th. In this way, a C major triad uses the notes C (root), E (major 3rd), and G (perfect 5th), but there's no need to be concerned about this

technical detail just yet – at this stage it's more important to focus your attention on playing those first chords.

THE FIRST CHORD

You are now about to learn an E major chord, which will be the first recognizably musical sound you make on the guitar.

The simplest chords that learners begin with are known as "open-string" chords, so-called because they can be formed by a combination of open (unfretted) strings, and the first two or three frets on the fingerboard. The E major chord is particularly significant, as the basic fingering can be moved along the fingerboard, creating a number of alternative chords.

E MAJOR

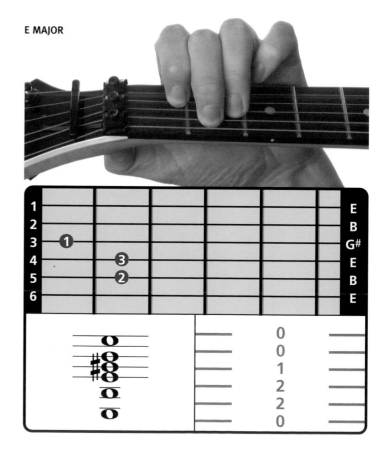

FRETTING

Below are four basic steps to play an open E major chord.
At first your fingers will probably feel very uncomfortable, but
don't worry, this is perfectly normal for the beginner. Just take it
easy, a step at a time.

- Put the 2nd finger of your left hand behind the 2nd fret of
  the 5th string.
- Put the 3rd finger of your left hand behind the 2nd fret of the
  4th string.
- Put the index finger of your left hand behind the 1st fret of the
  3rd string.
- Holdintg the pick in your right hand, strum all six strings.

You've done it – you've played your first chord.

THE THREE-CHORD TRICK

Next we're going to look at two chords, A major and D major,
both of which are closely related to the chord you've just played,
E major. These three chords are related to each other by the
intervals of their root notes, and some of the best-known songs in
rock, pop, blues and country use what are called "one-four-fives",
which is written in Roman numerals (I-IV-V).

A MAJOR

The 6th string is optional when playing the A major chord, which
is why the note is shown alongside the chord diagram in brackets.
Although a musically correct part of an A major triad, the "bottom
E", can create an imbalance to the complete sound because it's
lower in pitch than the chord's root note, and sometimes playing
this note simply makes the chord sound wrong.

D MAJOR

You can choose from a number of alternative ways of playing
a D major chord. One way is to play just the top four strings,
ignoring the bottom two. A more usual method is to play the
5th string, the chord still sounding satisfactory even though the
note A is lower in pitch than the root D. Both these approaches
can be tricky when strumming quickly in both directions with
a pick, and because of this a lot of players play a D major with
the thumb around the back of the neck to play the F# on the
2nd fret of the 1st string. As one can imagine, it's not a
technique approved of by classical tutors of the instrument,
but has worked in the hands of many great non-classical players
including Jimi Hendrix, and has to be worth considering as
another option.

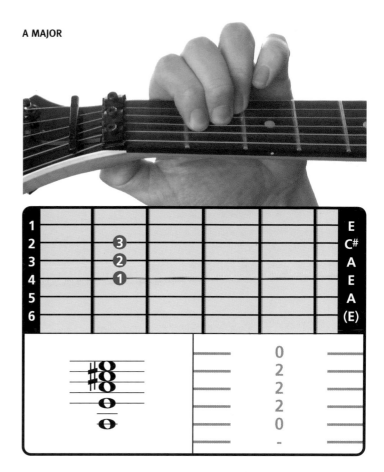

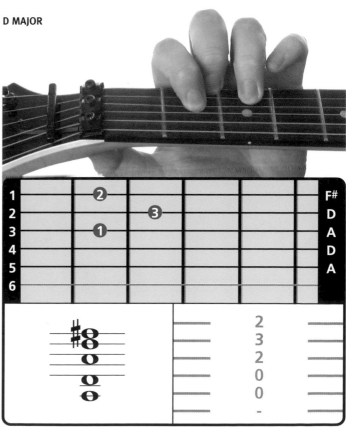

SIX MORE OPEN-STRING CHORDS

Another six open-string chords are illustrated below, including this time three "minor" chords. Minor chords are created by "flattening" the third note of a major triad – in other words reducing it by a semitone, or one fret on the fingerboard. Take, for example, a C minor triad which consists of the notes C (root), E♭ (minor 3rd), and G (perfect 5th). You can hear the dramatic difference between major and minor chords perfectly when you simply alternate the E major and E minor chords by removing the 1st finger.

G MAJOR

C MAJOR

F MAJOR

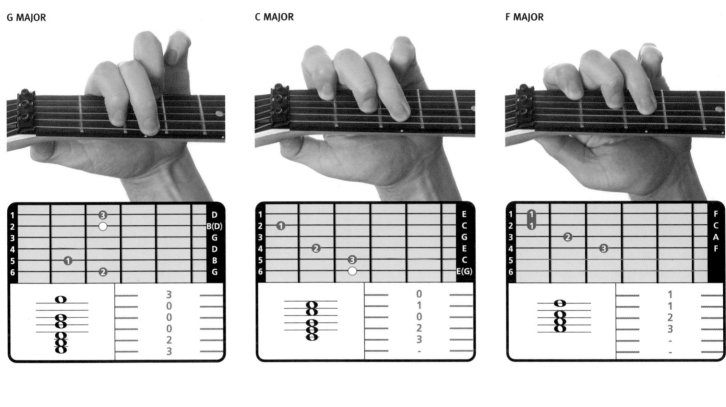

E MINOR

A MINOR

D MINOR

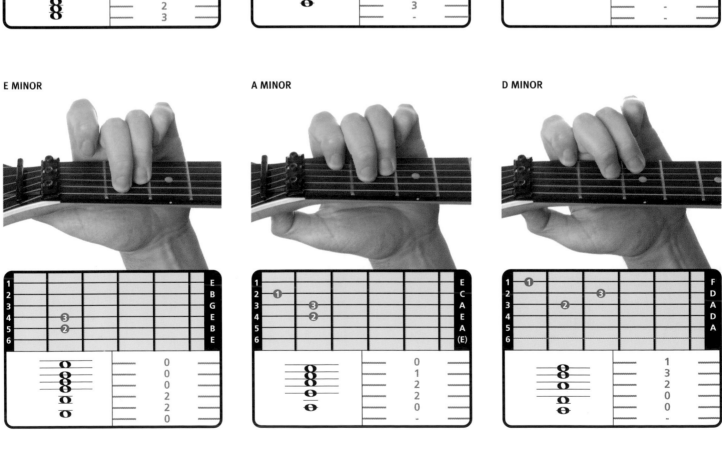

CHANGING CHORDS

Here below are some exercises that will help you learn to move around the three chord shapes that you've just practiced. At this stage there's no need to worry about keeping time, just fretting the notes correctly is all that's needed. This will be a really tough exercise for the complete beginner, so it's advisable to spend some time on this section before moving on to the other chords. But don't be put off – every player from Segovia to Santana has gone through this stage,, and they will almost certainly have found it just as difficult.

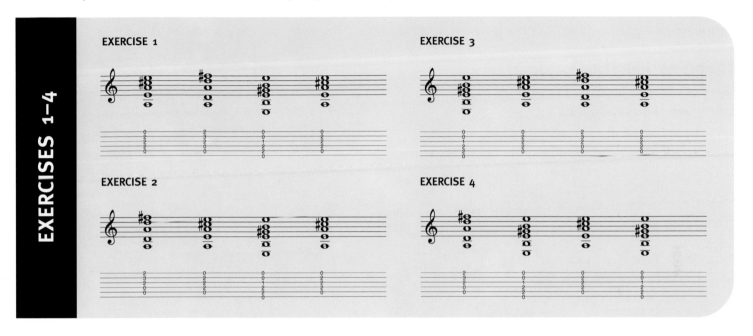

FLUENCY

Next are four exercises that integrate some of the new chords which you've just seen. Trying to play each one as smoothly as possible, see if you can also begin to keep time. Count out aloud "one-and-two-and-three-and-four-and..." while you're playing, hitting a new chord each time you get to "one." Or to keep time you can play along to a drum machine or metronome. These four sequences are known as "turnarounds", which means that when you get to the end of the sequence you go back to the beginning and start again.

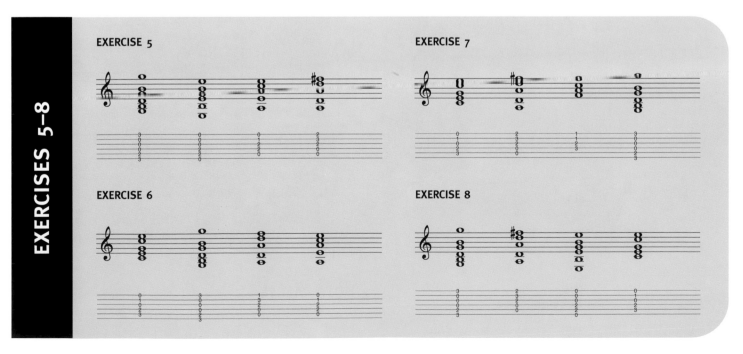

PLAYING IN TIME

One essential skill that every musician has to acquire is playing in time, i.e. playing a piece of music or accompanying other musicians at precisely the correct speed, without speeding up or slowing down. It can be one of the hardest skills to accomplish for beginners on the guitar, not least because there is so much concentration on making sure the left hand-fingers are in the correct position. The basic difficulty is that your right hand has to anticipate the exact moment that the pick will strike the string whenever you play a note or chord.

TEMPO AND RHYTHM

There are two basic elements of timing, tempo and rhythm. Tempo refers to the actual speed of a piece of music, this usually being measured in "beats per minute" (bpm). In printed guitar music we will often see a tempo instruction above the staffs at the top of the page. This example is a tempo instruction for a piece of music to be played at 120 beats per minute.

 = 120

CLASSICAL TEMPO TERMINOLOGY

Much written music specifies only a general tempo to be adopted, and these instructions are traditionally expressed by the use of Italian names. Here below are the terms (known as "tempo marks") along with the approximate beats per minute associated with each. We can see that within these ranges there is scope for individual interpretation on the part of a player or conductor. For instance, a piece to be played *Andante* would sound a lot different played at 75 bpm rather than 100 bpm. We can see some of the tempo ranges overlap because tempo marks can also indicate the character of the music.

TEMPO MARK	DESCRIPTION	BPM RANGE
Grave	Very slow, serious	Below 40
Lento	Slow	40–55
Largo	Broad	45–65
Adagio	Slow (literally, at ease)	55–75
Andante	Walking speed	75–105
Moderato	Moderate speed	105–120
Allegro	Fast (literally, cheerful)	120–160
Vivace	Lively	150–170
Presto	Very fast	170–210
Prestissimo	As fast as possible	Above 210

THE RHYTHM GUITAR

It is the rhythm that creates the "feel" in a piece of music, the term itself referring to the way in which notes are played or accented. The rhythm guitar had been prominent in many forms of ensemble group playing since the earliest days of jazz, blues and folk music, long before amplification gave the instrument a "lead" voice. Then, in the 1930s, enterprising jazz musicians such as Charlie Christian were the first to experiment with electronic pickups, so enabling the guitar to join keyboard, woodwind and brass instruments in playing solo parts that could be heard clearly in a jazz group or large dance orchestra.

PERFECTING A SENSE OF TIMING

Among the many different ways a beginner can develop a sense of timing is the much-used approach of playing along with records and CDs. The drawback with this is the recording may not be tuned to concert pitch, so it may be necessary to tune the guitar. A more traditional method is to use a metronome, a clockwork "ticking" apparatus that can be set at a tempo of your choice, while more recently drum machines have performed a similar function.

PLAYING WITH FEELING

A group of musicians can creatively use rhythm to establish a mood or "feel", with the ensemble pushing and pulling against the base tempo. This isn't a sign of shoddy musicianship, but the essence of a group playing with real feeling. Compared to music played against a mechanical rhythm backing, we only have to listen to some of the great house bands on R&B and soul records from the Motown or Stax labels, or outfits like James Brown's 1970s backing band, the JBs. The sheer feel demonstrated by musicians like these is something that can never be equalled by modern technolgy and electronic devices.

NOTE VALUES

A note played on the guitar comprises three elements: pitch, volume, and duration. Pitch is created by the fret position; the volume by how hard one strikes the string; duration by how long the note is sustained. In written manuscript music, the basic tempo is governed by how many "beats" are played every minute, with the value of individual notes being in relation to the length of that beat.

DIVISIONS

The longest note value is a note sustained for four beats, known as a "whole note". Subsequent notes may be halved in value until we get to the "sixty-fourth note", with a value of a sixteenth of a

beat – though a note of such short duration is very, very rarely to be found in guitar music.

The table below shows the symols for each different type of note, as they appear in written music. Every note below a quarter note has a series of "flags" attached to the stem, which are replaced by "beams" which join the notes together when groups of these notes appear on the staff.

Strumming the same sequence using chords with different time values can help the learner to find it easier to understand the breakdown of note values.

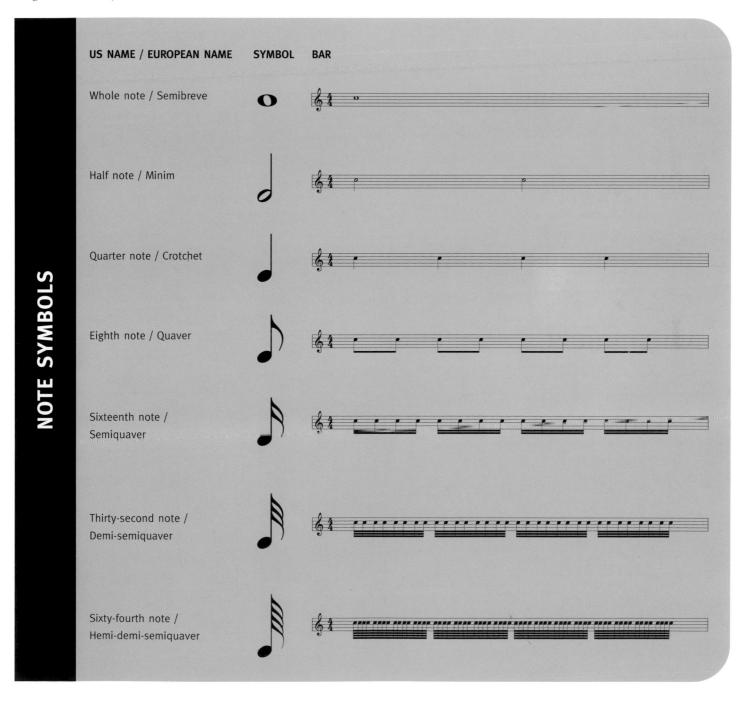

NOTE SYMBOLS

US NAME / EUROPEAN NAME	SYMBOL	BAR
Whole note / Semibreve		
Half note / Minim		
Quarter note / Crotchet		
Eighth note / Quaver		
Sixteenth note / Semiquaver		
Thirty-second note / Demi-semiquaver		
Sixty-fourth note / Hemi-demi-semiquaver		

TIME SIGNATURES

In written music, groups of notes are divided into little blocks known as "bars", each of which has a set number of "beats". The best way to appreciate this idea is by counting numbers out aloud: steadily and regularly counting out "1-2-3-4-2-2-3-4-3-2-3-4-4-2-3-4" means you have counted out four bars, with four beats in each single bar. Keep practising until you can do it without thinking.

COMMON TIME

If you look at the written music on these and previous pages, you'll see that some of it begins with two numbers, one on top of the other, on the staff to the left of the notes. This tells us the "time signature" of the particular piece of music, with the top number indicating how many beats are in each bar, and the bottom one telling us the time value of the beats.

In the example illustrated above there are four beats in the bar. Each beat has a value of a quarter note, because it lasts for a quarter of the bar. What can be quite confusing for musical beginners is the fact

that each bar doesn't necessarily *have* to comprise four quarter notes, but that regardless of how many notes are played in the bar, the total value of those notes *has to* add up to the top figure, which in the example is four.

Where we have four beats (quarter notes) in the bar, the music is said to have

a time signature of "four four", and is usually written down as as "4/4."

Because it is by far the most commonly used time signature, four-four time is also widely referred to as "common time" and is sometimes abbreviated on the staff as the letter "C," or in its its more formal manuscript form – ¢.

SIMPLE TIME

Known as "simple time", there are three basic time signatures in music: 2/4, 3/4, and 4/4. The examples on the left show the four-bar groupings for each of these time signatures. Remembering to accent the first beat of each bar, try counting along with each line of music. Counting for the four bars of 2/4 would go "one-two-one-two-one-two-one-two."

And with an unmistakable feel, the 3/4 time signature (also known as "waltz time" or "triple" time) has three beats in each bar.

It might be noticed that the examples in 2/4 and 4/4 have essentially the same time signatures. But the feel of the way the beats are counted is naturally altered by the fact that the 2/4 example would need twice as many bars in order to produce the same number of notes.

TWO-FOUR TIME
There are two beats to the bar, with all the beats being quarter notes.

THREE-FOUR TIME
There are three beats to the bar, with all the beats being quarter notes.

FOUR-FOUR TIME
There are four beats to the bar, with all of the beats are quarter notes.

COMPOUND TIME

The simple time signatures – which are also known as "meters" – in the examples on the previous page can also be grouped into triplets, or groups of three. In this way we get what is known as a "compound" time signature.

In the first example on the right, using 2/4 time, the two beats are played as two groups of three, thus creating a bar made up of six beats. This is a time signature of 6/4 (or 6/8 if eighth notes are being used).

In the same way, bars of triple time (3/4) can be played in groups of three, thus making a compound time signature of 9/4 or 9/8 – both with nine beats to the bar.

When bars of 4/4 time are grouped in this way, we get a compound time signature of 12/4 or 12/8, which has twelve beats in each bar.

COMPOUND TIME

SIX-EIGHT TIME
There are six beats to the bar, with all the beats being eighth notes.

NINE-EIGHT TIME
There are nine beats to the bar, with all the beats being eighth notes.

TWELVE-EIGHT TIME
There are twelve beats to the bar, with all the beats being eighth notes.

ASYMMETRIC TIME

FIVE-FOUR TIME
There are five beats to the bar, with all the beats being quarter notes.

SEVEN-EIGHT TIME
There are seven beats to the bar, with all the beats being eighth notes.

ELEVEN-EIGHT TIME
There are eleven beats to the bar, with all the beats being eighth notes.

ASYMMETRIC TIME

Time signatures with their number of beats not being divisible by two or three are less common, but the most usual of what are called "asymmetric" times are composed of five or seven beats in the bar. Less often we might find eleven- and thirteen-beat time signatures. Although these kind of rhythms are usually found in complex or "difficult" music, the actual rhythms are normally accented so that they can be broken down into groups of two, three, or four. A piece of music in 5/4, for example, can be heard as a group of two beats followed by a group of three – the accents falling on beats one and three. Alternatively, they can be heard as a group of three beats followed by a group of two, with the accents falling on beats one and four, these accent points being indicated by marks above the staff .

SUSTAINS AND RESTS

We can think of note values as our basic unit of musical currency, ranging from the smallest sixty-fourth note to the largest, the whole note. But we can also add to the core value of a note by adding "dot" or "tie" symbols. These dot and tie effects, which can be applied to any kind of note, fulfill a vital function in the creation of the mood, atmosphere and rhythm of a piece of music.

DOTS

We can increase the length of a note by half its value again by following it with a dot. The value of a half note, for example, with a value of two beats, is increased to three beats when followed by a dot.

TIES

The number of beats-to-the-bar in a piece of music are indicated by a time signature. So when we see a piece of music written in 4/4, we know that whatever combination of note lengths we have in that bar, they must total four beats, the value of a whole note. But we sometimes need to hold a note across a bar line – if, for example, a chord struck at the fourth beat of bar one has to be sustained until the second beat of the second bar. In these instances, the value of the notes in each bar are indicated on the staff by being "tied" together with a curved bar. What is vitally important to remember is that whenever you see a note or chord tied in this way, the second note must never be played – we merely sustain the previous note of the last bar for its own values plus the value of the second note. As we will find using the example illustrated above, a half note tied across the bar to a quarter note is sustained for three beats.

RESTS

One other element that has an important role in musical rhythm is the "rest" which, as the name implies, is simply an instruction not to play. There is a rest symbol associated with every type of note and, when this is written on a piece of music, it tells the player to rest for the same duration as the note would have lasted had it been played.

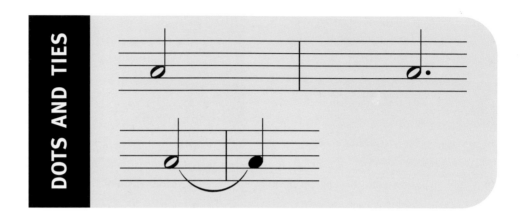

DOTS AND TIES

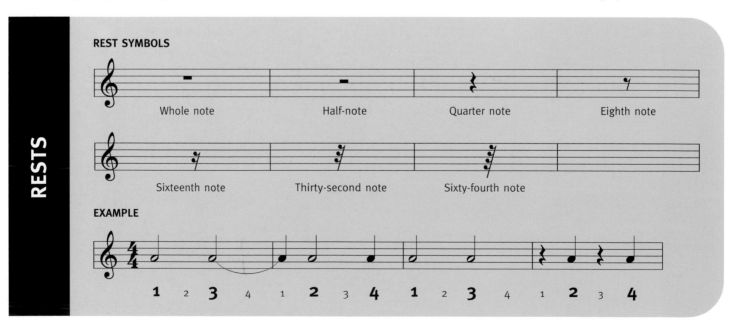

RESTS

REST SYMBOLS

| Whole note | Half-note | Quarter note | Eighth note |

| Sixteenth note | Thirty-second note | Sixty-fourth note |

EXAMPLE

1 2 **3** 4 · 1 **2** 3 **4** · 1 2 **3** 4 · 1 **2** 3 **4**

Rests are supremely important in bringing subtlety and nuance to the performance of a piece of music, as you can hear in the example at the bottom of the previous page. The second two bars insert a pair of quarter-note rests in the second bar, affecting the sound in a very noticable way. The note values in beats are written beneath the staves in order to stress how ties and rests are counted within the bar.

DYNAMIC EFFECT

By simply modulating the volume of a chord or note within a bar we can dramatically change the tone, rhythm and emotional feel of a piece of music. This dynamic effect can be created by either striking the strings harder with the right hand (indicated in manuscripts as an upward-pointing arrow above the note) or by muting them.

To mute or dampen the strings the player can use one of two techniques. You can release the tension of the fingers on the left hand immediately the notes have been played, or you can bring the edge of your right hand down over the strings above the bridge.

And you can still pick notes while the strings are being dampened. This can prove an extremely effective technique, particularly when it is played on an electric guitar using processing effects such as delay.

VOLUME INSTRUCTIONS

Italian phrases are used in written music to describe the dynamics of a piece of music (or a section of a piece of music), some of which are listed below.

pp	Pianissimo	Very soft
p	Piano	Soft
mp	Mezzo piano	Moderately soft
mf	Mezzo forte	Moderately loud
f	Forte	Loud
ff	Fortissimo	Very loud

CRESCENDO AND DIMINUENDO

Gradual modulations in volume are indicated by "crescendo" and "diminuendo" marks, horizontal arrows written above the staff telling the player that the range of notes directly beneath should be gradually played louder or softer.

CRESCENDO   DIMINUENDO

STACCATO

"Staccato" is an Italian word that literally means short and sharp, and is an instruction for a note to be played for half its value, but adhering to the overall rhythm. Indicated on the staff with a dot above or below the note, it's shorthand for showing a note followed by a rest of the same value. The opposite of "staccato" is "legato", where notes are slurred together with little space in between.

DIATONIC SCALES

A "scale" is a series of related notes, and every type of scale follows a set pattern of intervals played in sequence from a particular note to the octave of that note. The "key" of the scale is indicated by first note or "root", and the scales most commonly used are the diatonic major and the three relative minors.

MAJOR SCALE INTERVALS

In a major scale, the pattern of intervals (an "interval" being the distance in pitch between any two notes) that define the scale is made up either of "steps" (which are two frets apart on the fingerboard), referred to as "tones" in Europe, or "half-steps" (one fret apart), which are called "semitones" in Europe. The major scale moves in the following sequence from the root:**STEP•STEP•HALF-STEP•STEP•STEP•STEP•HALF-STEP**. In the key of C, the notes are the "white" notes on a piano – C, D, E, F, G, A, B, and C.

Once we know the root, and therefore the key, of a scale, every note – referred to as a "degree" – can be named both in its own right and as an interval between itself and the root. The diagram below illustrates in a C major scale how the notes are named in terms of the guitar fingerboard.

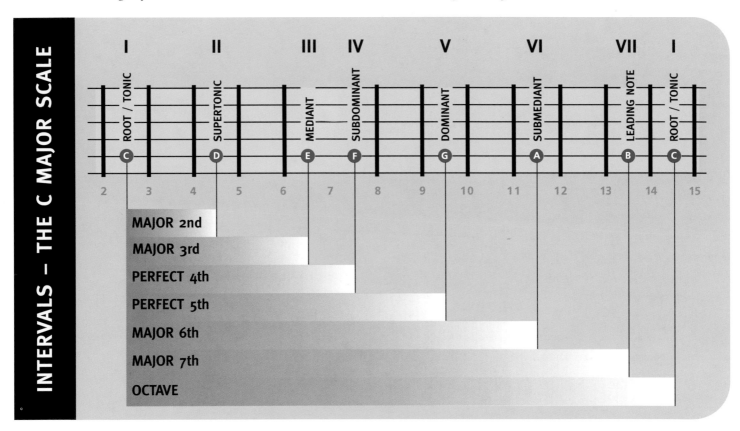

FINGERING

Although it is possible to play scales on a single string, it makes much more sense, and is far easier, to play them across the fingerboard. You will find it's possible, by using the correct fingering, to play all the notes of a major scale without actually moving the left-hand position at all. In classical training players are encouraged in the economic use of fingering by ensuring that each fret, in the range being played, is covered by only one finger of the left hand.

This idea can be demonstrated on a C major scale, where the range of notes to be played are all found from the 2nd to 5th frets on the fingerboard. Regardless of which strings are being used, the notes played on the 2nd, 3rd, 4th, and 5th frets are only held in position by the 1st, 2nd, 3rd, and 4th fingers respectively. You should play each note of the C major scale, making sure you use the correct left-hand fingering. This is not an easy exercise for the learner, making heavy use as it does of the 4th finger. Trying to master the interval between the "leading note" and the "octave," necessitating the co-ordination of the 3rd and 4th fingers, can be torturous in the extreme. But it's of no cause for concern, every budding guitar player has had the same problem. It's another instance of the little finger of the hand getting little or no vigorous exercise apart from musical activity.

Because the major scale, and indeed all scales, follows an exact pattern of intervals, it's easy to see that when your left-hand fingers have become used to the positions on the fingerboard, you to do to

play a scale in another key by sliding your hand until you find the appropriate position of the root-note required. In fact this same pattern, starting on the 5th string, can be used to play a major scale in any key, anywhere on the fingerboard.

If you move your whole hand with the fingers of your left hand covering the 9th to the 12th frets, and repeat the pattern above but starting on the 10th fret of the 5th string, you will find you can play the scale of G major.

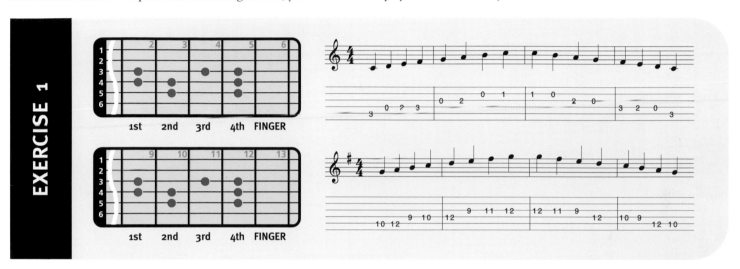

ALTERNATIVE FINGERING

There are two alternative major-scale patterns that are also in common use. One starts on the 6th string, the other on the 3rd. Both are illustrated below playing a C major scale. As we saw earlier, we can play in alternative keys by moving them along the fingerboard. Using the sixth-string scale positions you can play two full octaves straight through from the 1st string to the 6th.

Learners on the guitar often wonder why there isn't a major scale pattern that starts on the 4th string, and this is simply

because playing one would be extremly uncomfortable and consequently isn't recommended. As the interval between the 2nd and 3rd strings is different from the others, it would require a range of five frets, making it necessary for one of the fingers of the left hand to cover two frets.

It's essential to master these three fingering patterns – both playing ascending and descending scales – if you wish to acquire the kind of fluidity that will be necessary for you to develop your skills as a lead player.

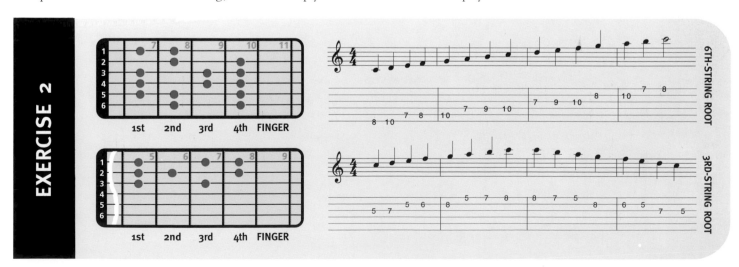

MINOR SCALES

A major scale and minor scale differ primarily in the interval between the 1st and 3rd notes. This interval is a major 3rd (two steps) on a major scale, while on a minor scale it is a minor 3rd (a step and a half step). The three distinct types of minor scale – the natural minor, harmonic minor and melodic minor – differ only in the 6th and 7th degrees of their respective scales.

NATURAL MINOR SCALE

The natural minor scale has the following intervals from the root: **STEP•HALF-STEP• STEP•STEP•HALF-STEP•STEP•STEP**. In the key of C the notes are C, D, E♭, F, G, A♭, B♭, and C. The fingering options are shown below.

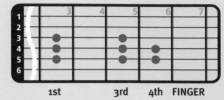

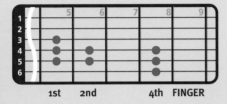

HARMONIC MINOR SCALE

The 6th note of the harmonic minor is raised by a half-step from that of the natural minor. The notes on the harmonic minor scale consist of the following intervals from the root: **STEP•HALF-STEP•STEP•STEP•HALF-STEP•STEP PLUS HALF-STEP•HALF-STEP**. In the key of C these notes are C, D, E♭, F, G, A♭, B, and C.

As can be seen on the fretboard diagram below, in order to play a harmonic minor scale from the 6th string you need to break the one-finger-per-fret rule. In this case the index finger, the strongest and most flexible finger, should be used as the most efficient way to cover the first two fret positions.

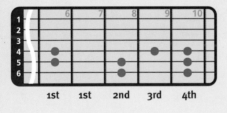

MELODIC MINOR SCALE

The 7th note of the melodic minor is raised by a half-step from that of the natural minor. The notes of the melodic minor scale consist of the following set of intervals from the root: **STEP•HALF-STEP•STEP•STEP•STEP•STEP•HALF-STEP**. In the key of C this uses the notes C, D, E♭, F, G, A, B, and C.

Important point: When playing a descending melodic minor scale, the notes revert to that of the natural minor scale, an important difference from the other minor scales.

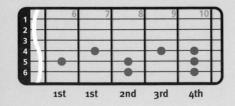

COMPARING THE SCALES

This table shows how the major scale and the three minor scales are different in terms of their intervals.

	ROOT / MINOR 2nd	MAJOR 2nd	MINOR 3rd	MAJOR 3rd	PERFECT 4th	AUGMENTED 4th or DIMINISHED 5th	PERFECT 5th	AUGMENTED 5th or MINOR 6th	MAJOR 6th or DIMINISHED 7th	MINOR 7th	MAJOR 7th	OCTAVE
	I	ii	II	iii	III	IV	V	V	vi	VI	vii	VII	I
MAJOR	●		●		●	●		●		●		●	●
NATURAL MINOR	●		●	●		●		●	●		●		●
HARMONIC MINOR	●		●	●		●		●	●			●	●
MELODIC MINOR	●		●	●		●		●		●		●	●

CONTRASTING SCALES

Play through the four scales shown below in the key of A in order to hear the differences between the scales. Use the fingering that is indicated in the examples for the key of C, starting from the 6th string. The player merely has to move the patterns three frets down the fingerboard. You will notice that the "three sharps" at the front of the A major scale are missing from the minor scale, this being because the A natural minor scale has no flats or sharps. Although starting from different roots, it's called the "relative minor" of the C major scale because it shares the same notes.

A MAJOR

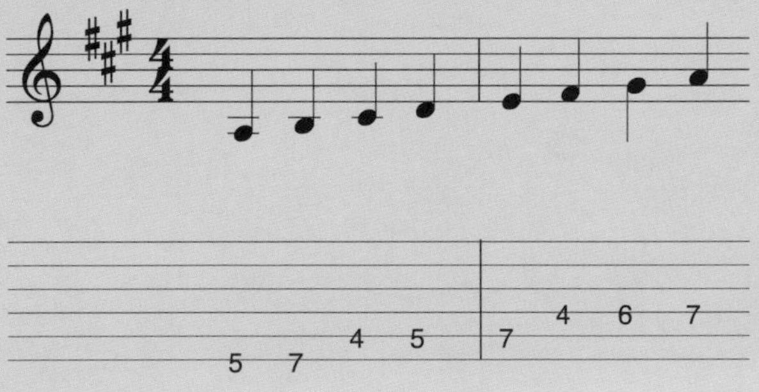

A HARMONIC MINOR

A NATURAL MINOR

A MELODIC MINOR

SCALE FINDER

The information on these pages could radically affect your progress on the guitar. These five tables show you the notes of the four scale types which have been featured on the previous pages, with each degree of each scale shown in all twelve keys. Use each scale as a practice exercise, and you will soon get acquainted with the characteristics of each type of scale. Play the notes in both ascending and descending sequence, not forgetting that you should switch to the notes of the natural minor for each key when you descend the melodic minor scale.

PRACTICING

For the beginner, practising scales can be one of the more tedious chores of learning an instrument, but it certainly pays off, and there are innumerable reasons why to ignore it would be detrimental. Familiarity with scales results in a clearer understanding of how notes relate to one another, which is indispensible as your repetoire of chords broadens. And if, later, you get round to writings songs, a knowledge of scales will be helpful in developing a melodic ear and in understanding why certain notes work best with certain chord sequences.

Scales are also all-important in progressing your lead guitar skills. In many ways this whole chapter can be seen as a first lesson in playing lead because a great deal of the solo work, heard in most areas of popular music, relies on a very limited number of scale types – basically, those that are already covered here and the major and minor pentatonics, which we'll discuss later. And most importantly from a soloist's point of view, an articulate and broad scale vocabulary is essential in developing really effective improvisation skills. The greater the knowledge of scales, therefore, the greater the playing options.

MAJOR	I	II	III	IV	V	VI	VII	I
	A	B	C#	D	E	F#	G#	A
	Bb	C	D	Eb	F	G	A	Bb
	B	C#	D#	E	F#	G#	A#	B
	C	D	E	F	G	A	B	C
	C#	D#	F	F#	G#	A#	C	C#
	D	E	F#	G	A	B	C#	D
	Eb	F	G	Ab	Bb	C	D	Eb
	E	F#	G#	A	B	C#	D#	E
	F	G	A	Bb	C	D	E	F
	F#	G#	A#	B	C#	D#	F	F#
	G	A	B	C	D	E	F#	G
	Ab	Bb	C	Db	Eb	F	G	Ab

NATURAL MINOR	I	II	iii	IV	V	vi	vii	I
	A	B	C	D	E	F	G	A
	Bb	C	Db	Eb	F	Gb	Ab	Bb
	B	C#	D	E	F#	G	A	B
	C	D	Eb	F	G	Ab	Bb	C
	C#	D#	E	F#	G#	A	B	C#
	D	E	F	G	A	Bb	C	D
	Eb	F	Gb	Ab	Bb	B	Db	Eb
	E	F#	G	A	B	C	D	E
	F	G	Ab	Bb	C	Db	Eb	F
	F#	G#	A	B	C#	D	E	F#
	G	A	Bb	C	D	Eb	F	G
	Ab	Bb	B	Db	Eb	E	Gb	Ab

Practising scales is also a useful warm-up exercise, helping you to improve the agility of the left hand and right simultaneously. A final note on scales: you may come across music books that look at what might seem to be impossible note names. This is because each scale is a specified pattern of intervals. In the key of E♭, for example, the natural minor flattens the 6th note of the major scale so, to be musically correct, a flattened C should be referred to as C♭, even though a flattened C is the same as B. In the tables below, to avoid unnecessary confusion, the notes C♭, B♯, F♭, and E♯ have all been referred to as B, C, E, and F respectively.

HARMONIC MINOR

I	II	iii	IV	V	vi	VII	I
A	B	C	D	E	F	G#	A#
B♭	C	D♭	E♭	F	G♭	A	B♭
B	C#	D	E	F#	G	A#	B
C	D	E♭	F	G	A♭	B	C
C#	D#	E	F#	G#	A	C	C#
D	E	F	G	A	B♭	C#	D
E♭	F	G♭	A♭	B♭	B	D	E♭
E	F#	G	A	B	C	D#	E
F	G	A♭	B♭	C	D♭	E	F
F#	G#	A	B	C#	D	F	F#
G	A	B♭	C	D	E♭	F#	G
A♭	B♭	B	D♭	E♭	E	G	A♭

MELODIC MINOR

I	II	iii	IV	V	VI	VII	I
A	B	C	D	E	F#	G#	A
B♭	C	D♭	E♭	F	G	A	B♭
B	C#	D	E	F#	G#	A#	B
C	D	E♭	F	G	A	B	C
C#	D#	E	F#	G#	A#	C	C#
D	E	F	G	A	B	C#	D
E♭	F	G♭	A♭	B♭	C	D	E♭
E	F#	G	A	B	C#	D#	E
F	G	A♭	B♭	C	D	E	F
F#	G#	A	B	C#	D#	F	F#
G	A	B♭	C	D	E	F#	G
A♭	B♭	B	D♭	E♭	F	G	A♭

MELODIC MINOR (DESCENDING)

I	vii	vi	V	IV	iii	II	I
A	G	F	E	D	C	B	A
B♭	A♭	G♭	F	E♭	D♭	C	B♭
B	A	G	F#	E	D	C#	B
C	B♭	A♭	G	F	E♭	D	C
C#	B	A	G#	F#	E	D#	C#
D	C	B♭	A	G	F	E	D
E♭	D♭	B	B♭	A♭	G♭	F	E♭
E	D	C	B	A	G	F#	E
F	E♭	D♭	C	B♭	A♭	G	F
F#	E	D	C#	B	A	G#	F#
G	F	E♭	D	C	B♭	A	G
A♭	G♭	E	E♭	D♭	B	B♭	A♭

KEYS

In the same way that a root note provides a scale with its key, so a piece of music can be similarly identified. For instance, if a melody is made up of notes from the G major scale, it's said to be "in" G major. In other words, it has a "key signature" of G major.

SHARPS AND FLATS

As you will remember, the notes that appear on the lines of a treble staff and E-G-B-D-F, and those set in the spaces between lines are F-A-C-E. This works fine for a piece of music that is written in the key of C major, which has no flats or sharps, but nothing – as they say – is that simple. Far from it, all the other major keys contain at least one sharp or flat. You could, of course, mark sharp and flat symbols alongside each note as they happen, but then a piece written in F♯ (which has a scale with six sharps) would probably just appear as a confusing jumble of sharp symbols. What is used instead is the system of marking an instruction at the beginning of the staff indicating that any occurance of a particular note should be sharpened or flattened accordingly, unless indicated otherwise. In this way the key signature of a piece of music can be instantly recognized by the number of sharps and flats appearing after the clef at the beginning of the music.

4ths AND 5ths

As you may have noiced by now, some types of chord sequences seem to gell more harmoniously than others, and in this respect there is a particularly dynamic relationship between the chords formed on the root, 4th and 5th degrees of the major scale. See how smoothly the four sequences shown below work as they flow together, by trying them out.

Then, by way of an experiment, sing the root note of the first chord all the way through the full sequence – in the first example,

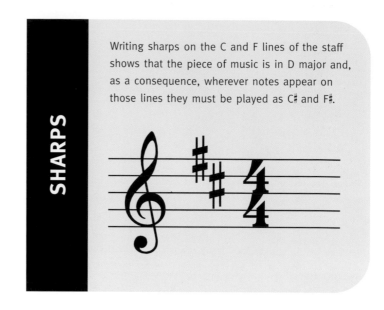

SHARPS

Writing sharps on the C and F lines of the staff shows that the piece of music is in D major and, as a consequence, wherever notes appear on those lines they must be played as C♯ and F♯.

sing the note C, even while you are playing the F and G chords. You'll notice that the note you're singing still seems to fit, even when the chords change. This is because the note C appears in the major scale for all three of the chords. And if you look at the notes of each scale, you can see exactly how closely the three are related: F major and G major have only one note that differs from the C major scale.

THE CIRCLE OF 5ths

This relationship of keys is illustrated most effectively in what has become known as the "circle of 5ths". This comprises a diagramatic

4TH AND 5THS

EXERCISE	I	IV	V	I
	C Major	F Major	G Major	C Major
	E Major	A Major	B Major	E Major
	D Major	G Major	A Major	D major
	G Major	C Major	D Major	G Major

CONTRASTING C MAJOR, F MAJOR, AND G MAJOR

	I	II	III	IV	V	VI	VII	I
C Major	C	D	E	F	G	A	B	C
F Major	F	G	A	B♭	C	D	E	F
G Major	G	A	B	C	D	E	F♯	G

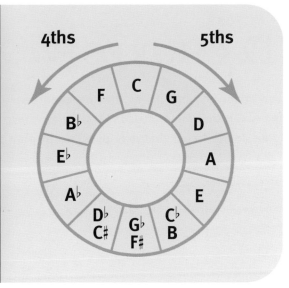

circle of twelve segments, the key of C being at the top. In intervals of a 5th, key signatures are added to each segment in a clockwise sequence. Moving clockwise in 5ths around the circle, you will find each major scale differing from the preceding scale by one note. Each time, the subsequent major scale is created by sharpening the note on the 7th degree –the leading note – by a semitone or half-step. As you will notice in the diagram on the right, there is an additional sharp in the scale on each of the subsequent segments.

Likewise, you will find there is also just one note difference between each pair of scales if you move counterclockwise around the circle in 4ths. In these instances, the new scale is formed by flattening the note on the 4th – the subdominant – degree of the previous scale.

ENHARMONICS

There can be more than one designation for certain notes. If D is lowered by a half-step it becomes D♭ and if C is raised by a half-step it becomes C♯ – yet both notes are an identical pitch. This is called an enharmonic relationship. In this case, if the note occurs in a "sharp" key it will be called C♯, and if it is a part of a "flat" key it will be known as D♭. The other two enharmonic keys are F♯/G♭ and C♭/B. In practice, particularly in popular music, the use of G♭ is rare and C♭ is almost unknown, even though the above rules apply equally to them.

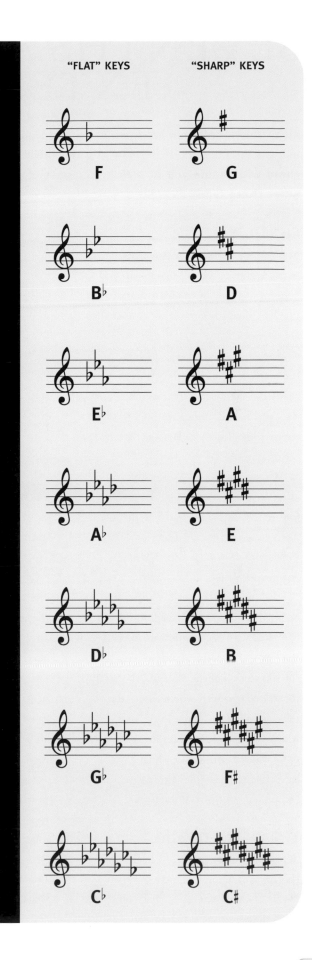

FLAT AND SHARP KEYS

SEVENTHS AND EXTENDED CHORDS

All of the chords that we have considered up to now have been major or minor types, having been constructed using combinations of the 1st, 3rd and 5th notes from both the major and minor "triads". Although these types of chord will enable you to play or compose a wide variety of tunes, don't forget that it is possible to play numerous other chord types as well.

CHORD BUILDING

You need to know about two other forms of triads known as the "augmented" and "diminished" triads, in order to understand the way in which some of these "extended" chords work.

The augmented triad is different from the major triad in that the 5th note is sharpened by a half-step or semitone; in the same way, in the diminished triad we see both the 3rd and 5th notes flattened by a semitone.

We can create a rich variety of alternative chord types by taking the four triads and notes related to the root. The "families" described here and in the pages following are the "7ths", "suspended 4ths", "6ths", "9ths", "11ths", and "13ths". All of these new chord types can be described in terms of a triad with added intervals. If this is a difficult concept to follow, refer to the top section of the table of 7th chords illustrated opposite, which names the relationship of each note to the root. It also designates the notes for the key of C, which is the key in which all of the 7th chord examples are shown throughout this part of the book.

THE FAMILY OF 7ths

With ten possible types of 7th chord, the 7th is certainly the most common family of chord extensions. Each one of them is created by adding either a

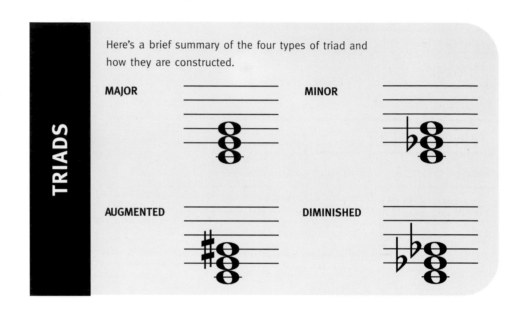

diminished 7th, a minor 7th, or a major 7th to one of the four types of triad.

The three 7ths which we find most often used in popular forms of music are the "dominant 7th", "minor 7th", and "major 7th", with the diminished forms also being quite common. You will find a full set illustrated over the next four pages, but bear in mind that some of the more obscure members of the 7th family are not to be found much in use outside the jazz world.

The table opposite illustrates the way in which these ten chords are constructed in terms of the relationship of each of the notes to the root.

DOMINANT 7th

Usually simply known as a "seven" or "7th" chord, the dominant 7th is formed

by adding a minor 7th to a major triad. In the key of C, the notes utilized are C (root), E (major 3rd), and G (perfect 5th) with an added B♭ (minor 7th). Its abbreviation is C7.

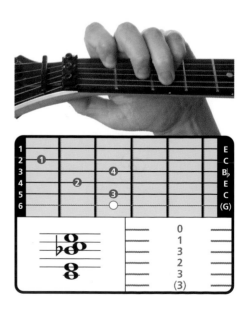

	ROOT (C)	MINOR 2nd (C♯/D♭)	MAJOR 2nd (D)	MINOR 3rd (D♯/E♭)	MAJOR 3rd (E)	PERFECT 4th (F)	AUGMENTED 4th or DIMINISHED 5th (F♯/G♭)	PERFECT 5th (G)	AUGMENTED 5th or MINOR 6th (G♯/A♭)	DIMINISHED 7th or MAJOR 6th (A)	MINOR 7th (A♯/B♭)	MAJOR 7th (B)
	I	**ii**	**II**	**iii**	**III**	**IV**	**IV+/V°**	**V**	**V+/VI**	**VI/VII°**	**VII**	**VII**
DOMINANT	●				●			●			●	
MINOR	●			●				●			●	
MAJOR	●				●			●				●
DIMINISHED	●			●			●			●		
DIMINISHED 5th	●				●		●				●	
AUGMENTED 5th	●				●				●		●	
MINOR/MAJOR	●			●				●				●
HALF DIMINISHED	●			●			●				●	
MAJOR DIMINISHED 5th	●				●		●					●
MAJOR AUGMENTED 5th	●				●				●			●

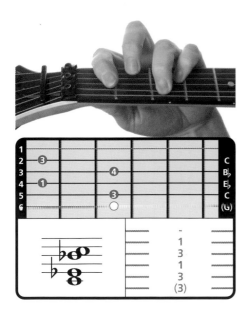

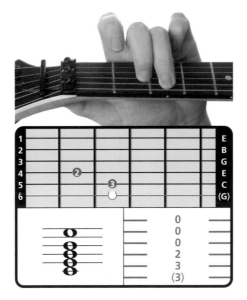

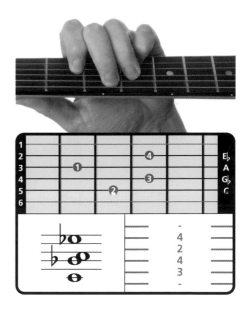

MINOR 7th

We form minor 7th chords by adding a minor 7th note to a minor triad. In the key of C, this chord uses the notes C (root), E♭ (minor 3rd), and G (perfect 5th), with an added B♭ (minor 7th). Its abbreviation is Cm7.

MAJOR 7th

Major 7th chords are formed by adding a major 7th note to a major triad. In the key of C, the notes used are C (root), E (major 3rd), G (perfect 5th), with an added B (major 7th). Its abbreviation is Cmaj7 or CΔ.

DIMINISHED 7th

The diminished 7th is usually simply known as a diminished, and is formed by adding a diminished 7th note to a diminished triad. In the key of C, this adds the note A to C, E♭, and G♭. Its abbreviation is Cdim or C°.

SEVENTH DIMINISHED 5th

7th diminished 5th chords are usually called "seven flat fives". They are formed by adding a minor 7th to the root, major 3rd and diminished 5th. In the key of C, this adds B♭ to the notes C, E, and G♭. Its abbreviation is C7-5.

SEVENTH AUGMENTED 5th

7th augmented 5th chords are commonly known as "seven sharp fives". They are formed by adding a minor 7th to an augmented triad. In the key of C, this adds a B♭ to the notes C, E, and G♯. Its abbreviation is C7+5.

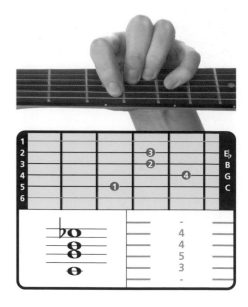

MINOR/MAJOR 7th

We form minor/major 7th chords by combining the root, perfect 5th, major 7th, and minor 3rd notes. In the key of C, the major/minor 7th chord uses the notes C, G, B, and E♭. The abbreviation is Cm/maj7 or Cm/Δ7.

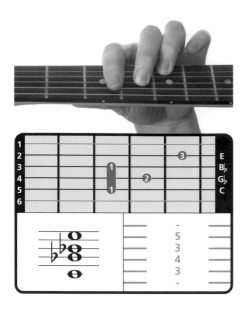

HALF-DIMINISHED 7th

Half-diminished 7th chords are created by adding a minor 7th to a diminished triad. Consequently the chord C7 half-diminished uses the notes C, E♭, G♭, and B♭. Its abbreviation is Cm7-5.

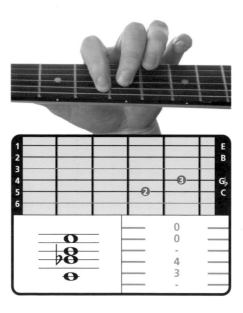

MAJOR 7th DIMINISHED 5th

A chord that is formed by combining the root, major 3rd, diminished 5th, and major 7th notes. In the key of C, the notes used are C, E, G♭, and B. Its abbreviation is Cmaj7-5 or CΔ7-5.

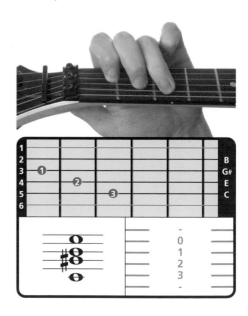

MAJOR 7th AUGMENTED 5th

We form the major 7th augmented 5th by combining the root, major 3rd, augmented 5th, and major 7th notes. In C, the notes C, E, G♯, and B are used. Its abbreviation is Cmaj7+5 or CΔ7+5.

The ten 7th chords you have just played are probably the most difficult you have yet come across. This is partly because they involve some demanding work with the 4th finger. One problem that all beginners on the guitar come across is the difficulty in getting the little finger to respond properly. Because the muscles in the little finger don't usually have much to do, it's hardly surprising that they may well be underdeveloped.

Work through the eight-bar exercise shown below slowly, it will help you to become more fluid in playing the basic 7th chords. Don't worry too much about your timing to begin with, you'll have enough to think about just getting your fingers in the right position.

The progression of the first three chords – from major to major 7th to dominant 7th – is a very familiar, and almost clichéd, sequence which stresses the movement to the three highest notes. In relation to the root, the notes move from the octave, to the major 7th, and then to the minor 7th.

We have seen all the chords in the key of C over the previous three pages. You have yet to come into contact with open-string voicings for D minor 7th and G dominant 7th, and are both illustrated below.

◀ D MINOR 7th

This is formed by adding the minor 7th to a minor triad. In the key of D, the notes used are D (root), F (minor 3rd), A (perfect 5th), and C (minor 7th). This voicing may seem similar to an F major with the 3rd finger released so that the open D can be heard.

▶ G DOMINANT 7th

This chord is created by adding the minor 7th to a major triad. In the key of G, the chord comprises the notes G (root), A (major 3rd), C (perfect 5th), and F (minor 7th).

FOURTHS AND SIXTHS

A major or minor scale is made up of seven different notes. All of the chords we have considered so far have used the four types of triad (the root, major or minor 3rd, and diminished, perfect or augmented 5th notes). The family of 7ths also uses all of these triads with an added major or minor 7th note. We can create further interesting and commonly used chord voicings using the perfect 4th and major 6th notes of the scales. When the perfect 4th appears in a chord, it invariably replaces the major 3rd; the major 6th is simply added to the basic triad. Chords utilizing these notes are suffixed "suspended 4ths" and "6ths" respectively.

SUSPENDED CHORDS

The complexion of a major chord can be radically altered by replacing the major 3rd in a major triad with a perfect 4th, producing what is known as a "suspended" chord. If we apply this principle to a major chord we get a "suspended 4th" chord (commonly referred to simply as a "sus4"). We can also apply the same idea to a dominant seventh chord, in which case it is known as a "seventh suspended fourth" (or "7sus4").

Esus4

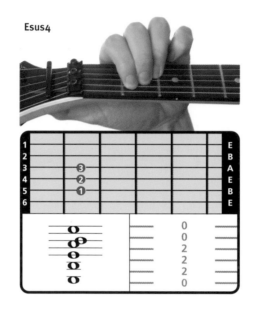

E7sus4

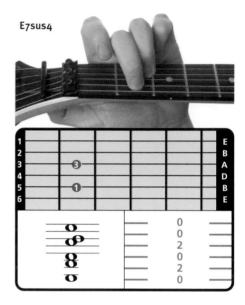

SUSPENDED 4th

By replacing the major 3rd in a major triad with a perfect 4th, a suspended 4th chord is created. In the key of E, this uses the notes E (root), A (perfect 4th), and B (perfect 5th). The chord is usually described as "Esus4."

SEVENTH SUSPENDED 4th

7th suspended 4th chords are created by adding a minor 7th to a suspended 4th chord. In the key of E, this comprises the notes E (root), A (perfect 4th), B (perfect 5th), and D (minor 7th). Its abbreviation is E7sus4. A very well-known example of where suspended 7th chords are used can be heard in the introduction to "A Hard Day's Night" by the Beatles.

SUSPENDED CHORD EXERCISE

Apply the rhythm, which is only shown over the first two bars, to each pair of chords listed directly above the music. In each case, the movement is from the suspended chord back to the equivalent major or dominant 7th in the same key. This type of progression, that has been widely used in all types of music through the ages, from classical to rock'n'roll is known as a "full close".

| Esus4 | E | A7sus4 | A7 | Esus4 | E | A7sus4 | A7 |
| Dsus4 | D | A7sus4 | A7 | Esus4/E | D7/D | Esus4 | E |

THE 6th FAMILY OF CHORDS

When we add the 6th note of the major scale to a major triad, it produces what is known as a "6th" chord (commonly known as a "six"). Likewise, when the 6th is added to a minor triad, a "minor 6th" chord ("minor six") is produced. 6th chords are commonly used in progressions that lead from a major chord to a dominant 7th, passing through the 6th, within the same key.

The two examples shown here (A6 and A minor 6) are the most basic of the 6th chords. More complex variations are to be found in the Chord Dictionary (see pages 212–249).

6th

6th chords are formed by adding a major 6th note to a major triad. The chord A 6th uses the notes A (root), C♯ (major 3rd), E

A6

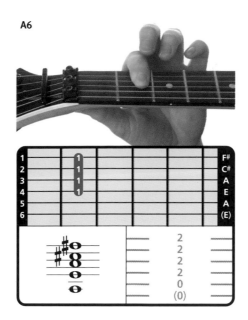

(perfect 5th), and F♯ (major 6th). Its abbreviation is A6.

MINOR 6th

Minor 6th chords are created by adding

Amin6

the major 6th note to a minor triad. The chord A minor 6th is made up from the notes A (root), C (minor 3rd), E (perfect 5th) and F♯ (major 6th). It is abbreviated as Am6.

PETE TOWNSHEND

Born: May 19, 1944, Chiswick, England

Guitars: Rickenbacker 330 and "signature model"; Gibson Les Paul and SG; Fender Stratocaster and Telecaster

Recorded Highlights: *The Who Sell Out*; *Quadrophenia*

Pete Townshend carved a name for himself in the rock hall of fame as a great guitarist in The Who, one of the greatest British bands of the 1960s.

Like a lot of UK musicians, he was a product of the post-war art-school system, and this probably influenced his instinct to experiment in the context of pop music. Following The Who's early classics like "My Generation" and "I Can't Explain", his musical horizons opened up with ambitious singles such as "I Can See For Miles" and the concept albums *Tommy* and *Quadrophenia*.

The Who also gained a well-deserved a reputation as one of the greatest live acts of the era, producing an awesome degree of dynamic power without the over-indulgent soloing which was a hallmark of much rock music at the time. In fact, when punk first exploded on the scene, Townshend was one of the few "old guard" musicians who greeted the new music with respect, gaining a new generation of fans as a consequence.

Like the Rolling Stones' Keith Richards, Townshend has always called himself a rhythm player. And, like Richards, he is known both for his powerful playing and the creation of some of the most memorable riffs in rock music, such as the "sus4" chords at the beginning of "Pinball Wizard."

EXTENDED CHORDS

We can create what is known as an "extended" chord by adding the 2nd, 4th, and 5th notes beyond the octave. Playing a 2nd note added above the octave creates a "9th" chord – the seven notes of the scale plus the first two notes of the extended scale. Similarly, the 4th and 6th notes can be added to create "11th" and "13th" chords. Some of these chords are among the trickiest to play on the guitar, with the player obliged to omit certain notes at his or her discretion, but still retain the flavour of the extension.

NINTHS

The "9th" series of chords is created by adding a major 2nd an octave above a chosen 7th chord. In this way, the three principle 7ths – dominant, minor, and major – all have their equivalent 9ths. In the key of C major, the major 2nd note is D – to create a ninth chord, the note D is added on top of the 7th chord. The music below illustrates how the chords are formed. The chords shown here do not, in fact, include the root note (D). In an ensemble situation the full chordal effect would, in most cases, be completed by other instruments; typically, the bass would play the root note. One of the keys to mastering chords comprising more than a triad is deciding which notes it might be appropriate to omit in certain musical contexts.

  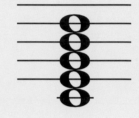

9th

A 9th chord – usually called a "nine" – is formed by adding the major 2nd above the octave to a dominant 7th chord. In the key of D, the chord comprises the notes D (root), F♯ (major 3rd), A (perfect 5th), C (minor 7th), and E (major 2nd/9th). Its abbreviation is D9.

MINOR 9th

Minor 9th chords are created by adding a major 2nd above the octave to a minor 7th chord. In the key of D, the chord comprises the notes D (root), F (minor 3rd), A (perfect 5th), C (minor 7th), and E (major 2nd/9th). Its abbreviation is Dm9.

MAJOR 9th

Major 9th chords are created by adding a major 2nd above the octave to a major 7th chord. In the key of D, the chord comprises the notes D (root), F♯ (major 3rd), A (perfect 5th), C♯ (major 7th), and E (major 2nd/9th). Its abbreviation is Dmaj9 or DΔ9.

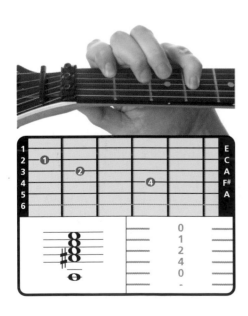 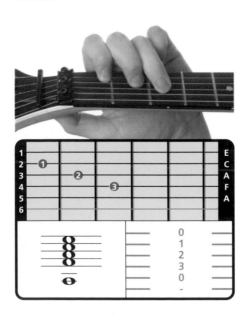 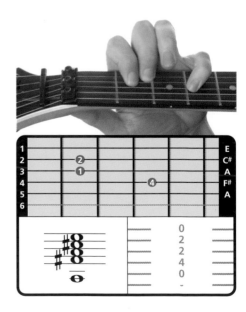

To form "eleventh" and "thirteenth" chords we apply the same principles as with the 9th chords shown on the previous page. To create 11th chords we add a perfect 4th to an existing 9th chord and, similarly, with 13th chords we add a major 6th note to the 11th chord. The two chords below illustrate how they are constructed in relation to the 9th chords described on the previous page.

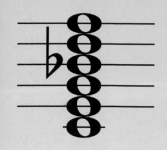

◀ **C 11th**
The chord comprises the root (C), major 3rd (E), perfect 5th (G), minor 7th (B♭), 9th (D), and perfect 4th/11th (F).

▶ **C 13th**
Root (C), major 3rd (E), perfect 5th (G), minor 7th (B♭), major 2nd (D), perfect 4th (F), and major 6th/13th (A).

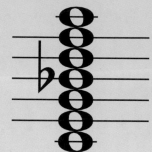

THE 11th

In the key of G, the note C (perfect 4th) is added to the 9th chord to form G 11th. Its abbreviation is G11.

The notes needed to create a full 11th chord in the key of G are: G (root), B (major 3rd), D (perfect 5th), F (minor 7th), A (major 2nd/9th), and C (perfect 4th/11th).

To play a full 11th chord we have to use six notes (see the example above for the key of C). But, although it is technically possible to play a full voicing on the guitar, it will often simply be impractical. When you are trying to use open-string voicings, in the majority of cases the notes just don't work happily together – it might be possble to play all the six notes comprising the chord, but you are likely to end up with a weird inversion that doesn't sound particularly attractive. The way to avoid this is to leave out one or more of the notes. This will often be the 5th and 9th notes, although the voicing on the right omits the 3rd and 5th notes.

It is possible to produce a wide variation of alternative chords that include the extended major 6th – some of which can be found later in the book.

THE 13th

In the key of G, the note E (major 6th) is added to the 11th chord to form G 13th. Its abbreviation is G13.

The notes that are required to create a full 13th chord in the key of G are G (root), B (major 3rd), D (perfect 5th), F (minor 7th), A (major 2nd/9th), C (perfect 4th/11th), and E (major 6th/13th).

The guitarist needs to be careful when using 13th chords. As can be seen from the chord on the staff at the top right-hand corner of the page, we need to use seven different notes to play a full 13th chord, which on a guitar is simply impossible. The voicing for the guitar illustrated on the right leaves out the 5th and 9th notes. Another alternative in common use is to omit the 9th and 11th notes, making the chord in essence a 7th with an added 13th note. In other words, as long as the root, 3rd, and 13th notes are sounded, the complexion of the 13th chord will be retained.

It is also possible to create minor and major 13ths by adding the major 6th above the octave on a minor or major 11th chord.

11th

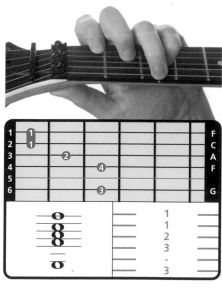

13th

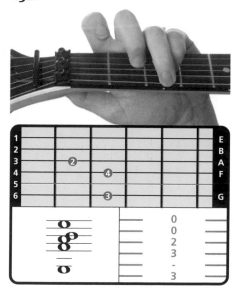

BARRE CHORDS

Every one of the chords that we have considered up to this point has been formed around the open strings of the guitar. However, you will have only a limited opportunity to play in many of the sharp or flat keys if you restrict your playing to these chords. Although many pieces of popular music can be played just using open-string chords, ignoring the full range of chords available is rather like a painter rejecting certain colours.

BARRE CHORDS

To solve this problem we have what are known as barre chords, which are open-string chord shapes formed at different positions on the fingerboard. To form a barre chord, the index finger is stretched across the width of the fingerboard, with the remaining three fingers used to form the chord shape. In this fashion, the index finger functions like the nut when playing open-string chords. We are able in this way to play open-string chord shapes in any key. The most common barre chords are variations on the E- and A-shaped open-string chords, although the C and G shapes can also be played as barre chords, but constitute a more difficult exercise for the fingers of the left hand.

The E-shaped barre chord is basically the same as an open-string chord shape. However, the 4th finger must be used in the formation of the chord shape because the index finger is now being used as the barre.

1 Form an open-string E major chord, but this time use the 3rd, 4th, and 2nd fingers to fret the 5th, 4th, and 3rd strings respectively, making sure your index finger is well clear of the strings.

2 Slide your left hand five frets along the fingerboard.

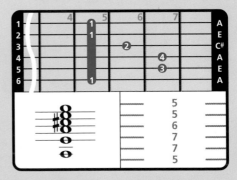

A MAJOR

3 Placing the index finger firmly behind the 5th fret, play across all six strings of the chord. This is an A major played using an E-shaped barre on the 5th fret.

We can convert any major chord in this way, the chord taking its key name from the note barred on the 1st and 6th strings.

THE E-SHAPED BARRE

EXTENDING THE E-SHAPED BARRE

As has been demonstrated on the previous pages, the basic major and minor chords can be "extended" to give us a rich choice of alternative sounds. We can also extend barre chords, although in some of the more complicated instances you will find that one or more of the strings should not be played. Among the most common extensions are the six shown below, which are all shown in the key of G, the barre being held on the 3rd fret.

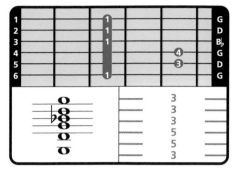

G MINOR (Gm)

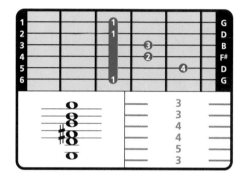

G DOMINANT SEVENTH (G7)

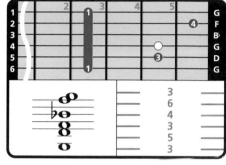

G MINOR SEVENTH (Gm7)

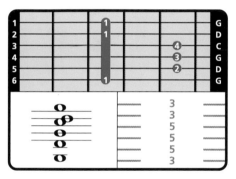

G SUSPENDED FOURTH (Gsus4)

G MAJOR SEVENTH (Gmaj7)

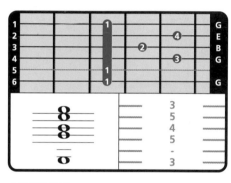

G SIXTH (G6)

BREAKING RULES

The maximum flexibility to switch between playing chords and single notes can be attained by using the correct left-hand posture for the E-shape barre shown above. Some guitarists, however, also use an alternative technique, with the index finger used to barre the top two strings and the thumb stretched around the back of the neck to fret the 6th string.

While most guitar tutors would frown on this, more creatively minded people might adopt a more flexible attitude. While it it can make changing chord shapes a little more difficult, it does enable us to alter the muting of the 6th string. Also it enables some players – with a big enough fingerspan – to reach over to fret the 5th string.

The view of this writer is that, basically, anything goes. If you get the idea that rubbing sandpaper up and down the fingerboard, for instance, will make your playing sound a whole lot better, then try it out – although that's not a recommended technique. As with many activities, we often only make progress if we're willing to rethink the rules. And that isn't meant as some kind of inverted snobbery. Although the tried and tested classical system provides everything you should require to become a good guitarist, if you come across other approaches that might produce results then you should at least give them a try.

THE A-SHAPED BARRE

Barre chords can also be contructed using the open-string A major chord shape.

1 First form an open-string A major chord using the 2nd, 3rd, and 4th fingers to fret the 4th, 3rd, and 2nd strings respectively.

2 Then slide your left hand seven frets along the fingerboard, so that the 9th fret is being held on the 4th, 3rd, and 2nd strings.

3 Place the index finger firmly behind the 7th fret, playing across all the six strings of the chord. This is an E major played using an A-shaped barre on the 7th fret.

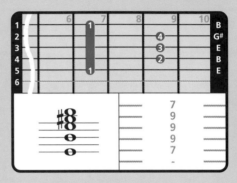

E MAJOR

EXTENDING THE A-SHAPED BARRE

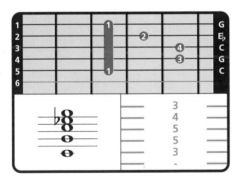

C MINOR (Cm)

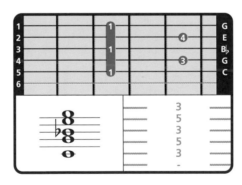

C DOMINANT SEVENTH (C7)

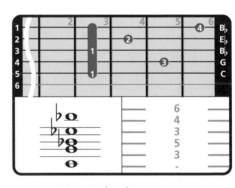

C MINOR SEVENTH (Cm7)

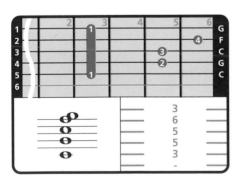

C SUSPENDED FOURTH (Csus4)

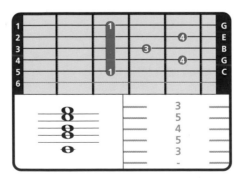

C MAJOR SEVENTH (Cmaj7)

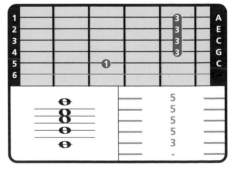

C SIXTH (C6)

ALTERNATIVE A-SHAPED BARRE

When playing an A-shape barre chord, many players today find that it is more convenient to play a kind of double-barre, using the 3rd finger to cover the 2nd, 3rd, and 4th strings. This is a highly effective technique, as long as the tip of the 3rd finger is bent back at a sufficiently obtuse angle so as not to accidentally mute the 1st string. An option is to avoid playing the 1st string, although that may prove difficult if you are strumming.

C-SHAPED BARRE

The C-shaped barre puts a lot of strain on the little finger – not only does it involve a good stretch, but the finger also has to fret a bass note which, because of the higher gauge, needs more pressure to hold it down on the fret. Because of this, practicing the C-shaped barre can be a helpful exercise in strengthening the little finger.

1 To form the C-shaped barre, play an open C major chord with the 2nd, 3rd, and 4th fingers playing the 2nd, 4th, and 5th strings respectively.

2 Slide the fingers four frets along the fingerboard, placing the index finger behind the 4th fret. This produces an E major chord.

G-SHAPED BARRE

The G-shaped barre is possibly the least commonly used of open-string shapes. It's simply not possible to play a complete open-G chord on the barre owing to what would be an impossible stretch between the 2nd, 3rd, and 4th fingers, and that's why the 1st string is not used.

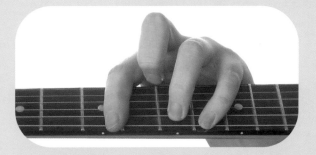

1 Form a partial open-G major chord using the 3rd and 4th fingers to fret the 5th and 6th strings.

2 Slide your hand five frets along, placing the index finger behind the 5th fret, thus creating a C major chord.

Use the chart below as an at-a-glance reference for playing chord types in any key, using the four barre shapes described on the previous four pages. The fret on which the index finger is positioned to create the barre is indicated by the numbers along the top row, with the individual cells in the four subsequent rows showing the key of the chords produced by using the various barre shapes. If you wish to play A-shaped barre chords in the key of G, for example, look along the second row until you reach the key of G – following the column up to the top row will tell you that the barre must be placed on the 10th fret. If you are familiar with the notes on the fingerboard, the positioning of the barre for E and A shapes will become almost automatic – they simply follow the notes of the 6th and 5th strings respectively.

	OPEN STRING	FRET ON WHICH BARRE SHOULD BE POSITIONED											
		1	2	3	4	5	6	7	8	9	10	11	12
E-SHAPED BARRE	E	F	F♯	G	A♭	A	B♭	B	C	C♯	D	E♭	E
A-SHAPED BARRE	A	B♭	B	C	C♯	D	E♭	E	F	F♯	G	A♭	A
C-SHAPED BARRE	C	C♯	D	E♭	E	F	F♯	G	A♭	A	B♭	B	C
G-SHAPED BARRE	G	A♭	A	B♭	B	C	C♯	D	E♭	E	F	F♯	G

INVERSIONS

You will be aware by now that that we can use a variety of finger positions to play the same chords. However, the same set of chords played on any instrument can sound very different if we reorganize the register in which one or more of the notes appears by raising or lowering the pitch by an octave. When playing through the exercise shown below, which consists of an open C major chord played as three major triads, just listen to the difference between the three chords.

All of the chords in the exercise are C major chords, each being made up of the notes C, E, and G. However, the second and third chords are different in that the lowest pitched notes in either triad are not the root note (C). This principle is what we refer to as "inversion". The second chord, whose lowest note is E, is known as a "first inversion". The third chord, whose lowest note is G, is known as a "second inversion".

However, the fact that the same note can be played on different strings uniquely complicates the inverting of chords on a guitar or other guitar-related instruments. In fact, if your guitar has a two-octave fingerboard, the note E played on the open 1st string can actually be played on every other string. In this way the choice you have at your disposal is made even greater – and at the same time far more complex.

A mastery of utilizng inverted chords is one of the secrets of arranging guitar music, and it's worth taking the trouble to experiment in this area, particularly if you are hoping to write or arrange your own material.

BARRE PROGRESSIONS

Practising the barre-chord progression exercise shown at the top of the page on the right will help you form an understanding of chord inversions while, at the same time, making you familiar with the different barre shapes.

The exercise uses a simple sequence of two alternating chords (E major and D major), all of which are played using each of the four barre shapes shown on the previous four pages: the E-shape is

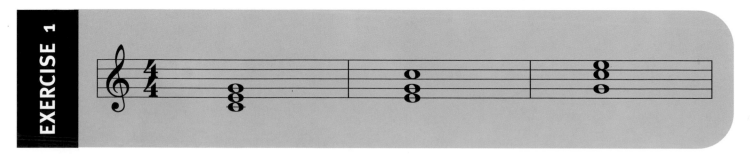

used in bars one and two; the G-shape in bars three and four; the A-shape in bars five and six; and the C-shape in bars seven and eight. Having mastered this exercise, you can then have a shot at a more demanding alternative by using the same chord types with different extensions – for example, you could try it out using minor voicings and then with sevenths.

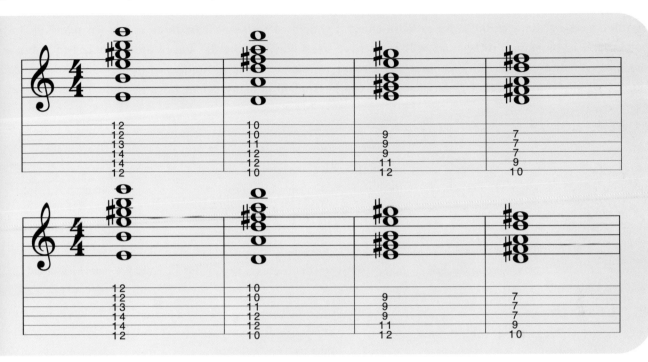

EXERCISE 2

THE CAPO

There's a definite tonal difference between playing barre chords and open-string chords which is noticeable in the playing of all but the most accomplished guitarists. And on some kinds of instruments, the 12-string guitar for example, barre chords often simply don't sound as good. This is largely because some strings are partially muted as a result of the index finger failing to exert pressure evenly across the fingerboard. Some players use a mechanical device called a capo to overcome this problem. The capo, which fits around the neck of the guitar, effectively creates a new zero fret at a different position on the fingerboard. This makes it possible to play the open-string chords in different keys.

In the photograph on the right, the capo is fitted behind the 4th fret.

The basic open-string fingering now produces the following chords:

OPEN STRING	4TH-FRET ROOT
Open E major	G♯ major
Open A major	C♯ major
Open D major	F♯ major
Open C major	E major
Open G major	B major

When using a capo, care should be taken fitting it around the neck. Too tight and it may detune the guitar or damage the strings; if it's too loose, the strings will be able to move across the fret, resulting in an unpleasant scraping effect each time you strum a chord.

The capo is a cheap and useful addition to the guitarist's tool bag, despite being looked down upon by some musicians, and can be a life-saver during a long, arduous recording session when your index finger has become numb with pain.

THE ROOT AND THE PERFECT FIFTH

Strictly speaking, for a chord to be called a chord it should comprise at least three notes. For many years however, particularly in blues and rock music, guitarists have been playing "chords" based around only two notes – a pairing of the root with the perfect fifth. Whether you choose to refer to these groupings of notes as chords, or call them by the technically correct term of "intervals", they can be applied in many useful ways in contemporary music.

POWER CHORDS

Sometimes known as "fives", "fifths", or simply "power chords", chords formed around the root and an interval of a perfect fifth are very widely used, and can be highly effective.

But what makes these chord types something of a headache for theorists is that they are tonally ambiguous. The basic differences between a major and minor triad revolve around the second note – whether the chord contains a major 2nd or a minor 2nd wholly defines the chord

either as a major or a minor in this context. The "five" chord has only the first and third notes of the triad, allowing for both major and minor scales in the same key to be played over the chord. Or alternatively, in an ensemble setting, the major 2nd or minor 2nd notes could be played on another instrument, creating the full triadic effect.

Because of its simplicity, this type of chord is particularly popular in heavy metal and similar rock music. When played through a heavily distorted

amplifier, or using heavy electronic effects, "five" chords emphasize the harmonious nature of the two closely related notes and tend to retain their character.

IMPLIED HARMONIES

Any accompanying instruments or vocals tend to render the chords implicitly "major" in tone. But if the guitarist were to create the full major triad by adding the major 2nd, the result could be a "muddy" overall sound, and a reduction in the "cutting" effect of the guitar chords.

THE BARRE TO THE FIVE CHORD

The simplest examples of five chords are those based around the E- and A-shaped barre forms, and are extremely easy to play. Try the following examples, using both clean and heavily distorted sounds to get the full effect.

EXAMPLE 1
The fingering is taken from a standard E-major barre chord shape. However, in this example you only need to play the bottom three strings. The chords are A, C, B, and D, and are formed by placing the barres on the 5th, 8th, 7th, and 10th frets respectively.

EXAMPLE 2
This example uses the fingering for both an A-shaped barre and an E-shaped barre. Remember that you should only play the 3rd, 4th, and 5th strings when playing the A-shape, so make sure you mute the other strings if you want to avoid some unwelcome additional noise.

You can also be create full six-string "open" versions of these five chords. On the right are chord diagrams for the keys of E and A. The example below illustrates how these two chords can be used in practice.

DOUBLING UP

Some of the notes will be doubled up when two different notes are played across six strings. If you like the sounds that this can create, the section on alternate tunings will probably be of interest to you. Similarly, you may also find that experimenting with 12-string guitars is a worthwhile exercise .

The last piece in this section is included because it looks at a different approach to manipulating the basic open-string chord shapes, despite being slightly tangential to the subject of barre chords. Here we will be taking the basic finger position and moving it along the fingerboard – rather like playing the barre chord but leaving the barre off. This will allow you to create some interesting new chordal effects, most of which – though rarely to be found in standard chord books – you can hear often enough on well-known records.

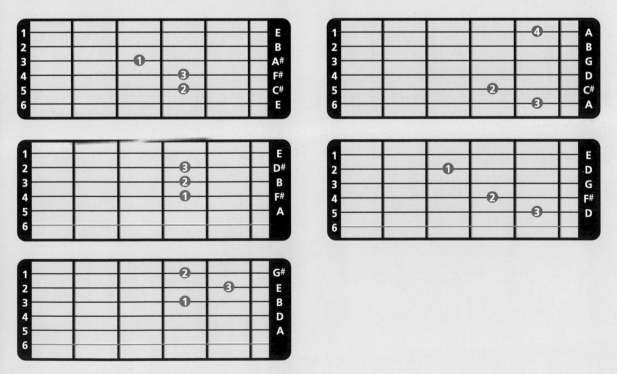

MOVING KEYS

Life would be a whole lot simpler if all music was written in one key – C major, for example – and if you were only using chords based around the major scale, there wouldn't even be any of those troublesome sharps and flats to worry about. But it would also make music extremely dull, apart from the fact that there are a number of practical reasons why we choose to play a piece of music in one key rather than another.

There are two musical terms you are most likely to come across in conjunction with key changes, and they are "transposition" and "modulation". Although some people use these terms interchangeably, they actually represent two very distinct musical concepts. Transposition refers to the playing of the same piece of music in different keys, while modulation describes when we have a deliberate change of key taking place within a piece of music.

TRANSPOSITION

Among a variety of reasons why one might want to play the same piece of music in a different key, the most common is simply to accomodate the range of a particular vocalist. All singers have a specific range in which they operate, and even the best singers feel more comfortable with certain keys. In other words, to allow singers to give their best you need to accompany them in a key most appropriate to each voice.

Another time you may want to change keys is when playing with other musicians, as using certain voicings on particular instruments can change the whole the mood of a piece of music. Remember the exercise on barre chords, you will recall the various ways a C major chord could sound for instance, determined by which chord voicing you played. A further reason, that has to be born in mind when arranging for a large ensemble, is that certain instruments – especially brass and reeds – are much harder to play in particular keys or registers.

TRANSPOSING CHORDS

At this stage you should have a reasonable understanding of the basic way in which intervals work – especially how the unique relationship between the 1st (I), 4th (IV), and 5th (V) degrees of a scale can be used to create chord progressions which, when played together with each other, sound harmonious and instinctively "right". A set of chords can be built on each degree of a scale in the same way that a scale is constructed from its own unique set of intervals. These patterns of chords are called "scale tone" chords, and each chord can be given a Roman numeral relating to the degree of the scale on which it falls. The pattern of chords for C major is: C major (I), D minor (II), E minor (III), F major (IV), G major (V), A minor (VI), B diminished (VII), C major (I). The three sequences to play below show the chords on the major scales in the keys of C, F, and G.

We can also use these scale degrees as a musical shorthand for playing chords, or writing down a song structure. A sequence which progresses from I through IV to V, for instance, can be notated as a "I-IV-V" sequence. If the I chord is C major, you therefore know that the IV chord is F major, and the V chord is G major. You can get an instinctive feel for the way notes and chords sound in relation to one another once you are familiar with thinking in this way, enabling you play any chord sequence in any key with far less difficulty. It's a way of dealing with notation that is very popular with jazz musicians, but is worth considering regardless of what kind of music you play.

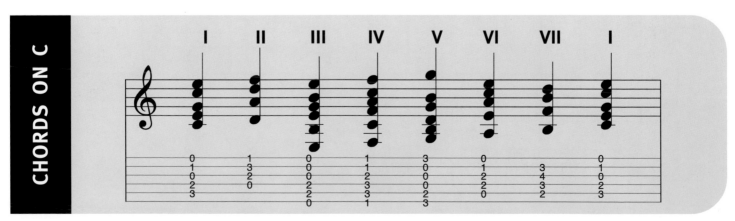

CHORDS ON F

I	II	III	IV	V	VI	VII	I

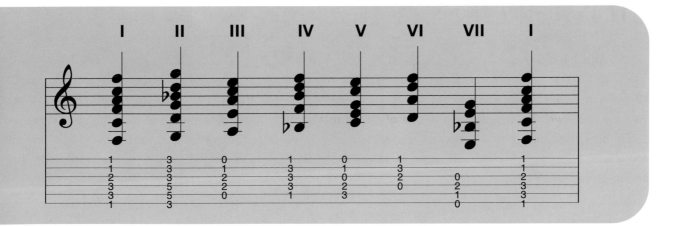

CHORDS ON G

I	II	III	IV	V	VI	VII	I

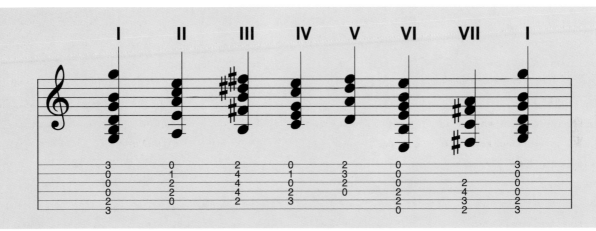

TRANSPOSING WITH A CAPO

The capo is a useful piece of machinery which creates a "mobile nut" or zero fret when clamped around the fingerboard. We've already discussed how it can be used to make an artificial barre for playing open-string chords along the fingerboard, and the capo can also come in handy when transposing chord progressions. If, for instance, you have a chord progression that moves from D major to A major, to E major, all played as open-string chords, then if you want to transpose the sequence from D to G, by fixing the capo at the 5th fret, the same open-string voicings can be used to play the chords G major, D major, and A major.

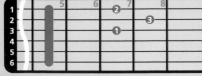

TRANSPOSING USING
SCALE DEGREES

In order to transpose a sequence using scale degrees, the first thing is to write down the chords as their equivalent Roman numerals. For example, in a C major–E minor–D minor–G major chord sequence the root chord is C major, so the progression could be described as "I-III-II-V". To transpose the chords to G, all you need to do is work out the chords on the 2nd, 3rd, and 5th degrees of the G major scale, and you will arrive at the new chord sequence of G major–B minor–A minor–D major.

ROMAN NUMERALS

For practical purposes, you should remember that different extensions can be used even though the chord types created from each degree of the scale are musically correct in their use of major, minor, and diminished voicings. An alternative method, with each scale degree being just associated with a note name rather than a chord type, is also adopted by some people. In these instances, a II chord would automatically be a major chord, and if a minor chord was needed it would be signified as IIm.

TRANSPOSING SEQUENCES

With the aid of the table below you will be able to easily transpose chord sequences from one key to another.

KEY	I	II	III	IV	V	VI	VII
A	A	Bm	C#m	D	E	F#m	G#dim
B♭	B♭	Cm	Dm	E♭	F	Gm	Adim
B	B	C#m	D#m	E	F#	G#m	A#dim
C	C	Dm	Em	F	G	Am	Bdim
C#	C#	D#m	Fm	F#	G#	A#m	Cdim
D	D	Em	F#m	G	A	Bm	C#dim
E♭	E♭	Fm	Gm	A♭	B♭	Cm	Ddim
E	E	F#m	G#m	A	B	C#m	D#din
F	F	Gm	Am	B♭	C	Dm	Edim
F#	F#	G#m	A#m	B	C#	D#m	Fdim
G	G	Am	Bm	C	D	Em	F#dim
A♭	A♭	B♭m	Cm	D♭	E♭	Fm	Gdim

ODDITIES

For anyone intending to arrange music for other instruments, a working knowledge of transposition is essential – and never more so than with brass and reed instruments. For obscure and complicated reasons, a middle C on certain instruments is not actually the same note as the middle C in concert pitch. It might seem crazy, but there are a number of "transposing instruments" in music. An example is the trumpet, which transposes down a tone to B♭; so if a trumpet player is looking at a piece of music instructing an F to be played, the note you hear will be the equivalent of E♭ on a piano keyboard. If the arranger wants to hear concert pitch F, the note G will have to be on the trumpet player's sheet music!

Strictly speaking, because music written for the instrument is an octave higher than it really sounds, the guitar is also a transposing instrument. This is often signalled on the staff with a small "8" written below the treble clef. Instruments that require transposition include:

TRUMPET	down to B♭
PICCOLO TRUMPET	up to D
FLUGELHORN	down to B♭
FRENCH HORN	down to F
COR ANGLAIS (ENGLISH HORN)	down to F
CORNET	down to B♭
CLARINET	down to B♭
SOPRANO SAXOPHONE	down to B♭
ALTO SAXOPHONE	down to E♭
TENOR SAXOPHONE	down over the octave to B♭
BARITONE SAXOPHONE	down over the octave to B♭

CHORD CHARTS

In most types of music apart from strictly classical, ensemble arrangements are not always written out in full, allowing the players the flexibility to interpret the music as their taste and inspiration dictates.

Probably the most common mode of working in rock, pop and jazz music is to use a chord chart. We've already seen how scale tone chords are utilized to transpose chord sequences – this is a form of chord chart in itself. But in practice, chord instructions are usually a lot less formal.

SOME OTHER SHORT CUTS

There can be many different forms of chord charts. The most basic and widely used example is a scrap of paper with chord names simply scribbled on it, while indicating a time signature and a series of chord names written within the musical bars – often written out on manuscript paper for convenience – is a slightly more sophisticated approach. The latter can also include, of course, various other embellishments of standard musical notation, such as rests and repeat signs. Although some of these instructions can seem a bit confusing to begin with, they are

worth aquainting yourself with because they can save you a considerable amount of time in the long run.

The simplest embellishment – which we have already come across – is the bar repeat sign, which signifies the start and end points of a piece of music which has to be repeated. There are also simple instructions for repeating chords and bars, some of the most common of which are illustrated here:

/

REPEAT PREVIOUS CHORD WITHIN BAR

✗.

REPEAT PREVIOUS BAR

Indicated below are four, four-bar examples, which are all displaying the same information, but at varying levels of complexity. On the top line of bars we see the staff with the chord written out. The second line shows just the chord names, to be played on each beat of the bar. The third line illustrates the stroke symbol being used as an instruction to play the same chord as the last within the bar, while the fourth shows the bar repeat symbol, telling the player he is to repeat the previous bar exactly.

EXAMPLES OF SHORT CUTS

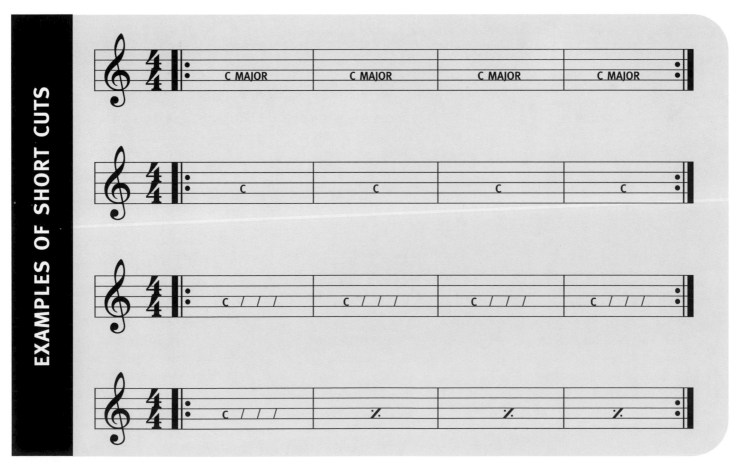

AMENDING CHORDS

All of the chords we have used up to now have been more or less straightforward, in so far as they are all, in one way or another, extensions on the four triadic forms – major, minor, augmented and diminished. The actual definition of these chords can often be more ambiguous, however. Take "polytonal" chords, for example, which comprise the basic elements of two separate chords played at the same time. A similar effect to this – which is extremely common in all types of music – can be heard in the sound of a chord played over a bass note which differs from the root.

ALTERED BASS NOTES

In order to hear the effect of a chord played over an altered bass note, play a regular open-string D major chord and shift the root note – the open 4th string – up to E on the 2nd fret.

The notes of the D major chord are D (1st), F♯ (3rd), and A (5th).

Treating the new chord as having a root of E rather than D, the notes of the chord and their relationship to the root become: E (1st), F♯ (9th), A (11th), and D (flat 7th). All these notes are from the chord E11; by adding an E root to a D major chord, you have created E11.

Now compare that first chord with the more usual E11 voicing illustrated below. As with any alternative voicings, it will always sound a little bit different, but here there's something of more basic importance going on. By simply adding the flattened 7th and 11th notes to a root we can produce the "flavour" of an 11th chord – however, the first chord you

In the sequence of chord diagrams below we can see a full set of altered bass notes. From left to right, an E major chord is played on the guitar, the root note descending in half-step intervals. Some of these familiar sounds are very harmonious, as you will hear when you try to play them for yourself, while others create discordant effects. The principle of altered bass notes does not only apply to major chords, but

E MAJOR
No altered bass note
E (1st), G♯ (3rd), B (5th).

E MAJOR OVER E♭ (E/E♭)
Bass note dropped by
half-step (semitone)
E♭ (1st), B (sharp 5th),
E (flat 9th), G♯ (11th).

E MAJOR OVER D (E/D)
Bass note dropped by step (tone)
D (1st), A♯ (flat 5th), B (6th), E (9th).

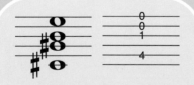

E MAJOR OVER C♯ (E/C♯)
Bass note dropped by step plus
half-step (tone plus semitone)
C♯ (1st), G♯ (5th), B (flat 7th),
E (sharp 11th).

E MAJOR OVER C (E/C)
Bass note dropped by
two steps (two tones)
C (1st), E (3rd),
G♯ (sharp 5th), B (7th).

E MAJOR OVER B (E/B)
Bass note dropped by two steps plus a
half-step (two tones plus a semitone).
Playing E major over a B just creates
an inversion of the same chord.

played was without the 3rd and 5th notes which give the full-bodied sound to the eleventh. In these circumstances, therefore, it's usually of more use to refer to the original triad with an altered bass note. Here the chord would, more often than not, be referred to as "D major over E" and would be written down quite simply as "D/E".

We might think this distinction is rather contrived, but it does make sense in practice. Not least, it makes things simpler, it being a lot easier calling a chord "D/C" rather than "C6/9/♭5" or "C/6/9♯/11" – and, of course, most amateur guitar players would have to look at a chord dictionary before they could work out the fingering. But in many ways, converting discrepancies between chords and bass lines, although technically correct, will not always give a true picture of what's really happening.

For example, in many cases, particularly in rock or pop bands, chords such as these will often be the result of interplay between the the guitar and another instrument, typically a bass guitar. In this example, the guitarist in virtually every case would not be playing either of the C6/9 chords. He or she would be more likely to be playing D major, and the bass the note C. The actual effect of this is something very different.

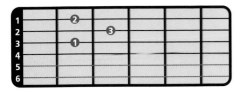

D MAJOR

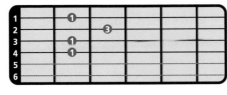

D MAJOR OVER E

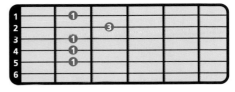

E11

can also be utilized with any other chord type. In order to play every one of these 12 examples, use the fingering for the top four strings of an open E major chord. The root (starting on the 3rd string) descends gradually over the bottom three strings. But remember that you should only ever play four strings – that is the top three, plus whichever string the new root note is on.

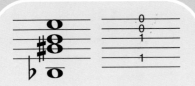

E MAJOR OVER B♭ (E/B♭)
Bass note dropped by
three steps (three tones)
B♭ (1st), A♭ (flat 7th),
B (sharp 7th), E (sharp 11th).

E MAJOR OVER A (E/A) (A MAJOR 9TH)
Bass note dropped by three steps plus
a half-step (three tones plus a semitone)
A (1st), E (5th), G♯ (7th), B (9th).

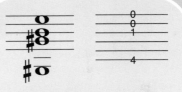

E MAJOR OVER G♯ (E/G♯)
Bass note dropped by
four steps (four tones).
Playing E major over a B creates
an inversion of the same chord.

E MAJOR OVER G (E/G)
Bass note dropped by four steps plus a
half–step (four tones plus a semitone)
G (1st), B (3rd), G♯ (flat 9th), E (13th).

E MAJOR OVER F♯ (E/F♯)
Bass note dropped by
five steps (five tones)
F♯ (1st), E (flat 7th),
G♯ (9th), B (11th).

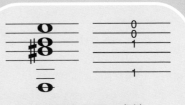

E MAJOR OVER F (E/F)
Bass note dropped by five steps plus a
half–step (five tones plus a semitone)
F (1st), E (7th), G♯ (sharp 9),
B (sharp 11).

LEAVING OUT NOTES

The guitar is inherently limited as a chordal instrument in that the maximum number of strings you can play at the same time is six. When playing some of the more "full-bodied" extensions – such as variants on 9ths, 11ths, and 13ths – the voicings are sometimes so demanding that you may only be able to play four or five of the strings. Indeed, as you've already seen, to play a full 13th chord requires seven notes to be played at once. Therefore, on occasions, the guitarist will be called upon to exercise skill and judgement in deciding exactly which notes within a chord need to be played.

GRASPING CHORD CONSTRUCTION

In order to make the best possible decision in omitting notes from a chord, the guitar player needs to have not only a very good grasp of the way in which chords are constructed – which, assuming you have worked hard through this book, you should be well on the way to attaining – but, in ensemble group settings, a feel and general understanding of what the other instruments are playing.

An element of this understanding is also a knowledge of groups of chords or chord types that share the same notes. Here's a simple example: as we've learnt, the chord C major 7th consists of the notes C, E, G, and B. However, leaving out the root note and just playing the notes E, G, and B, creates a new chord – E minor. If you were playing the guitar solo, it's unlikely you would ever think of substituting these chords – it would obviously change the whole feel of the particular music you were playing. But if you were playing with other musicians, the effect of playing an E minor chord while the keyboard or bass was playing the root note C would still create the C major 7th chord overall.

SHARED NOTES

MINOR 9th TO MAJOR 7th
Omitting the root of any minor 9th chord produces a major 7th chord whose root is a minor 3rd higher than that of the original chord. For example, C minor 9th becomes E♭ major 7th by leaving out the note C. Likewise, G minor 9th converts to B♭ major 7th by subtracting the note G.

SEVEN FLAT NINE TO DIMINISHED
Omitting the root of any 7-9 chord creates a diminished chord with a root that is a major 3rd higher than that of the original chord. In diminished chords, because of their very nature, the remaining notes can be inverted to create alternatives with any of the notes as a root.

NINTH TO HALF-DIMINISHED
Omitting the root of any 9th chord produces a half-diminished chord with a root that is a major 3rd higher than that of the original chord. In the key of C, C7-9 becomes E half-diminished by subtracting the root (C). Similarly, G7-9 becomes B half-diminished by leaving out the note G.

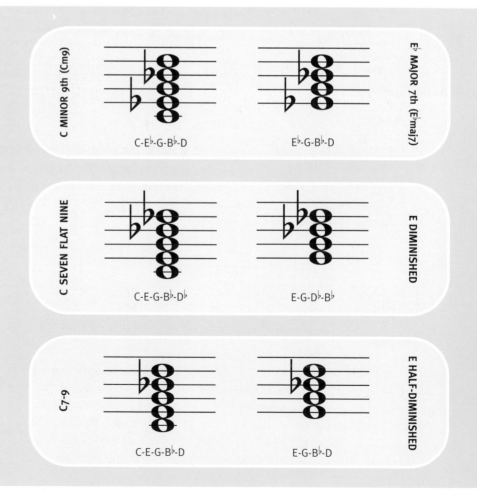

C MINOR 9th (Cm9)   C-E♭-G-B♭-D   E♭-G-B♭-D   E♭ MAJOR 7th (E♭maj7)

C SEVEN FLAT NINE   C-E-G-B♭-D♭   E-G-D♭-B♭   E DIMINISHED

C7-9   C-E-G-B♭-D   E-G-B♭-D   E HALF-DIMINISHED

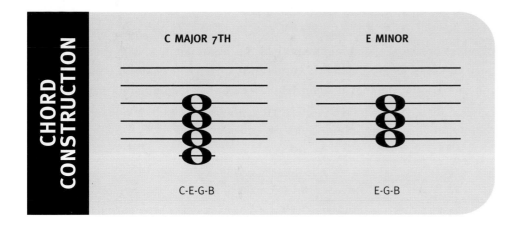

CHORD CONSTRUCTION

C MAJOR 7TH

C-E-G-B

E MINOR

E-G-B

SHARED NOTES

A good method of working out chord synonyms is by playing the full chord then leaving out the root. In this way you will create a new root, usually starting on the 3rd (although other notes can be used), and therefore a new chord type.

You can adopt this approach with chords formed on top of the major and minor triads, although in most cases an unacceptable level of discord is likely to be produced.

A good grasp of the process of chord synonyms will increase your familiarity

with chords generally, and can also be very useful in composition, enabling the player to move between chord positions with a great deal more ease. Basically, this is another firm move on the route to understanding the way in which notes relate to each another.

Below are examples that illustrate how pairs of chords can start in one key and end up in another, simply by the removal of one or more notes.

All of the six chord pairings begin in the key of C, and yet produce new voicings in the keys of E, E♭, G, and G♭. Obviously, these can be converted into other keys – look at the circle of 5ths diagram to see how the keys relate: for example, Cadd9 to Gsus4 transposes to Gadd9 to Dsus4.

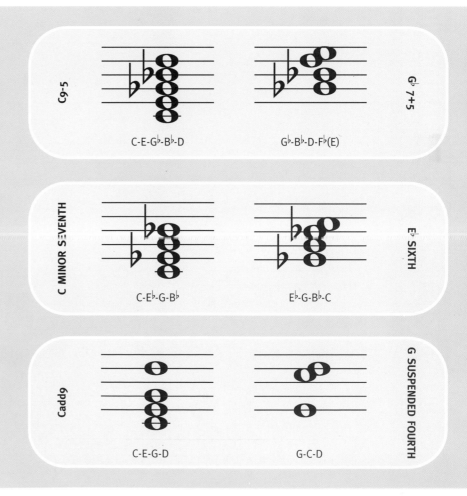

NINTH DIMINISHED 5th TO SEVENTH AUGMENTED 5th

Omitting the root of any 9th diminished 5th chord creates an inversion of a 7th augmented 5th chord whose root is a diminished 5th higher than that of the original chord. In actual practice, the 3rd of the first chord becomes the flattened 7th of the synonym.

C9-5 — C-E-G♭-B♭-D

G♭7+5 — G♭-B♭-D-F♭(E)

MINOR SEVENTH TO 6th

The 6th can be viewed as a simple inversion of a minor 7th with a root that is a minor 3rd higher than that of the original chord. The root, minor 3rd, perfect 5th, and minor 7th notes of the minor 7th chord therefore become the major 6th, root, major 3rd, and perfect 5th of the 6th chord.

C MINOR SEVENTH — C-E♭-G-B♭

E♭ SIXTH — E♭-G-B♭-C

ADD NINE TO SUSPENDED 4th

Omitting the 3rd from an "add9" chord and inverting the root so that the 5th is the lowest note creates a suspended 4th chord whose root is a perfect 5th higher than that of the original chord. Therefore, Cadd9 becomes Gsus4 when E is not played.

Cadd9 — C-E-G-D

G SUSPENDED FOURTH — G-C-D

PLAYING LEAD GUITAR

Playing a guitar solo is, for many guitar players, the most glamorous aspect of the instrument, giving even the most modest and humble musicians a chance to stand in the limelight. Although it doesn't have to be limited to a succession of crisply played single notes, in one way or another playing lead is all about manipulating scales. There are many playing effects which can add a distinctive characteristic to your playing by giving you greater freedom of expression and "feel", such as hammering, pulling, string bending and vibrato.

HAMMER-ON AND PULL-OFF

The "hammer-on" – known as *ligado* in the classical world – is to be found in every style of guitar playing. Produced by moving a left-hand finger to a fret further along the fingerboard on the same string, while that string is playing, it produces a higher note, and is indicated on a written manuscript as two notes joined by a slur with a letter "H" alongside.

The opposite of the hammer-on is known as a "pull-off" or "descending *ligado*," and is produced by playing a fretted note and releasing the left-hand finger to sound a lower note. It's indicated on sheet music in the same way as the hammer-on, but with the letter "P" alongside.

You can use both hammering and pulling techniques for playing either single notes or chords.

HAMMERING A SINGLE NOTE

Follow the steps below to practice using the hammer-on technique:
- Place your 1st finger on the 5th fret of the 3rd string – this is the note C.
- Play the note.
- Position the 3rd finger on the 7th fret of the 3rd string – the note D – while the note is still ringing.
- Let the note sustain.

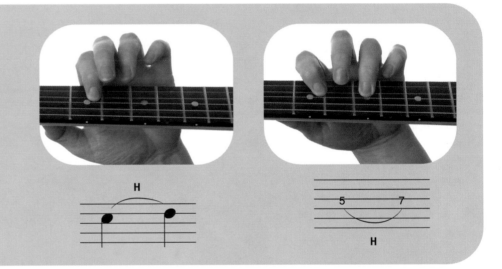

PULLING OFF A SINGLE NOTE

Follow this example to practice the pull-off:
- Position the 4th finger on the 10th fret of the 6th string – this is the note D.
- Place the 1st finger on the 7th fret of the 6th string – the note B.
- Play the D note.
- Release the 4th finger, allowing the B to sustain while the note is ringing.

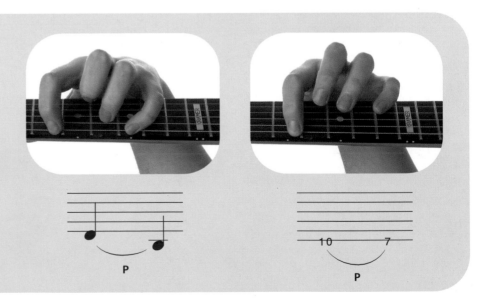

Here are two exercises to get your fingers working across the full width of the fretboard. As a central part of all guitar playing it's vital you master these two effects. Be careful to watch out for the letters "H" and "P" on the sheet music, and don't forget the one-finger-per-fret rule – for instance, in the first exercise the 1st finger plays all the notes on the 5th fret of each string.

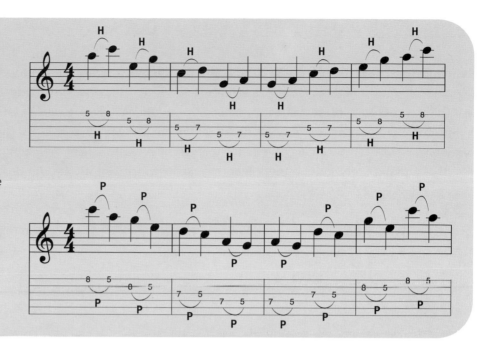

We can also apply the hammering and pulling technique on the previous two pages to chords. This is often done by using an incomplete open-string chord along the fingerboard. One technique is to barre the 2nd, 3rd, and 4th strings – forming a partial A-shaped barre – with the 1st finger. A second barre can then be hammered-on with the 3rd finger, two frets along the fingerboard or – a little more tricky – with the 4th finger three frets along.

You can try this example for yourself:

- Place the barre on the 7th fret with the 1st finger.
- Play just the 2nd, 3rd, and 4th strings with the right hand – the chord is a D major triad.
- Hammer-on a barre on the 9th fret with the 3rd finger – this is the chord E major.

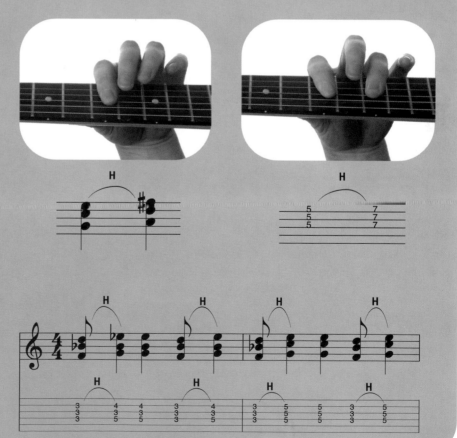

EXERCISE

Practice this chord-hammering exercise. The starting position uses an index-finger barre on the 3rd fret. In the first bar, the first move hammers-on what appears to be an open A minor chord shape, but which is actually an inversion of E♭. This progression is used extensively in rock music.

STRING BENDING

Bending the strings is one of the most basic but effective techniques utilized by electric guitarists, which normally involves playing a note and then bending the string to alter the pitch. The tremolo arm fitted to many instruments also allows you to achieve the effect mechanically. String bending, which has become a central part of modern guitar playing where it can provide richer texture to the sound as well as an extra emotional dimension, was originally developed by blues and country music players to mimic the sound of a bottleneck guitar or, in later times, the pedal steel guitar. The governing factor which will dictate the degree to which you can actually bend a string is its "gauge" or thickness.

SINGLE NOTE BENDING

This exercise entails playing the note F on the 2nd string and then bending it up to a G on the same string.

- Play the 6th fret of the 2nd string with your 3rd finger.
- Sound the string with your right hand.
- While the note sustains, pull the string downwards until the pitch increases by a whole tone.
- You should now be playing the note G.

Although initially it might prove tricky to stop bending at the correct pitch, you will master it with practice. What is more, a pitch-perfect bend is not even necessary or even really appropriate in some types of playing – in blues, for instance, slightly flattening the second note can be effective. But be careful not to push the string too far, or you will end up making the note sharp.

An alternative way of bending the string is to push upwards rather than pull downwards.

SECOND STRING BENDING

The effect of this basic bending technique can be enhanced to by playing to, or with, a second string. A trick which is common in rock and blues playing is to bend a note on one string up to the same note played on an adjacent string. In the exercise illustrated on the right we bend a D to an E, and while that note is still ringing play an E on an adjacent string. The secret in mastering this technique is to make sure you have the correct fingering for the second note in place before you actually start to play the initial note.

- Place the 1st finger on the 5th fret of the 2nd string (E), and the 3rd finger on the 7th fret of the 3rd string (D).
- Strike the 3rd string and bend the note up by a step (tone).
- While that note is still ringing, make the two notes sound together by playing the 2nd string.

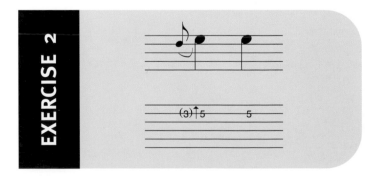

BENDING TWO NOTES INTO ONE

Another variation we can try is to play the two notes at the same time and then bend the 3rd string, bringing the pitch of the two strings together, so producing the same note.

The exercise above, while helping to get your fingers working, will also get you used to bending to the correct pitch. Here we play a C major scale by moving the hand along the same two strings (2nd and 3rd) and bending the notes together.

Using the 2nd the 3rd strings like this is relatively straight-forward. The interval of a major 3rd between the two strings means that, using the one-finger-per-fret rule, the 3rd string can be bent by the 3rd finger (the original notes being two frets apart). For other combinations using adjacent strings, however, the original notes will be three frets apart, so the bend has to be made by the 4th finger – a far more demanding exercise.

These kind of string-bending techniques are particularly effective when played with "distorted" sounds, the resulting variation of pitch making for interesting textures, such effects being further exaggerated by the addition of vibrato.

"PRE-BENDING" STRINGS

We can also bend a string to play a note which is lower in pitch than the starting note. This is done by bending the string into position before it is struck; the tension is released when you sound the string, the string returning to its natural position.

- Place your 3rd finger on the 7th fret of the 3rd string (the note D), and push the string upwards. Or, if you prefer, you can pull the string downwards .
- Holding the finger in position, play the note with a plectrum.
- While the note is still ringing slowly release the string, leting it rest at its natural position.

As you won't hear the first note to judge whether it is at the correct pitch before striking the string, pre-bending will call for constant practice before you can use it accurately.

NOTATION OF BENDS

The bend is indicated on the staff as two notes joined together by a line called a "slur". The first note – which is referred to as an "appoggiatura" – is much smaller than the second note, which can be quite confusing for learners who are trying to count out note values within a bar. It's important to remember that the duration value of the appoggiatura is not to be counted within the bar, and is simply to indicate the starting pitch. The value of the second note governs the overall duration of the note from the start of the bend to the finish, although the appoggiatura can be seen as "eating into" the duration value of the second note.

MULTIPLE BENDS

Another set of techniques worth mastering involves bending more than one string, or one or more of the notes of a chord. As when bending to a second note, these effects will often utilize the 2nd and 3rd strings, where we have a convenient interval of a major 3rd between the two strings. Try out the exercise which is illustrated below.

- Place the 3rd finger on the 7th fret of the 3rd string and the 4th finger on the 7th fret of the 4th string.
- Play both notes simultaneously.

- Push both strings downwards while the notes are still ringing.

Another method is to barre the 2nd and 3rd strings with the 3rd finger, pushing the barre downwards. Whichever method is used, controlling the pitch of both strings accurately can be difficult. In this example, you bend the 3rd string by a step (tone) and the second string by a semitone or half-step. This is used more often than bending both strings by an equal pitch because the difference in string gauges means that bending each string by the same amount will not alter the pitch to an equal degree.

BENDING CHORDS

A country-sounding flavour can be achieved in a solo by bending one or more notes of a chord. The example below involves fretting the three treble strings of an E-shape chord. Here, the second note of the chord is bent from a major 2nd up to the major 3rd to create the chord.

- Position the 2nd finger on the 9th fret of the 3rd string.
- Position the 3rd finger on the 10th fret of the 2nd string.
- Position the 4th finger on the 10th fret of the 2nd string.
- Sound the three strings together.
- Bend the 3rd string so that it increases in pitch by a tone.

It is possible to play this position using the first three fingers – in fact you would probably find it easier to play in this way. But by allowing the 1st finger to "float" above the action you will make it easier to combine this style of playing with the use of barre chords.

There is a mechanism, popular with country-rock guitarists in the 1970s, which can be used to create the same kind of sounds, called the Parsons-White system. Fitted to most models of the Fender Telecaster, it involved the 1st and 2nd strings being connected by a strong spring mechanism to the strap buttons. With this system the guiatrist can push the body of the instrument downwards at either end of the strap, causing the the pitch of either string to be altered. The system is highly effective, particularly when imitating pedal steel sounds, but to be fitted involves a lot of alteration to the structure of the guitar – not a good idea if you have a vinatge instrument.

Another pitch-altering technique – the effectiveness of which varies from guitar to guitar and which is only possible on guitars without locking nut systems – is to press on the treble strings behind the nut.

VIBRATO

"Vibrato" is a sound created by invoking small variations in pitch either side of a note which is used on all types of stringed instruments, and is one of the most expressive of single-note playing devices. The word itself comes from the Latin verb *vibrare*, which literally means "to shake." The effect of this "shaking" can be used to great effect in increasing the impact of the music.

There are various ways in which vibrato can be achieved on the guitar. The classic technique – utilized in many types of music – involves the finger "rocking" back and forth along the string. The hand movement, amounting to little more than a vibration, is extremely slight, and so the variation in pitch is hardly perceptible. However, some musicians prefer to produce a more extreme-sounding vibrato – in fact a very gentle form of string bending – by moving across rather than along the string.

CLASSICAL TECHNIQUE

The execise on the right illustrates a vibrato effect played on the note D on the 5th fret of the 6th string. Take note that the movement comes from the entire wrist action, not just from the fingers. On the other hand, the motion comes entirely from the finger when playing vibrato by bending the string.

The terms vibrato and tremolo are often used interchangeably. This is not actually correct, but seems to have come about during the 18th century, when the latter was widely used in describing left-hand vibrato effects on the violin. Although technically it means a rapidly repeated succession of notes, in practice, the term tremolo is often used to refer to an exaggerated vibrato.

EXERCISE 3

THE TREMOLO ARM

The tremolo arm was developed during the 1940s to produce vibrato effects on the guitar. It was during the 1950s that the term "tremolo" came to be applied to these mechanisms, and the name, though technically incorrect, simply stuck – although some purists still refer to them as vibrato arms.

It was during the late 1950s that guitarists like Duane Eddy and Hank Marvin began integrating them into their playing styles, and during the following decade some guitarists explored the potential to execute string bends that would be completly impossible to achieve using conventional methods.

The original designs, as produced by Fender and Bigsby in the 1940s and 1950s, were barely modified over the next three decades, even though they created tuning problems on even the best models. This finally improved in the 1980s, when the guitarist Floyd Rose developed the modern locking tremolo.

He devised a system that allows strings to be detuned to the point of laying slack on the fingerboard before being tuned back to perfect pitch. The Floyd Rose tremolo arm has proved so effective that every major guitar manufacturer now uses a variation of it in their instruments.

ADDITIONAL EFFECTS

We have already looked at the most common types of ornamentation to lead guitar playing – including effects like hammering-on, pulling-off and string bending – which add character and individual style to a performance. Here we will consider some more advanced techniques which, when adopted, should add further flair to your solo playing.

SLIDES

A "slide" means altering the pitch of a string by running one or more of the fingers of the left hand along its length. There are various types of slide commonly used, all producing their own individual effects. The term can also refer to an actual style of guitar playing, which achieves the same kind of effect with a glass or metal tube fitted over one of the fingers of the left hand.

The four examples illustrated below all move between the 3rd and 10th frets of the 1st string – the notes G and D. Particular attention should also be paid to the different ways in which each type of slide is signified in written music. And it should be remembered that written music does not recognize the difference between using your fingers or a glass bottleneck to slide, as the musical effect is just the same.

SLIDING BETWEEN NOTES

The most commonly used type of slide involves positioning the 1st finger on the 3rd fret of the 1st string and playing the note. While it is still ringing, slide the 1st finger up to the 10th fret, ensuring the pressure is consistent throughout. Releasing the pressure from the string while you move your hand will dampen the sound, this being true of all types of slide.

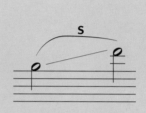

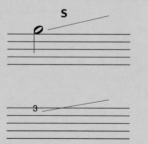

SLIDING TO A STRUCK NOTE

Though essentially the same as the previous exercise, this time when your 1st finger reaches the 10th fret the note should be played again with the pick. The difference is indicated in written music by the removal of the tie symbol that joins the two notes.

OPEN SLIDE TO A NOTE

You can also make what is termed an "indeterminate" slide to or from a note. In this exercise, place the 1st finger on the 3rd fret of the 1st string. Then quickly move your left hand along the fingerboard, avoiding playing the string with your right hand until you reach the 10th fret.

OPEN SLIDE FROM A NOTE

The same operation can be done in reverse. Place your 1st finger on the 3rd fret of the 1st string and play the note, moving your left hand along the fingerboard, releasing pressure gradually. The sound should gently fade away, but not on any one note in particular.

TRILLS

The trill is a very fast form of hammering and pulling between two different notes. It can be shown in written music in a variety of ways – in fact, for some odd reason, music scholars have been engaged in lively debate for many years as to whether the starting note should be considered as the main note or the auxiliary. Trills are usually indicated as a single movement, with the notes sounding virtually "blurred" or indistinct.

TRILL EXERCISE

This exercise moves between D and E on the 7th and 9th frets of the 3rd string.
- Position the 1st finger on the 7th fret of the 3rd string.
- Play the note and hammer-on the 9th fret with the 3rd finger.
- Immediately pull-off with the 3rd finger.
- Repeat the last two steps in quick succession as often as you wish.

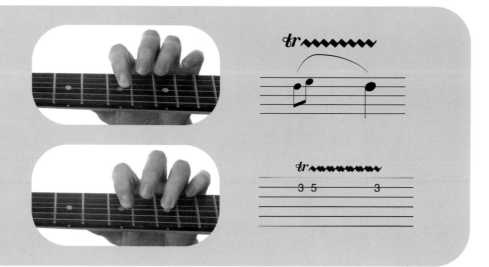

FINGER TAPPING / FRET TAPPING

Finger tapping, also referred to as fret tapping, is an extension of the single-note technique of hammering-on and pulling-off, which also "taps" out notes along the fingerboard using the right-hand fingers. The technique is used to play solos at a blistering speed in the hands of prime exponents like Eddie Van Halen and Joe Satriani. Although it rose to prominence during the 1980s, finger tapping is no new idea – session players such as the jazz-funkster Harvey Mandel demonstrated the effect on albums in the early 1970s. Jazz musician Stanley Jordan can be see using a related technique, in which he places the the guitar in a more or less horizontal position on his lap and plays it a bit like a piano keyboard, pressing down on the strings with both hands. Both these techniques – which require great technical skill – only really work effectively on amplified instruments, where notes can be sustained all over the fingerboard. They are valued by rock players because a consistency of volume to individual notes can be given by the extreme levels of compression and distortion.

TAPPING EXERCISE

The technique of tapping is similar to hammering-on and pulling-off, in that notes are hammered when moving up a scale and pulled-off when moving down. The main difference is that the pull-off played by either hand can be achieved with a gentle sideways pluck, to give extra volume for the next hammered note.

1 Position the 1st finger of the left hand on the 7th fret of the 1st string. Place the 1st finger of your right hand near to the 11th fret and pluck the note.

2 With the note sustaining, hammer-on the 9th fret of the 1st string with the 3rd finger of the left hand.

3 Pull-off the 11th fret by plucking the string alongside the fret and releasing the finger. In a similar fashion, pull-off with the other two fingers.

HARMONICS

By damping specific frets on the guitar fingerboard we can get bell-like sounds that are referred to as "harmonics". We have come across harmonics in the tuning section, and although for some players that might be the full extent of their knowledge about them and their use, harmonics can provide a guitarist with some handy effects.

CHARACTERISTICS

The exact sound you hear every time you strike a guitar string is the result of a number of different elements which, taken together, are known as the "harmonic series". The dominant sound you hear is referred to as a "fundamental", and is the string vibrating along the full length of the fingerboard between the bridge and the nut, which defines the pitch of the note. But, in addition, there are other components that we can also hear, and they are the result of shorter frequencies vibrating along different parts of the string. These frequencies are always strict multiples of frequency of the fundamental, and are known as harmonics or overtones. The tonal characteristics of an acoustic note produced by any musical instrument is created by the balance between the the various harmonics and the fundamental.

1ST TO 5TH HARMONICS

We can hear the sound of the harmonic on its own by playing a note muted by the left hand at specific positions on the fingerboard, the 12th fret being most commonly used. When we do this, the fundamental is muted, leaving only the harmonic to sound. The mathematical divisions that are allowed to resonate in this way dictate the pitch of the note we hear. By muting the fundamental

THE HARMONIC CAN BE HEARD WHEN THE STRING IS GENTLY MUTED ABOVE SPECIFIC NODES ALONG THE FINGERBOARD.

at the 12th fret you divide the string in half, and this causes the string to resonate in two equal measures (the distance between the nut and the 12th fret being identical to the distance between the 12th fret and the bridge saddle). This is known as a 1st harmonic, creating an identical note to the fretted note at the 12th fret.

There are other possible types of harmonic: the 2nd harmonic divides the string into three equal lengths; the 3rd harmonic causes the string to vibrate in four equal lengths; and the 4th harmonic divides the string into five equal lengths.

PLAYING HARMONICS

The various types of harmonic can be played at different points on the fingerboard. The diagram below clearly illustrates where they can be found.

● **1ST HARMONIC**
Place the finger above the 12th fret, causing the string to vibrate in two equal segments. This produces a note one octave higher than the open string.

● **2ND HARMONIC**
Place the finger above the 7th or 19th fret, causing the string to resonate in three equal segments. This produces a note one octave and a perfect 5th above the open string.

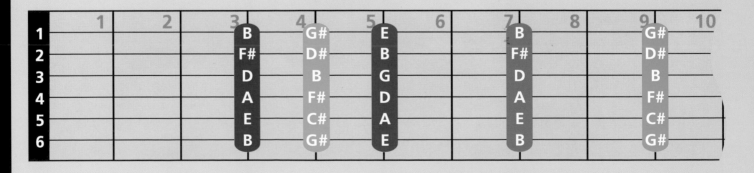

FRETTED HARMONICS

We can play harmonics for any note on the fingerboard. While the left hand frets notes in the normal way, the right hand mutes the string with the 1st finger of the right hand and simultaneously plucks the note either with the thumb or 4th finger. An excellent knowledge of the fingerboard is needed to pitch a note in this way. Fretting a note is, in effect, creating a new "nut" position. Harmonics are played relative to the shift between the nut or zero fret and the fretted note.

To demonstrate this for yourself, place the 1st finger on the 2nd fret of the 2nd string. Now place the 1st finger of the right hand lightly on the string above the 14th fret, plucking the note with the thumb of the right hand. This creates a first harmonic of C♯.

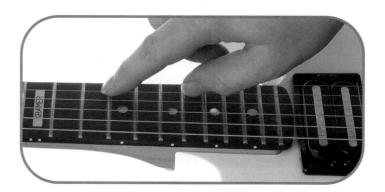

With the left hand still in position it is possible in the same way to hear second harmonics – the note G♯ – on the 9th and 21st frets, and a third harmonic (C♯) on the 7th fret.

FRETTING A CHORD

With some practice it should be possible to play a simple melody using fretted harmonics. One particularly pleasant style is to pick out the notes of a chord and play them as an arpeggio of fretted harmonics. Practice this example using an open C major chord.

- Hold an open C major chord with the left hand, remembering that the 1st finger holds the 1st fret of the 2nd string; the 2nd finger holds the 2nd fret of the 4th string; the 3rd finger holds the 3rd fret of the 5th string.
- Hold the 1st finger above the 15th fret of the 5th string and pluck the note with the thumb.
- In a similar way, play the 14th fret of the 4th string, the 12th fret of the 3rd string, the 13th fret of the 2nd string, and the 12th fret of the 1st string. Try to play the notes of the chord as evenly as possible, both in their timing and volume.

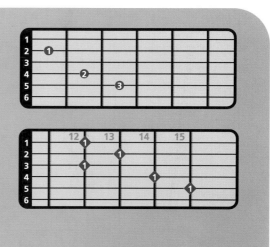

● 3RD HARMONIC
Place the finger above the 5th (or 24th) fret, causing the string to vibrate in four equal lengths. This produces a note two octaves above the open string.

● 4TH HARMONIC
Place the finger above the 4th, 9th, or 16th frets, causing the string to resonate in five equal lengths. The note is two octaves and a major 3rd above the open string.

● 5TH HARMONIC
The 5th harmonic falls between the 3rd and 4th frets, and produces a note two octaves and a perfect 5th above the open string

11	12	13	14	15	16	17	18	19
	E B G D A E				G♯ D♯ B F♯ C♯ G♯			B F♯ D A E B

THE SYNTHETIC SCALES

The diatonic scales that we have covered up to now – the major and minor series – are the most extensively used in most types of music. Having said that, there are various other scale types which constitute different combinations of intervals from the twelve half-step or semitone steps that make up an octave. Known as "synthetic" scales, the three most common types are pentatonic, augmented ("whole-tone") and diminished. We find pentatonic scales very widely used in blues, jazz and rock music, with the minor pentatonic scale often referred to as the "blues" scale. And there are many other more exotic scale types, often more commonly associated with ethnic music from around the world. By experimenting with some of these alternative note combinations, you will be better equipped to create your own distinctive lead parts, and avoid having to draw continually from the same musical resources.

PENTATONIC SCALES

Pentatonic scales are among the oldest known – and certainly the most widely used – type of synthetic scale, with variations having been found in the diverse ethnic musical cultures of Asia, Eastern Europe, the Far East and Native America.

As the name suggests, the pentatonic scales are constructed using five different notes from the root to the octave, with the two most commonly found forms in Western music being the major and minor pentatonics. Primarily because of their strong melodic feel, they are the most commonly heard of any non-diatonic scales.

ROCK, BLUES, AND THE PENTATONIC SCALES

Pentatonic scales are most familiar from their use in popular music, especially rock and blues, although they have been used in some 20th-century classical music. In fact, over the past 30 years or so, there have been numerous classic rock riffs that have been derived from pentatonic scales, famous examples including "Layla" by Derek and the Dominos, "Black Night" by Deep Purple and "Whole Lotta Love" by Led Zeppelin.

But the use of pentatonic scales is not restricted just to rock music, they are also frequently found in both folk and country music.

MAJOR PENTATONIC

The major pentatonic scale utilizes the same set of notes as a regular diatonic major scale, with the exception of two notes which are omitted, these being the 4th and 7th notes of the scale.

Consequently the set of intervals that define the major pentatonic scale is as follows: **STEP•STEP•STEP+HALF-STEP•STEP•STEP+HALF STEP**. In the key of C, the notes used are C, D, E, G, and A. This set of intervals can be transposed to every other key as with all scales. On the right we see the notes of the major pentatonic scale in the seven principal scales.

A	•	B	•	C♯	•	E	•	F♯	•	A
B	•	C♯	•	D♯	•	F♯	•	G♯	•	B
C	•	D	•	E	•	G	•	A	•	B
D	•	E	•	F♯	•	A	•	B	•	D
E	•	F♯	•	G♯	•	B	•	C♯	•	E
F	•	G	•	A	•	C	•	D	•	F
G	•	A	•	B	•	D	•	E	•	G

| **I** | STEP | **II** | STEP | **III** | STEP + HALF-STEP | **IV** | STEP | **V** | STEP + HALF-STEP | **I** |

PLAYING THE MAJOR PENTATONIC

To work through the major pentatonic scale, study the fingering diagrams shown below. They illustrate three alternative sets of positions, the first two of which start with the root note played on the 6th string and extend a full two octaves across the width of the fingerboard. The third pattern (below, right) has the root positioned on the 5th string and covers a single octave. In each case, the scale is played in the key of C, and the left-hand finger number is indicated on the diagram.

SWITCHING TO OTHER KEYS

To play these major pentatonic patterns in other keys, all you need do is move the pattern accordingly after choosing a new root note along the fingerboard.

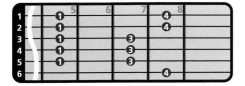

ROOT ON THE 6TH STRING

ROOT ON THE 6TH STRING

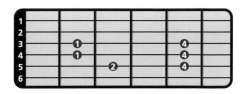

ROOT ON THE 5TH STRING

MINOR PENTATONIC

The minor pentatonic scale utilizes the same notes as a natural minor scale, but leaves out the 2nd and 6th notes. It is sometimes known as the "blues scale". The set of intervals is **STEP+HALF-STEP•STEP•STEP• STEP+HALF-STEP•STEP**. On the right we see the notes for the seven main keys.

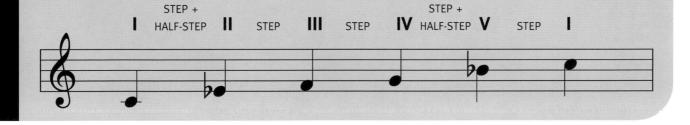

PLAYING THE MINOR PENTATONIC

Again there are three alternative fingering patterns as shown below, this time for playing the minor pentatonic scale in the key of C. The first two patterns illustrated start with the root note on the 6th string and extend over two octaves, while the third has the root positioned on the 5th string and plays through a single octave.

For all would-be blues guitarist, a good understanding of – and feel for – the minor pentatonic scale is an absolute must. Without it, we just wouldn't have the blues!

ROOT ON THE 6TH STRING

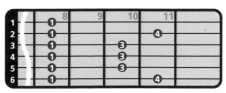

ROOT ON THE 6TH STRING

ROOT ON THE 5TH STRING

EXTENDING THE PENTATONICS

We've seen how the minor pentatonic scale is widely used for improvisation in blues, jazz and rock. With the following set of exercises we can continue the idea of moving notes from a scale around, taking the notes from a pentatonic scale and then extending it by adding some "unrelated" notes from the scale.

The first two bars illustrate the scale played in the key of C. Like any other scale it can be extended by adding notes from outside. These can be used to create a wider range of melodies, or just notes whose role is simply to connect two notes within a phrase – "passing notes".

ADDITIONS

There are three main additions we can make to the minor pentatonic: the addition of a flattened 5th (the note F♯ in the key of C), the addition of a major 3rd (E in the key of C), and the addition of a major 2nd and major 6th (D and A in the key of C). We can see all of these in the exercises below, the final example of which converts the minor pentatonic scale into what is referred to as the Dorian mode. We will deal with Modes in more detail on pages 178–181.

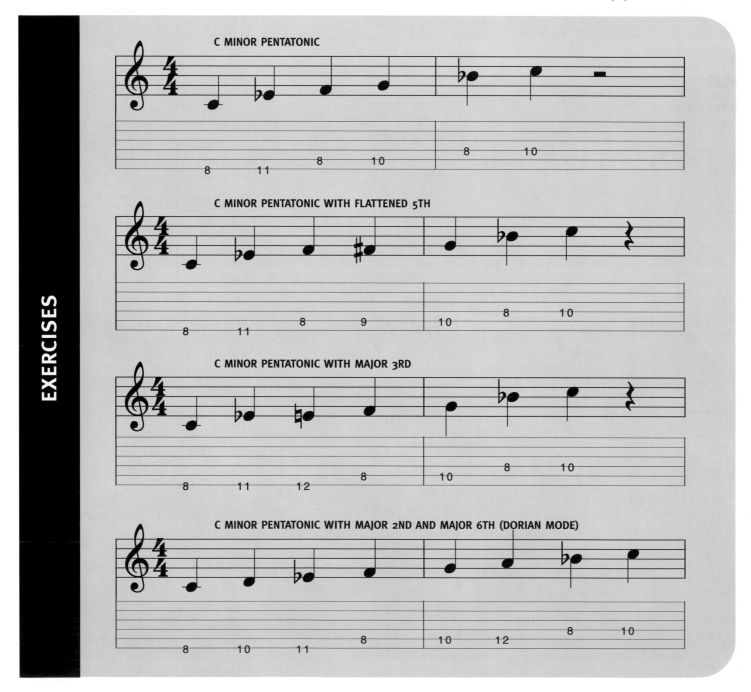

The exercise below is a typical example of how we find the notes from a minor pentatonic scale used in rock music. Begin by taking it easily, the hammered 16th-note runs in bars 5 and 8 are particularly tricky, being played at high speed. You will also notice the slide between the 3rd and 4th notes of bar 2, an effect that is very common in rock and blues.

SOME OTHER SYNTHETIC SCALES

As well as the pentatonic scales that have come to dominate blues and a big proportion of rock music, the augmented and diminished synthetic scales also proliferate in Western music. There is often a mysterious lilting or floating feeling to melodies that have been created using augmented scales. Diminished scales, on the other hand, are to be found in the work of jazz musicians rather than in other areas of non-classical music.

AUGMENTED SCALE

The augmented scale is also known as a "whole-tone" scale, this being because it moves from the the root to the octave through six steps or tones. The pattern of intervals is therefore **STEP● STEP● STEP●STEP ●STEP●STEP**.

Given the nature of the intervals, the effect of the scale will sound the same whatever note you start from. Because of this, only two different combinations of notes are needed to play an augmented scale in any key. They are C-D-E-F♯-G♯-A♯ and C♯-D♯-F-G-A-B.

PLAYING THE AUGMENTED SCALE

Shown here, in the key of C, is a fingering pattern for the augmented scale covering two octaves. This position lets you play the scale in half of the possible keys, and you will be able to play the other half by shifting the pattern one fret along in either direction.

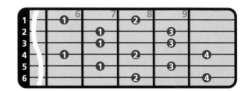

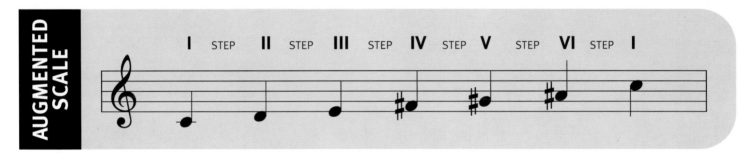

THE DIMINISHED SCALE

The diminished scale moves from the root to the octave using a pattern of eight separate intervals. They are: **STEP●HALF-STEP●STEP●HALF-STEP●STEP●HALF-STEP●STEP● HALF-STEP**. In the key of C this uses the notes C-D-E♭-F-G♭-G♯-A-B. The diminished scale has four key centers based around the 1st, 3rd, 5th, and 7th notes. Because of this, a diminished scale in any key will share the same notes with three other keys, and so three scale patterns will cover all twelve keys.

PLAYING THE DIMINISHED SCALE

Shown here in the key of C is a fingering pattern for the diminished scale covering two octaves, a position that allows you to play the scale in four possible keys. You will be able to play the eight keys simply by shifting the pattern by either one or two frets in either direction.

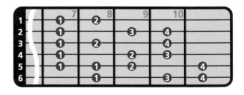

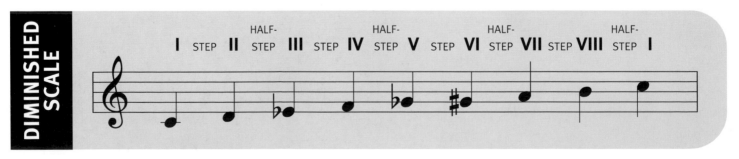

The examples below are just approximations of "world music" scales that can be used to create a flavour of their ethnic cultures. Many of them do not use chromatic tuning In their original forms, and to not conform to an octave comprising twelve equal parts. So, when played correctly, the scales will often sound alien or even out of tune to Western ears.

PELOG SCALE

INDIAN SCALE

HIRAJOSHI SCALE

KUMOI SCALE

NEAPOLITAN SCALE

HUNGARIAN SCALE

MODES

As with the scales that we have already seen and played, a mode is a series of notes with fixed intervals. You've quite possibly come across the term "mode" – maybe in the context of "modal jazz", which was fashionable in the late 1950s, for instance. But don't let this make you think that modes are some kind of musical curiosity or gimmick. In the context of musical history, modes actually pre-date the major and minor diatonic scales, that didn't evolve until as late as the 17th century. The modal system, on the other hand, was practiced by the Ancient Greeks before being taken up by the Christian church during the Middle Ages, after which it dominated Western music for several hundred years. Additionally, modes also feature in various types of folk and ethnic music.

Although the best-known exponents of modal playing are probably jazz improvisers like saxophone giant John Coltrane, as with other types of music theory the modes can be applied to any instrument. There are plenty of examples of modal guitar work to be found not only in jazz, but also in rock and blues. In fact the modes are used intuitively by some of these self-taught players, but there's nothing wrong with that! The guitarist is immediately attracted to the notes without necessarily realizing that they come from a specific mode.

HOW MODES WORK

Each mode comprises eight notes from root to octave, as in the diatonic scales. The notes used by every one of the modes are directly equal to the white notes of a piano keyboard – hence the equivalent to the notes of a C major scale. However, although it uses the same eight notes between root and octave, each mode starts on a different note. The result of this is that each of the seven modes has a different set of intervals, which means that each mode also has a unique sound characteristic. But as the notes are all the same, as long as you have mastered your major scale fingering, playing through these modes will be easier than you might anticipate.

MODAL INTERVALS

All this raises the question of whether all this is of any real use. We must realise that the modes were viewed as a fixed

The seven different modes are shown in the diagrams here and across the page. To hear how they work, just play them with the chords on the major scale – their "tonic" chords. These are illustrated in their simplest triadic forms of just three notes.

THE IONIAN MODE
(C TO C PLAYED OVER C MAJOR)

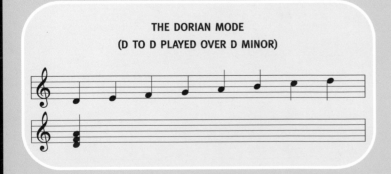

THE DORIAN MODE
(D TO D PLAYED OVER D MINOR)

THE PHRYGIAN MODE
(E TO E PLAYED OVER E MINOR)

series of notes, not a set of relative intervals, in their original forms. Before key signatures evolved, musicians were familiar with, and understood, the nature of each mode – pieces of music were written for the mode, and this in turn was to define the notes used. In modern times, however, each mode has been regarded as a scale with its own set of intervals as opposed to specific notes. This makes it possible to create seven new types of scale each with its own unique characteristics, by transposing of any of these sets of intervals into any key.

In reality you will find only five unfamiliar scales when you play through the set of modes below and on the next page. You will probably recognize that the Ionian mode is actually a major scale, and in the same way the Aeolian mode utilizes the same set of intervals as the natural minor scale.

INSPIRATION FROM OTHER INSTRUMENTS

Miles Davis and John Coltrane were two modal pioneers who brought a huge influence to the jazz world of the late 1950s and early 1960s, and it can still be heard today. Masters of the trumpet and tenor (and soprano) saxophone respectively, their work nevertheless was an influence on many instruments, musicians and composers, regardless of instrument.

It can come as a suprise to realise how many well-known guitar players have been influenced in their playing by listening to performers on other instruments. One of the originals of the electric jazz guitar, Charlie Christian, is known to have cited the great saxophonist Lester Young as one of his prime influences.

In the same way Ritchie Blackmore, the 1970s' guitarist made famous with rock bands Deep Purple and Rainbow, admits that his style of soloing developed by listening to, and indeed copying, jazz and R&B sax soloists. As he says: "They're all single notes, and therefore can be repeated on the guitar. If you can copy a sax solo, you're playing very well, because the average sax player can play much better than the average guitarist."

Different musical forms and unusual instruments found in other parts of the world have also proved an inspiration to musicians through the ages.

THE LYDIAN MODE
(F TO F PLAYED OVER F MAJOR)

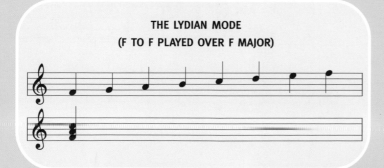

THE MIXOLYDIAN MODE
(G TO G OVER G MAJOR)

THE AEOLIAN MODE
(A TO A OVER A MINOR)

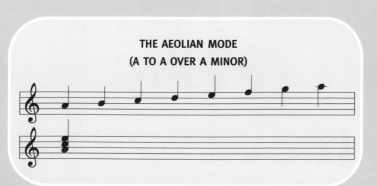

THE LOCRIAN MODE
(B TO B OVER B DIMINISHED)

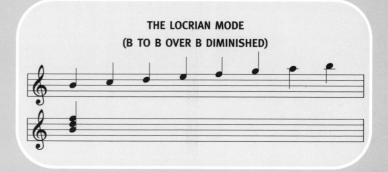

MODES IN PRACTICE

Taking a brief look at each one of the modes, we will see how they have been used in practice. The Ionian and Aeolian modes – the major and natural minor scales – can be ignored here as they've already been covered in some detail. All of these modes are an excellent basis for improvisation over different types of chord progression, just like the diatonic scales. A way of handling modal improvisation is to play over a pedal tone – a droning note or chords. The scales and chords illustrated on these pages can be used for this purpose. If you have a keyboard or sequencer, try programming an infinite D minor chord and improvising using only notes from the Dorian scale. This is the quickest method of experiencing various effects you can get from using the modes.

THE DORIAN MODE

The Dorian mode is a minor mode, although it differs from the natural minor scale (or Aeolian mode) in that the 6th note is sharpened. It has been widely used by jazz musicians since the 1950s.

A very well-known use of the Dorian scale is to be found on the first track of the classic 1960 Miles Davis album *Kind Of Blue,* "So What". One of the most recognizable bass lines in jazz, using notes from the Dorian mode, introduces the other instruments which cut in with a two-chord vamp consisting of intervals of 4ths, again from the Dorian scale (see the music across the page) – a harmonic departure from the usually played chords derived from triads. The faultless soloing by Davis and tenor sax player John Coltrane represents ensemble playing at its

most perfect – world-class musicians breaking new boundaries, and in doing so changing the complexion of jazz.

Coltrane subsequently took the form to an even more refined level when, in his later work with pianist McCoy Tyner, he was responsible for some of the most hypnotic music ever produced in jazz. He had, by this time, studied modal music for some years, both from traditional Eastern music and the early European church.

THE PHRYGIAN MODE

The Phrygian mode is another minor mode, differing from the natural minor in that the 2nd note is flattened – a note which can actually be heard as a flattened 9th. We can identify a minor mode by looking at the interval between the 1st and 3rd notes – they are two steps apart

THE SEVEN MODAL INTERVALS

On these two pages you will see all seven modal types written out in the same key – C. Practice through them one by one, and you should soon be able to familiarise yourself with their different characteristics.

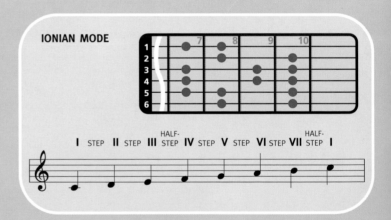

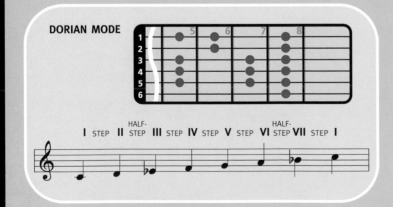

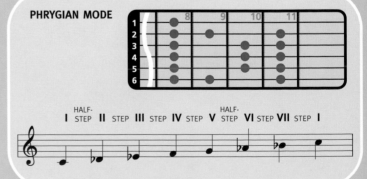

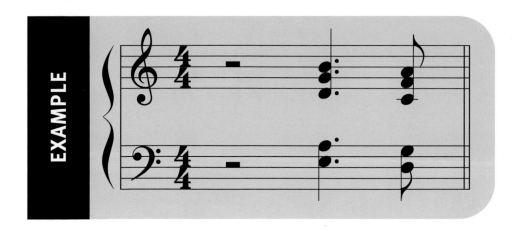

EXAMPLE

on all of the major modes. We can hear the Phrygian mode used extensively in flamenco music.

THE LYDIAN MODE

The Lydian mode is different from the diatonic major scale because the 4th note is sharpened. In fact the fashion for modal

music in the 1950s was triggered by the composer George Russell with his well-known work *The Lydian Chromatic Concept Of Tonal Organization*.

THE MIXOLYDIAN MODE

The Mixolydian mode varies from the Ionian (or diatonic major scale) by just one

note – the 7th which is a flattened 7th. It produces a mellow, "bluesy" effect, making it possibly the most popularly used mode in all types of modern music. With its flattened 7th, the Mixoldyian mode is especially useful in blues playing where it can be interchanged to good effect with a minor pentatonic scale in the same key.

THE LOCRIAN MODE

As the 7th degree of the scale, the Locrian mode is different to all of the others because it is a diminished scale. All of the notes are flattened except the 1st and 4th degrees, which results in a unique "exotic" feel. It is not commonly used in Western music – while being widely heard in the ethnic music of Asia – although it can easily be applied to give a stereotyped flavour of Middle Eastern music.

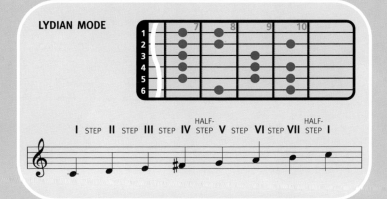

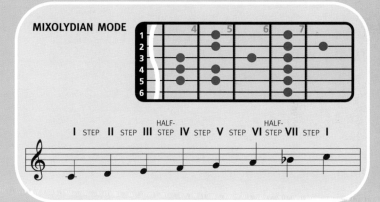

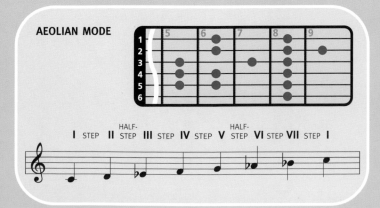

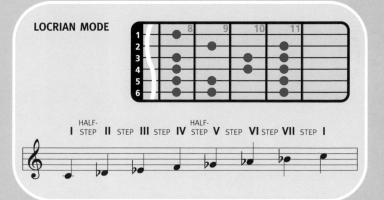

VARIATIONS

Since it first appeared in the Renaissance, the guitar has undergone some major changes although it wasn't until the end of the 18th century that the tuning system that we use today became standardized and six strings became the norm. And since that time variations – or altered tunings – have always been used in different types of guitar music.

Tunings for the lute and vihuela have been adapted for the guitar in classical music, to allow for the performance of pieces written for those instruments. In blues and folk music, there has been a long-standing tradition for the use of open tunings.

Similarly, when banjo players during the jazz age switched to the guitar in order to continue working, they brought their tunings variations with them. More changes came when the guitar was exported from America to the island of Hawaii, which witnessed the birth of "slack-key" tuning.

The slack-key trend was at its most popular during the late 1960s, when – inspired by the country and folk musicians of the period – famous names from the Beatles to Led Zeppelin were to experiment with this alternative. In fact Joni Mitchell, for one, has used open tuning on everything she has done – she simply never learned to play using standard tuning. And more recently we have seen a new generation of "ambient" guitarists, for whose "new age" musings altered tunings provide an ideal starting point.

USING ALTERED TUNINGS

There are a great variety of alternative tunings, a number of which will be shown here. Although most usually used by steel-string acoustic players, they can be equally applied to electric guitars. But be warned, if your guitar is fitted with a locking tremolo unit, you might possibly wear out a few Allen keys if you really get into this style of playing.

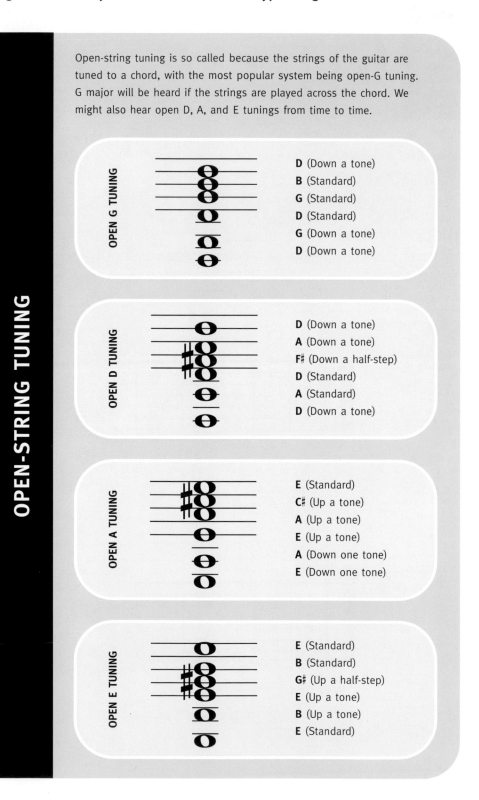

OPEN-STRING TUNING

Open-string tuning is so called because the strings of the guitar are tuned to a chord, with the most popular system being open-G tuning. G major will be heard if the strings are played across the chord. We might also hear open D, A, and E tunings from time to time.

OPEN G TUNING
D (Down a tone)
B (Standard)
G (Standard)
D (Standard)
G (Down a tone)
D (Down a tone)

OPEN D TUNING
D (Down a tone)
A (Down a tone)
F♯ (Down a half-step)
D (Standard)
A (Standard)
D (Down a tone)

OPEN A TUNING
E (Standard)
C♯ (Up a tone)
A (Up a tone)
E (Up a tone)
A (Down one tone)
E (Down one tone)

OPEN E TUNING
E (Standard)
B (Standard)
G♯ (Up a half-step)
E (Up a tone)
B (Up a tone)
E (Standard)

For the next set of exercises, you need to tune your guitar to an open G – the 1st, 5th and 6th strings all go down by a tone. The easiest way to use open-string tunings is with a barre. If you play the strings without fingering any frets, you will hear the chord G major, so if you hold a barre over the 2nd fret you will be playing an A major chord. Open-string tuning is very popular among slide players because of this simple approach to playing full six-string chords. The diagram shows which major chords can be created at different points along the fingerboard. Also indicated are the chords in the same positions using the other three open tunings shown on the opposite page.

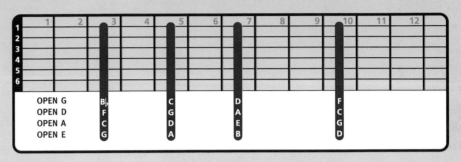

FINGERING

Producing totally unexpected chords is one of the most enjoyable aspects of using altered tunings. Here are two interesting chord positions to be used with an open G tuning – Cadd9 and G7. As an exercise play, the following two sequences. For the first, simply strum the chords any way you like; for the second, play the same chord sequence, but this time using right-hand fingerpicking.

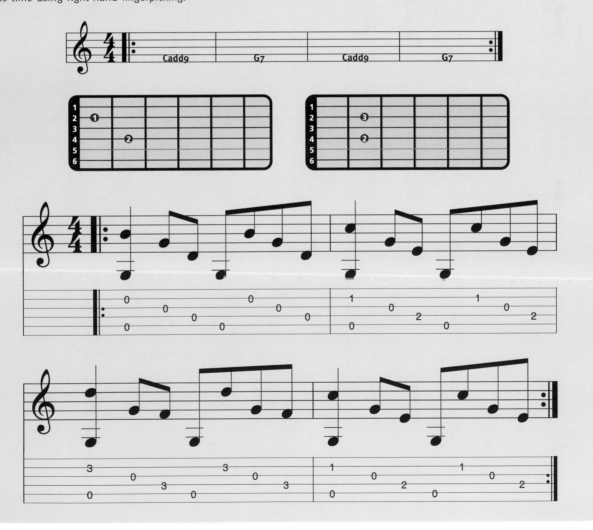

DROP D TUNING

One of the simplest tunings is Drop D tuning. All it entails is dropping the pitch of the 6th string by a whole tone, taking it down to D. Less popular, but still effective, is the Double Drop D tuning, which also takes the 1st string down to D.

In many cases, altered tunings have been developed to play in certain keys – in fact the very reason that they are not more widely used is because standard tuning allows for a greater degree of all-round flexibility. But in itself, a Drop D tuning is ideal for songs which use open D chords extensively, allowing for a full six-string chord with the root note on the lowest string. If you try it out for yourself you'll

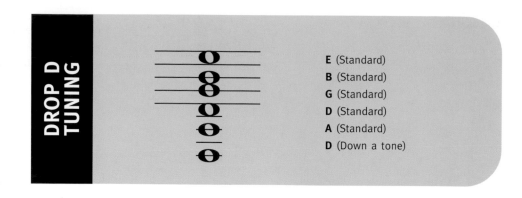

DROP D TUNING

E (Standard)
B (Standard)
G (Standard)
D (Standard)
A (Standard)
D (Down a tone)

hear no better-sounding voicing for a D major chord.

And as long as you remember that on the 6th string you must position your finger two frets higher than you would with standard tuning, Drop D tuning also works very well for other chords. On the

other hand you've got the option of simply not playing the 6th string if you don't want to learn new chord positions. To avoid tying your fingers up in knots with the alternative, it's also advisable at this point to discard the classical left-hand position and bend the thumb around the back of the neck to fret the 6th string.

In the chord positions shown here, the dots on the diagrams marked "T" should be played by the thumb. Also listen to the quality of the G major chord – like D, this is another very attractive alternative.

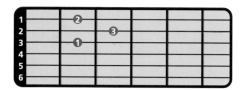

D MAJOR

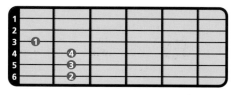

E MAJOR

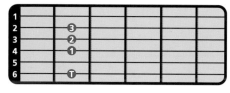

A MAJOR

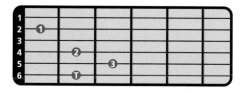

C MAJOR

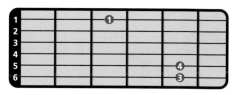

G MAJOR

WATCH THE TENSION

You will need to tune strings to a higher pitch for some of the alternate tunings shown in this lesson. Open A, for example, increases the pitch of the 2nd, 3rd and 4th strings by a tone. Any increase in the tension of the strings places a strain on the body and neck of the guitar, and if you are already using heavy-gauge strings, in extreme circumstances this could permanently damage your instrument. String breakage is also more likely to happen for the same reason, so it's a good idea to take precautions such as muting the fingerboard with a cloth – don't forget snapped strings have a tendancy to fly up towards the face. Using lower-gauge strings which can take greater tension is a viable alternative course of action.

On the other hand, the opposite is also true. The slackness from detuning a set of the lightest gauge strings by a tone can result in the vibrating strings hitting the fingerboard. In this situation, you should consider fitting higher-gauge strings in order to achieve a clean sound.

DADGAD

DADGAD tuning, which first emerged in the 1960s, was pioneered by the folk guitarist Davey Graham after he had experimented by playing with ethnic musicians from Morocco. This tuning is very effective on melodic work where the droning strings that underpin the sound – the pedal tones – are utilized to provide a harmonic framework to accompany tunes played either on single or double strings. In fact one of the most familiar popular examples of the use of the DADGAD tuning is possibly the Jimmy Page version of "Blackwater Side", even though it is more commonly used by folk musicians.

Fingerings for a small selection of chords you can play using the DADGAD tuning are illustrated on the right.

DADGAD TUNING

D (Down a tone)
A (Down a tone)
G (Standard)
D (Standard)
A (Standard)
D (Down a tone)

D MAJOR

D 5

G MAJOR

A MAJOR

DADGAD EXERCISE

Here we can clearly see how DADGAD tuning can be used to great melodic effect, and how the pedal tones can create an effect that is akin to many types of ethnic music heard throughout the world – from Celtic to North Indian.

The purpose of this exercise is for you simply to experiment with the eight chords, and for this reason only the tablature is shown.

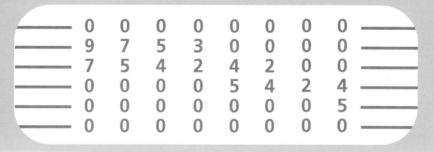

DROP G TUNING

E (Standard)
B (Standard)
G (Standard)
D (Standard)
G (Down a tone)
D (Down a tone)

DROP G (OR G6) TUNING

Drop G tuning is very effective for playing in the key of G, with the bottom two strings tuned down a whole tone. These bass notes are G and D, consequently there is rarely a time when you need to fret them with this tuning. Another advantage is that most standard chord voicings can be used or adapted because the top four strings still use standard tuning.

PLAYING SLIDE GUITAR

The evolution of the slide or "bottleneck" technique is closely related to the history of blues music. It started, and got its nickname, when early guitarists attempted to imitate the expression and emotion of the human voice by sliding the neck of a glass bottle along the guitar strings. A parallel development transpired in Hawaii, with the emergence of a style based on playing the guitar flat on the lap. Slide playing can be integrated with regular playing techniques and used with standard guitar tuning, but can also be used to good effect with altered tunings.

THE SLIDE OR THE BOTTLENECK?

Strictly speaking, a slide is made from metal and a bottleneck from glass, but the two terms have become largely interchangeable, so from here on we'll simply refer to "slides".

Choosing a slide with which you feel comfortable can be as important as finding a suitable pick. Slides can be found in all sorts of shapes and sizes, but as a rule glass produces a cleaner, more authentic sound than metal, which can sometimes make a grazing sound moving along the strings. But the type you opt for will be governed by the sort of guitar you play and the effect you wish to produce. It's worthwhile trying as many different types as you can find, as slides are relatively cheap, being no more expensive than a packet of strings.

SLIDE TECHNIQUE

The fact that you can no longer rely on the frets to provide perfect intonation is the trickiest aspect of slide guitar playing. So to make sure you play in tune – always to be advised – it is important for

SLIDE VIBRATO

Vibrato is one of the most expressive effects that we can achieve with the slide, and can be created with a slide just by gently moving the wrist backwards and forwards. You can produce different effects depending on how far you move either side of the note. A half-step or semitone in either direction would be the absolute maximum to get a pure vibrato, but other equally interesting effects can be produced by going further.

the slide to be positioned directly above the fret of the note required. To get this right requires considerable practice, especially as you will be more familiar with fitting your fingers behind the fret when pressing down on the strings. Quite simply, when the slide is placed behind the fret the note will be flat, and when it's positioned ahead of the fret, it will be sharp.

It's important to remember that the slide needs little more pressure than its own weight against the string. A problem that frequently plagues beginners is the unpleasant "buzzing" that can easily be produced when you press the slide too hard against the strings, which can even cause contact with the frets. If the "action" – the height of the strings above the fretboard – of your guitar is too low, buzzing may be unavoidable, even though the fingers behind the slide can be used to dampen fret rattle to a degree. Some guitarists raise the action on their instrument to avoid this happening, this being done by adjusting the height of the strings at the bridge, and/or increasing the height of the nut, or zero fret. But be careful when trying this – the intonation of your guitar can easily be ruined if you're not too sure what you're doing. Musicians who use slide a lot in their playing usually find it more convenient to have a separate instrument set aside for slide use.

Slides can be indicated in written music in a number of different ways. The most common version has two notes joined by a straight line with the letter "S" shown above, and is identical to the notation for regular slide when performed with one of the fingers of the left hand. Simply using curves and omitting the letter is preferred by some musicians.

Begin by positioning the slide above the nut in order to get your left hand accustomed to holding the slide. Play an open E on the 1st string, then slide up to the octave on the 12th fret while the string is still ringing. Then try the same exercise in reverse, starting on the 12th fret of the 1st string. Practice the exercise with all the six strings.

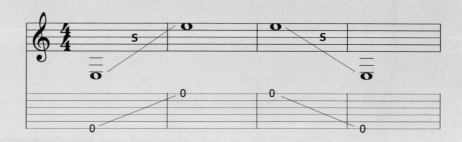

Test your intonation when playing with the slide with the following exercises. First we are looking at a complete scale played along one string. This time, start on the 3rd string and play a G major scale one note at a time. Again, try playing it with all six strings.

In the final example we see a staggered, descending major scale. Play the 12th fret; slide down to the open string; slide up to the 11th fret, then back down to the open string. Carry on like this until you complete the scale.

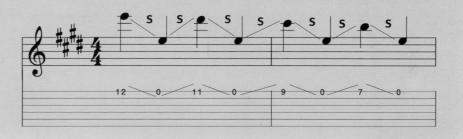

This A minor pentatonic scale starts on the 5th fret of the 1st string and descends to the 7th fret of the 5th string. This exercise should be attempted both descending and ascending the scales.

CHORDS AND ALTERED TUNINGS

Although many modern players integrate slide playing into their regular technique, there is a strong blues and folk tradition of playing slide using altered tunings. The most popular approach is to use open tunings; as the strings are tuned to a chord, you can play other chords simply by sliding the bottleneck along the fingerboard.

CHORDS USING OPEN-G TUNING

The most important thing to consider when playing chords with a slide, is that the point at which the slide touches the strings has to be absolutely parallel to the frets. If they are not, the chord will not be in tune.

The slide exercise opposite uses open-G tuning. Begin by retuning the strings of your guitar – this entails lowering the pitch of the 1st, 5th, and 6th strings by a whole step. From bottom to top, your guitar strings should be tuned to D, G, D, G, B, and D. Placing the slide above the nut, gradually move up in half-step

intervals until you reach the 12th fret. And don't forget to make sure the slide is parallel to the frets – you'll soon hear the less than pleasant result if you don't!

MISSISSIPPI FRED McDOWELL

Born: January 12, 1904, Rossville, Tennessee, USA
Died: July 3, 1972, Memphis, Tennessee, USA
Guitars: Hofner acoustic; National Resonator; Gibson "Trini Lopez"
Recordings: *In London*; *Sounds Of The South* (compilation)

One of many "unknown" blues pioneers who was discovered late in life, Fred McDowell spent his first 55 years as an itinerant labourer on farms around Mississippi, occasionally playing to local black audiences. It was the noted blues and folk archivist Alan Lomax who discovered McDowell's work, which he issued as a part of his seminal series of field recordings made in 1959.

Encouraged by Lomax, McDowell became part of the burgeoning US folk circuit, a home to many such "rediscovered" blues legends. McDowell was a popular attraction on the US college circuit with his combination of charismatic charm and unspoiled authenticity. A growing reputation, helped in part by the word-of-mouth generated by this new following, was to bring him to the notice of several prestigious folk and blues record labels in the early 1960s.

His first album was recorded in 1963 on the eve of his 60th birthday and – entitled *Delta Blues* – it featured a dynamic playing technique based almost entirely around the use of a steel slide and bass-string runs executed with amazing expertise. Fred McDowell's live concert repertoire included some notable compositions of his own, such as "Write Me A Few Lines," as well as a cross-section of blues standards.

He gigged and recorded extensively until his death from cancer in Memphis in 1972, having made a successful transition to the electric guitar in the mid-1960s that showed a surprising adaptability for a player of his age. McDowell enjoyed his greatest popularity with youthful white audiences, and he was also an important influence on young blues players who grew up through the 1960s – Bonnie Raitt, herself now acknowledged as one of America's finest contemporary slide guitarists, being among the most notable.

The exercise below involves playing fingerpicking with the right hand and slide chords with the left. With your guitar still tuned to open G, you're only concerned with three chords – D (7th fret), A (14th fret), and G (12th fret) – with the final chord being played as a harmonic on the 7th fret.

SOME ALTERNATIVES

Most of the musical styles and techniques that we have covered so far have been fairly conventional in the main, though not always quite as "by-the-book" as some formal tutors might prefer. To conclude the playing section we will consider some alternative approaches to guitar playing, not as a straightforward tutorial but as a brief look at an area that is largely ignored by guitar tuition of any complexion. It's an area of playing where there doesn't necessarily have to be six different strings tuned to E-A-D-G-B-E, or where fingers and picks are the only way of striking those strings. We'll also take a look on the spreads that follow at some hardware-based approaches to playing; these are areas of guitar playing where the hardware drives, and in some ways defines, both the music and its execution (other effects are discussed on pages 198–201).

SOME ALTERNATIVES TO STRINGING AND TUNING

We know that strings are manufactured in a variety of sizes (gauges) and materials, all designed to provide the most effective way of producing a consistent sound across approximately four octaves. However, certain musicians have experimented with modifications on the traditional approach, with varying degrees – depending on your musical point of view – of success.

A prominent practitioner in this area is the New York-based composer Glenn Branca, who is known for the sounds he produces with his guitar "orchestras". Many of Branca's works have been spectacular both musically and visually, performed in large-group ensemble settings comprising mainly electric guitars. The individual instruments, however, are either re-strung or retuned in order for them to be played over a limited range of notes or register.

To try for yourself the alternative approach to tuning described above – without having to restring your guitar – follow the retuning instructions on the right, tuning each string DOWN to a D. Strum across all six strings.

You will get some idea of the power of this approach by playing a D major scale, using an index finger barre on the top three strings and treating the open bass strings as pedal tones – notes that remain "droning" beneath the scale.

1ST STRING	D	(DOWN 1 STEP)
2ND STRING	D	(DOWN 4 STEPS PLUS A HALF-STEP)
3RD STRING	D	(DOWN 2 STEPS PLUS A HALF-STEP)
4TH STRING	D	(UNCHANGED)
5TH STRING	D	(DOWN 2 STEPS PLUS A HALF-STEP)
6TH STRING	D	(DOWN 1 STEP)

TUNING TO D

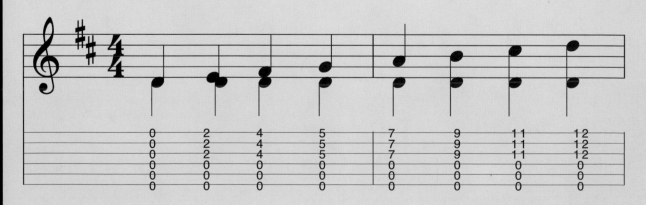

In the most extreme instance, the guitar is restrung so that all the strings are not only identical but also tuned to the same note, with changes in pitch being made by playing barres with the index finger. In other cases, the guitars will be strung conventionally but again all are tuned to a single note, although in different registers. Various guitars in the orchetsra are tuned to differing core pitches. The overall impact of full six-string "chords" played on a half-a-dozen or more of these guitars can, as you might imagine, be quite overwhelming for the audience.

BEYOND THE SIX STRINGS

Guitar makers have constantly tried looking beyond the concept of the six-string guitar, which has dominated the instrument's development for nearly 200 years. A number have aimed to address the question of the guitar's limited bass register, and one attempt at this was the Gibson "harp-guitar" produced in the 1920s, which was a standard guitar with the headstock extended to accomodate 12 bass strings – one for each key – each tuned at half-step intervals.

Not quite as radical was a seven-string instrument designed by jazz guitarist George van Eps in the 1940s, which was produced briefly by Gretsch in the 1960s. In a similar vein, the late 1980s saw Steve Vai collaborating with Ibanez to produce the Universe guitar. Both of these experiments included an additional bass string, usually tuned to a B – the same interval below E on the 6th string as those between the bottom four strings. As well as creating a significant addition to the range of notes available, this also opens up an entirely new set of chords based on the B string, or B-shaped barres.

But much of the basic attraction of the guitar, even though seven-string instruments have their enthusiasts, is that for many the beauty of guitar music is its simplicity – and the possibility for the lowliest beginner to learn a few chords almost immediately. At the end of the day, for most players a few extra bass notes just wouldn't make much difference.

SEVEN-STRING CHORDS

The two seven-string chord diagrams below give some idea of the possibilities that an extra string has to offer. The chord on the right shows a full seven-string voicing for an open B major chord, while the one on the left illustrates how the principles of barre chords can be applied to the 7th string. This B-shaped barre from the 7th fret creates an alternative E major chord over the bottom six strings – playing the bottom five strings alone will produce a very powertul "tive" chord.

In practical terms, the main advantage of seven-string guitars is in extending the player's single-note range. When playing chords, they are mainly used in the same way as six-string instruments, that is with the 7th string omitted.

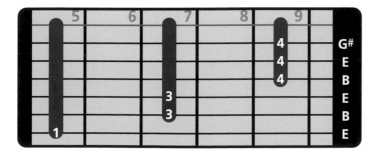

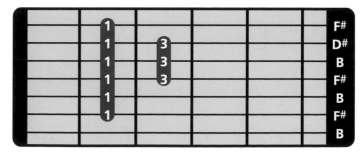

CHOOSING HARDWARE

The first thing you need if you are using an electric guitar will be a combination of an amplifier and loudspeaker to produce the sound. As well as their basic function of increasing the volume of your guitar, amplifiers also have the facility to produce various sounds and effects to enhance your playing. In terms of the overall influence it has on your sound, choosing an amplifier can in many ways be as important as choosing your guitar. In addition, electronic effects units, from simple foot pedals to expensive digital multi-effect units, can be used to produce a far greater range of sounds than you would achieve using just a guitar and amplifier. In fact, many of the sounds that we now take for granted as part of the standard repertoire are only possible with the aid of some kind of additional unit. It's fair to say that effects are now almost a necessity for many types of music.

TEN CHECKPOINTS WHEN CHOOSING AN AMPLIFIER

CHECKPOINT 1 – POWER
When you are about to choose an amplifier you should first consider how you want to use it, and how loud you are likely to want to play. You will probably need between 50 and 100 watts of power if you're planning to play in a live venue, but don't forget that high output doesn't always mean high quality in an amplifier.

CHECKPOINT 2 – COMPATIBILITY
Although any amplifier can function with any guitar in the basic sense of making the signal louder, you should always have your own instrument with you when testing an amplifier. Some pairings are simply more compatible than others, and this is the only way of testing whether a particular piece of equipment is the right one for the sound you're aiming for.

CHECKPOINT 3 – THINK WHAT YOU NEED
It's a good idea to think about what you really need before considering amplifiers with lots of special effects. As with guitars, some of the most reliable – and popular – amplifiers are quite basic models designed back in the 1950s. The best idea is to begin with a modest system, adding to it as and when new refinements become necessary.

CHECKPOINT 4 – SIZE
The size and weight of amplifiers can vary greatly. If you are choosing an amplifier "head" with a big, separate speaker cabinet, check first that you have space for it in your home. Bear in mind that damp garages or cellars are not ideal places to store sensitive electrical equipment. Also, if you have to struggle with a bulky "four-by-twelve" cabinet up and down flights of stairs, you'll soon have second thoughts about the choice you've made.

CHECKPOINT 5 – BUYING SECONDHAND
Be wary of amplifiers that look battered or damaged if you are buying one secondhand. It could mean that the equipment has been heavily used, has been "in transit" a lot, or has simply not been looked after properly, all of which can affect its reliability.

CHECKPOINT 6 – SILENCE IS GOLDEN
If you hear any excess buzzing or similar noise, either before you plug in or when you are not playing, beware – it could be a sign of worn or damaged circuitry.

CHECKPOINT 7 – CHECK THE SPEAKER
Any damage or flaw in the speaker can adversely affect the sound. If you are able to, remove the grille that covers and protects the loudspeaker and check the cone, making sure it's not dented or torn. You should also check the cone periphery for wear and tear.

CHECKPOINT 8 – CHECK THE ELECTRICS

You should check all of the switches, and volume and tone controls, satisfying yourself that they all function properly without emitting clicks or crackling noises. But as they can generally be repaired fairly easily, if you're being offered a real bargain it's still worth considering – getting a qualified technician to give it the once-over isn't going to cost a fortune.

CHECKPOINT 9 – LOOSE ENDS

A simple way of checking for loose valves or other circuitry is to stamp your foot on the ground next to the amplifier, with it switched on but not connected to a guitar. If you hear any electrical noise as a result, you probably have a problem.

CHECKPOINT 10 – DON'T TAKE AMPLIFICATION FOR GRANTED

It's easy to be too casual about choosing an amplifier. The amp not only increases the volume of your playing, it colours the entire sound, so be cautious before opting for a particular model. If you try out a variety of different types you'll soon be aware of the vast differences between them.

EFFECTS FOR BEGINNERS

With a new system it's very tempting to add the latest in electric gizmos and gadgetry as soon as you get started, but forget it. Your work will be cut out merely getting your fingers to do what you want, and you certainly won't need the added distraction of worrying about what weird and wonderful sounds are coming out of the loudspeaker. If you can't resist the temptation to purchase some kind of effect, choose something that is simple and versatile, such as reverb or delay or, if you're amplifier won't produce such sounds, distortion.

It's always a good idea to use the cleanest sound possible when you practice your basic playing techniques. Although shoddy or imprecise playing can be disguised by heavily processed sounds, in the long run they can be a liability, making it difficult for you to evaluate your progress on the instrument accurately.

AMPLIFIERS

To produce a sound, an electric guitar is connected to an input socket on an amplifier with a "lead" – a length of screened cable with jack plugs at either end. Amplifiers come in many shapes and sizes, with a variety of special features, but there are basic elements – input sockets, channel input level, tone controls (usually bass, mid-range, and treble), and a master volume control – that are found on almost all models.

AMPLIFIER STAGES

Amplifiers work in various ways, but there are a number of operations that all amplifiers have to be able to perform regardless of whether they are combos or heads and stacks, or whether they are using valve or solid-state circuitry, .

These functions include two fundamental stages: the pre-amplifier (more often referred to as the "pre-amp") determines the input volume and tone, while the power amplifier controls the overall volume. The pre-amp stage is crucial because that is when most of the tonal colouration takes place.

INPUT SOCKET

The process starts with an input signal from a guitar, which invariably comes via a jack socket. A lot of amplifiers have more than one input channel, which can be used to plug in a second guitar or another electronic instrument. It can also be used to go from one setting to another, which can be very useful when you want to set different volumes for playing, for example, lead and rhythm guitar.

CHANNEL INPUT VOLUME

Even though the level and tone of this signal can be adjusted on the actual guitar, the volume of the initial signal is controlled by the input channel volume control. The signal is boosted by this pre-amplifier stage, and is then passed to what is known as the equalization stage.

TONE CONTROLS ("EQ")

At its most basic, this part of the process might involve just a single bass and treble control, with classier models featuring a mid-range control. Some, such as the advanced Mesa Boogie combos, use a graphic equalizer instead of normal tone controls. This allows for very precise tonal programming at the amplifier stage by splitting the sound spectrum into five or more bands.

OUTPUT VOLUME

At the final stage of the process, the output signal from the pre-amplifier passes to the power amplifier, with the master volume being the final control before the signal is passed to the speaker. The overall output of the amp is governed by the master volume, regradless of the number of input channels or their settings.

VARIATIONS

More costly and sophisticated valve amplifiers often feature various intermediary stages. A lot of classic amplifiers have built-in sound effects such as reverberation, or, in the case of some vintage Vox AC30s, even tremolo. Some amps also have "lead" or "overdrive" channels separate from the usual volume channels.

VALVE, SOLID-STATE AND HYBRID

The classic valve amplifier sound, associated with a warmth and smoothness of tone, is favoured by most guitarists. However, unlike solid-state circuitry, valves – which also produce a pleasant distortion as the volume increases – can come loose, or may require replacing from time to time. Because different valves can produce different sounds, some guitarists will experiment endlessly with a variety of possible combinations.

Solid-state "transistor" amplifiers are characterized by a sharper, brittle sound, and are favoured by players who want a cleaner tone. Transistors can deal with a wider range of frequencies than valve amplifiers, and also distort less at higher volumes, which makes them more suitable and reliable for pure amplification purposes, like PA systems or studio monitors. Solid-state is basically more consistent, so any two similar models will always sound the same, though for this reason some guitarists regard them as lacking in character.

A hybrid of both systems which has emerged over the past decade has become a popular alternative. This generally uses a valve amplifier or pre-amp to provide the basic sound which is then amplified through an independent solid-state power amplifier.

COMBO, STACK AND RACK

The "combo" is the traditional guitar amplifier so-called because it combines an amplifier and loudspeaker in a single compact and portable unit. The trend towards using separate amplifier and loudspeakers grew during the 1960s; in this combination, the amplifier is usually referred to as the "head" and the speakers as the "stack". Though potentially able to produce greater volume than a combo, in a small venue it can prove hard to produce a high-quality distortion sound at a low enough volume. It does mean, however, that the player has the advantage of choosing his own combination of amp and speaker cabinet.

Pre-amplifiers and power amplifiers fitting into standard 19-inch (approx 0.5-metre) rack units are now being produced by some manufacturers. Although this might just be regarded as another way of storing the amplifier "head," in recent years MIDI has been utilized to enable different settings to be stored and controlled from a footswitch, or sometimes an external sequencer or computer.

PRACTICING AT HOME

Practicing at home can be a bit of a nightmare for an electric guitarist, the main problem being in achieving a satisfactory balance between volume and sound. You might have a 100-watt valve head and a four-by-twelve stack standing there in your bedroom, but it won't be practical to drive it at enough volume to get a decent sound – crank up the volume, and you'll alienate your family and neighbours, and damage your hearing. Using a practice amplifier is one way around this. A practice amp is a small combo – usually less than 5 watts in power – with all the features of a standard guitar amplifier, the best-quality models specifically designed to produce an excellent sound at low volumes.

Practicing using headphones is another popular solution, which can be done in several different ways. There are now multi-effect guitar pedals on the market which are equipped with headphone sockets, so to hear what you're playing you don't even have to have an amplifier, although the sound won't be particularly wonderful. A better solution is to use a speaker simulator or direct injection (DI) box, with which you can plug the speaker output of your amplifier into a line input on a mixing desk or hi-fi. But a word of warning, never, ever, plug the speaker output directly into your hi-fi amp unless you want to blow your sound system completely.

PRODUCING THE RIGHT SOUND

The wide range of sonic possibilities available means it is crucial that you are able to produce the right kinds of sound which are appropriate to the type of music you are playing, and you should be able to produce any kind of sound that you require once you become familiar with the way your equipment works. Illustrated below you will see six different but widely used amplifier settings – try them out for yourself. The letters on the knobs represent the following: I – input volume; B – bass; M – mid-range; T – treble; O – output (master) volume.

1. NEUTRAL SETTINGS

All of the controls are set in a central position, producing a clean sound, with very little or no distortion. These settings would be suitable for basic rhythm or chord work in most types of music, and you can alter the volume without changing the nature of the sound by using the master volume control.

2. TREBLE-HEAVY SETTINGS

We get a brighter, cutting, ringing sound by boosting the treble control (T) . However, as it also increases the overall volume, the master volume (O) needs to be reduced to compensate. Adding treble (and a touch of mid-range, M) might be necessary to produce a flat sound in a very sound-absorbent atmosphere, or if you are using certain types of humbucking pickup (see pg 197).

3. BASS-HEAVY SETTING

For a deeper, fuller sound, we boost the bass control (B). Once again, it might be necessary to reduce the master level (O) to compensate. Bass levels can vary depending on the speakers used, smaller speakers with limited low-frequency response benefitting from extra bass – though too much can cause distortion.

4. GENTLE DISTORTION

Boosting the input volume (I) in valve pre-amplifiers will gradually cause the sound to distort. Because this boosts the overall volume, the master volume (O) will have to be reduced to compensate. With the tone controls set equally, this is usually a good, general setting for lead-guitar .

5. CRUNCH

When the input volume (I) is on high, the pre-amplifier distorts, the increase in treble (T) producing a cutting sound. This kind of effect can only really be achieved with a valve amplifier – solid-state models will need an external effect unit. This setting can also create feedback, whether you want it or not, but this can often be controlled by reducing the treble on the guitar's control panel.

6. MUTE DISTORTION

When the input volume (I) is set to the maximum, reducing the treble (T) and mid-range (M) produces a "muffled" sound. This can result in an extremely effective "bluesy" lead effect when it's played with valve overdrive, possibly also using the rhythm pickup (see opposite page).

PICKUPS AND SOUND

Besides the amplifier and effects, the pickup also has a major effect on the sound produced by an electric guitar. Different kinds of pickup play a major role in the overall sound, as does the way they are actually positioned on the body of the instrument. There are two broad categories of magnetic pickups – single-pole and twin-pole, also known as humbucking (see picture, right), each having its own type of sound.

Originally pickups were all single-pole in design, until twin-pole pickups were introduced by engineers at Gibson in the 1950s as a device to reduce electrical hum, which is how they got the name "humbuckers".

Because of the different ways in which the string vibrates along its axis, the amplified sound alters depending on where the pickup is positioned. There are two or three pickups on most electric guitars. The best for lead work, because it produces the brightest sound, is the one positioned closest to the bridge, and is often known as the "lead" pickup. The one closest to the fingerboard is best suited for rhythm work (although commonly used by jazz players for playing lead) as it creates a more mellow, less cutting

tone. If there is a third pickup, it will be located between the lead and rhythm pickups. One or a combination of both pickups can be heard by using a mechanical switch on the body of the guitar.

Certain pickups on various well-known guitars (including Telecasters and Stratocasters) have a lead pickup angled in such a way that the poles on the top strings are closer to the bridge than those of the bass strings, thus altering the tonal balance and allowing the top strings to produce a more biting, treble sound.

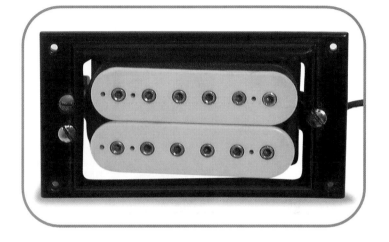

CONTROLS ON THE GUITAR

Nearly all electric guitars are fitted with at least a volume and tone control, and some models, like the classic Gibson Les Paul, have these two controls for each pickup, allowing the player to switch between settings easily. But many players hardly ever touch the controls, instead preferring to keep them set permanently on "full", using the amplifier for any tonal changes they wish to make. Having said that, it's always useful to experiment with the guitar settings. A good example is with heavy valve distortion, which can sound sweeter with the guitar treble tone set to a minimum value.

We can also produce a number of playing effects using the guitar controls, such as striking a note or chord with the volume turned off, then fading the volume up as the note sustains.

EFFECTS

Whether we are talking about simple foot pedals or expensive digital multi-effect units, all electronic effects units allow the guitarist to create a far wider range of sounds than he or she could have previously achieved with just a guitar and amplifier. In fact, there are a huge number of sounds which we take for granted as a normal feature of today's music repertoire which simply wouldn't exist were it not for some sort of add-on unit. In other words, for a lot of modern music, effects are now a necessity.

PEDALS

When you plug your guitar straight into an amplifier, the signal that emerges from the loudspeaker will have already gone through a wide range of tonal modification in the amplifier itself, like alterations in equalization, or deliberate distortion produced by overloading the pre-amplifier. And the nature of the sound can be altered further using a great number of other electronic processing effects.

Electronic sound processing effects were first created in the 1950s and 1960s. They were either mechanical or used analog electronics which seem primitive by today's standards. These days even the most simple and inexpensive effects are likely to be either digital simulations of natural phenomena, such as reverberation and echo, or wholly artificial effects based mainly on changes in pitch or a distortion of the original signal.

PLUGGING IN

A plug-in foot pedal is certainly the easiest – and least costly – way of obtaining an electronic effect, and most of the commonly used effects such as delay, chorus, phasing, and flanging etc., can be produced with dedicated foot pedals.

Foot pedals are very uncomplicated to operate, all that is needed is an extra guitar lead. Inserting the pedal between the guitar and amplifier, just plug the guitar into the pedal's "In" socket using one lead, the second lead being connected between the pedal's "Out" socket and amplifier.

POWERING EFFECTS

Footpedals are usually powered by a standard 9-volt battery, and although most modern units also include the option of using a mains converter unit, it's always a good idea to use transformers designed by the effect's manufacturers specifically for the job – "unregulated" units might not work, can create obtrusive hum, and can even do damage to the foot pedal.

REVERBERATION

Reverberation is a natural effect that occurs when a sound bounces off a surrounding surface like a wall or ceiling, before fading away. As you can hear if you shout in a large, empty room, the effect is heard as part of the original sound. "Reverb", as it is referred to, produces a warm, ambient effect of the sound spreading out when added to a guitar signal.

The original simulated reverb effects were produced by the use of a small spring that was vibrated by the guitar signal, making the "clunking" sound that you may have noticed on many a twangy-guitar vintage rock'n'roll instrumental.

A device still used in some modern studios, it produces natural reverb in acoustic chambers with microphones placed at different intervals from the sound source, a system first developed by studios in the 1960s.

A number of manufacturers attempted analog recreations of the sound during the 1970s, but these were unsuccessful in the main, and spring reverb was the standard until replaced by sophisticated electronic digital units in the 1980s. These days, even the most run-of-the-mill reverb unit gives you the luxury of programming parameters, based on characteristics of natural reverberation such as the size, shape, and sound-damping features of an imaginary room.

For the guitarist, top-quality reverb is the most essential effect, whether at home or in the most professional studio environment. Reverb is the magic quality that breathes life into "dead" sounds.

The quality of the effect found in the form of pedals on the other hand (or to a lesser extent, in multiple-effect units), tends to be significantly less, being designed more for playing live.

DELAY

Among the most popular electronic effects used by guitarists are those produced by repeating a delayed signal. As with reverb, delay is an effect of nature which is produced by a sound reflected from a distant surface.

When they were originally produced by mechanical means, delay effects used a cut-down version of a reel-to-reel tape recorder, with a loop of quarter-inch (5 mm) tape passed across a series of heads; the signal was produced by a record head, to be then replayed by a series of playback heads. First produced in 1954, the Watkins Copycat was the best known of the early models. These machines had the same problems as any lo-fi tape recorder – poor signal-to-noise ratio and limited frequency response – but neverthless they were popular right through to the 1980s. There are hi-tech versions still made today, some guitarists being adamant that you cannot duplicate the effect of a signal saturating the magnetic tape.

Delay, however, is now produced almost exclusively digitally, with different effects created depending on the length of the delay. They can be seen in the diagram below measured in milliseconds, 500 milliseconds being equal to half a second.

PHASING (7–12 MS) AND FLANGING (12–20 MS)

The effect of phasing happens when the same signal is played back simultaneously from two different sources. Every sound is composed of a soundwave which passes from peaks to troughs, and when two identical signals are out of alignment and the peaks on one signal coincide with the troughs on another, the effect is known as "phase cancellation", producing a "sweeping" sound. When the delay is greater, the sweep becoming more extreme and "metallic", the result is known as flanging.

CHORUS AND ADT (20–35 MS)

The original way that delay effects were created was by recording a signal on two tape machines and playing them back simultaneously. The overall sound was achieved by virtue of the inconsistencies in speed and pitch between the machines. These effects are emulated electronically by adding pitch modulation and speed controls to interfere with the delayed signal. ADT – "automatic double tracking" – and "chorus" are two of these effects. We can create the effect of doubling up the performance by adding variations in pitch to a delayed signal, this usually being used to "beef up" vocals or a thin guitar sound – it's a useful alternative to recording the same part twice on separate multitrack channels. It is especially effective when the original signal and the effect are panned to extremes in the stereo spectrum, used over a rhythm guitar part.

Chorus, modulating a number of repeats, extends this approach. The delay is so fast that it produces a full-bodied, rich, sustained sound which is particularly effective on chord work.

ECHO (OVER 35 MS)

Echo occurs when a delay is long enough for the repeated signal to be heard as a distinct sound in its own right. When a single fast repeat is played back at the same volume as the original signal it is known as "slap-back" echo – this was the sound used widely by early "rockabilly" rock'n'rollers, both on guitar and vocals. In more recent times, guitarists including Queen's Brian May and the folk-rock musician John Martyn have used delays of several seconds to build up, and play over, thick layers of sound. The approach was to reach a natural conclusion in the work of Robert Fripp, who used two tape recorders linked together by one spool of tape to create soundscapes constructed from delays of 10 seconds or even more.

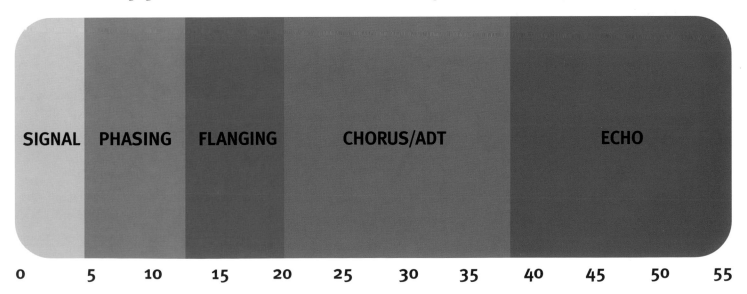

| SIGNAL | PHASING | FLANGING | CHORUS/ADT | ECHO |

0   5   10   15   20   25   30   35   40   45   50   55

PITCH-SHIFTING

A digital pitch-shifter, as the name suggests, alters the pitch of an incoming signal. Technically speaking, this is a delay effect, even though to be effective the delay needs to be as transparent as possible. The principle is cunningly simple (even if the technology behind it is staggeringly clever) – the original signal is delayed by the shortest possible time it takes to convert a sound into a digital sample and then that sample is replayed at a different speed. As far as guitarists are concerned, the most common use for a pitch-shifter is to generate automatic harmony lines which can be mixed with the original signal. Most units have a range of one octave above and below the original signal, with semitone steps in between. There is also usually some facility for fine-tuning the harmony, making it possible to create micro-tonal effects. Some of the more costly units are capable of generating multiple harmonies of up to four or five parts.

A similar technology is also used in digital recording systems that enable entire recordings to be replayed in a different key.

When this technology first became widely available in the early 1980s, the processing was relatively crude, and often resulted in an unpleasant digital effect known as "glitching"; modern-day systems should be capable of seamlessly reproducing intervals of a perfect fifth above or below the source note.

FOOT PEDALS CAN BE USED TO DELAY OR EVEN ALTER THE PITCH OF A SIGNAL.

ALTERNATIVE DISTORTION CAN BE ACHIEVED USING AN OVERDRIVE PEDAL.

TONAL EFFECTS

Effect units can also be used to alter the tone of a sound either by altering the "EQ" or creating distortion effects. We've already seen how amplifiers can be used to create distortion – using an external effect offers an even wider range of sounds. Although amplifier overdrive had appeared on many blues tracks recorded in the 1950s, the first well-known solo played through a fuzz box was by Jeff Beck, who used a Sola Sound Tone Bender on The Yardbirds' "Heart Full Of Soul" in 1964. There are numerous different distortion effects available.

There are a number of effects that manipulate the "EQ" of the guitar signal. The most famous of these is the wah-wah pedal. This is a foot pedal which alters the tone as the foot moves the pedal. It can either be used as a tone control in its own right, or rocked back and forth while playing.

stored and recalled at the click of a footswitch. It may even be possible, on some of the more sophisticated units, to alter parameters via MIDI or a USB link to a computer system.

AMPLIFIER SIMULATION

The most important development in guitar technology over the past decade has been the emergence of the digital amplifier simulator. As the name suggests, this technology "models" the tonal characteristics of classic amplifier and speaker combinations, and makes it possible for a guitarist to "Direct Inject" the output from the unit into a mixing desk without necessarily having to use an amplifier at all. If you understand that different amplifiers and speakers have characteristics of their own then a box of tricks that can, say, transform your sound at the touch of a button from a 1960s Vox AC30 to a modern-day Mesa/Boogie has clear appeal; if you add effects to the equation its usefulness is multiplied.

Like other methods of simulation used in music technology – such as playing back digital samples of a concert grand piano – the sounds need to be used with care if they are to sound convincing. Frankly, an amp simulator will never be able to sound exactly like a Fender Twin Reverb when played in isolation, but in the context of a recording it may well sound pretty well indistinguishable from the real thing.

Amp simulators are especially good for guitarists working in project home studios, allowing not only limitless choice, but a way of getting big sounds without having to work at painfully high volumes. Since units are also invariably stereo, sounds can be created that would only otherwise be possible if recorded conventionally in a studio with a multiple microphone set-up. Digital outputs on the more expensive units also ensure the highest quality sound.

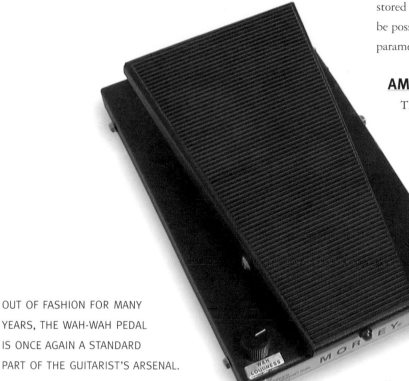

OUT OF FASHION FOR MANY YEARS, THE WAH-WAH PEDAL IS ONCE AGAIN A STANDARD PART OF THE GUITARIST'S ARSENAL.

MULTIPLE-EFFECT UNITS

One of the great things about foot pedal effects is that they are relatively cheap and easy to use. They can also be daisy-chained to provide combinations of different effects. However, a major drawback is that complex combinations – all of which, remember, may require specific parameters to be set on each pedal – may well be too complex to operate. This is especially true in a live context, or if you want to refer to a combination of effects at a future date. The modern solution to this problem started to appear in the early 1990s with the first multiple-effect units. These are high-quality digital units capable of producing all the traditional foot-pedal effects simultaneously. Furthermore, they're invariably programmable, meaning that dozens of complex settings can be

THE LINE6 POD REPRESENTS THE CUTTING EDGE OF AMPLIFIER MODELLING TECHNOLOGY.

THE RECORDING OF THE GUITAR

One issue that you can be sure will always be the subject of much debate among recording engineers is the question of recording with microphones. As you might expect, most engineers have their own favorite microphones and their own ideas as to how to best position them. Such widespread disagreement on the matter merely goes to prove that – just like with playing the guitar – at the end of the day there are no hard-and-fast rules. The examples discussed below can all be considered good, sensible methods, but the only way you will ever achieve the sound that you personally want is by experimenting.

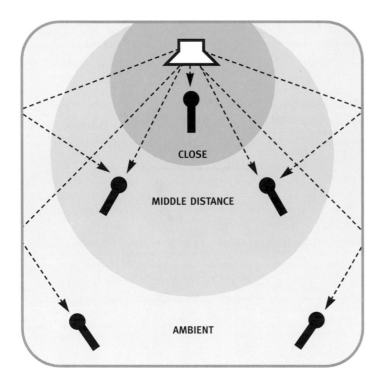

CLOSE-MIKING

Different effects can be produced, determined by how far away the microphone is from the sound source. The techniques most used in in the studio situation are known as "close-miking". Setting up a microphone between 2 and 18 inches (5 and 46 cm) away from the instrument or voice gives us the most detailed sound, because the signal captured is, in the main, the sound coming from that source rather than the ambiance of the room, with soundwaves reflecting off walls and ceilings etc. This is why close-miked recordings can often sound unnatural, in that they contain little or no ambient reverberation. To compensate for this, artificial studio digital reverb is usually added to make it sound more "real".

Simply repositioning the microphone by a few inches can make the way an instrument is recorded sound vastly different, as you will find out for yourself as you experiment, and your hearing becomes more sensitive to the subtle nuances of a sound. If we

move a microphone closer or further away from a source it can have unpredictable results, although you should bear in mind a couple of rules when placing microphones. The first is that when we move a microphone away from the source it not only reduces the volume but also the bass response; the second is that, in the same situation, the volume does not drop in a consistent way. Subject to the sensitivity of the microphone, the relative signal may decrease drastically between the space of 12 to 24 inches (30 to 61 cm).

DISTANCE MIKING

This occurs when microphones are placed a distance of 3 feet (1 meter) or more from the sound source. There is a natural balance between the sound of the instrument and the ambience of the surrounding room in recordings made at between 3 and 10 feet (1 and 3 meters) away from the sound source, this effect being magnified by the use of omni-directional microphones.

AMBIENT MIKING

Placing microphones at a distance of further than 10 feet (3 meters) from the source will produce a signal that is largely made up of ambient room reflections.

We can often achieve the most effective guitar sounds by recording with the microphones positioned in a combination of all three of these modes, as shown in the diagram.

MIKING AN ACOUSTIC GUITAR

Beacuse the character of the instrument is extremely subtle, the sound of the acoustic guitar is always difficult to capture with a microphone. Traditionally, the position for miking an acoustic guitar is around the loudest point on the guitar, the soundhole. If we move the microphone along the strings to the bridge it will modify the tonal balance, increasing the bass, whereas moving it toward the top of the fingerboard will boost the treble. The actual type of music being played will determine to some degree the final positioning of the microphone.

A frequent problem that arises in recording acoustic guitar concerns variations in volume. A lot of players, beginners in particular, have little understanding of dynamics, and studio work requires a more subtle and accurate touch than does most live performance. Although most reasonable engineers would expect a musician to change his or her playing to make a recording easier, a working awareness of which techniques might be most appropriate can make things a lot easier for everyone concerned.

RECORDING ELECTRIC GUITARS

It should be possible to plug an electric guitar directly into the mixing console, given that a guitar fitted with a pickup has an electrical signal just like any other piece of equipment. Suggesting this approach – referred to as "DI-ing" or direct injection – will almost always antagonize any guitarist in the studio, most of whom quite rightly consider their amplifier as being an integral part of their overall sound. It is more usual, therefore, to mike-up the amplifier's loudspeaker. However, there are alternatives and compromises, as will be demonstrated.

The easiest set-up is to position a single directional microphone at a distance of between 2 and 6 inches (5 and 15 cm) and at the same height as the center of the loudspeaker. If the dynamic of the signal varies, try introducing compression into the recording chain: a ratio of around 2:1 will help level out a clean sound, and for a heavily distorted sound, you can go as far as 8:1.

Another approach is to add a second microphone placed above the first and pointing downwards at a 45° angle, with the slightly different sounds then mixed together on the desk before being recorded on a single track. If there are enough spare channels on the recorder, it's possible to record them on separate tracks then balance them during the mixdown.

Many guitarists and producers have experimented with more unusual ways of recording a guitar sound in the studio. Sometimes microphone signals from close, natural, and ambient positions are mixed together, or the sound from the loudspeaker is channelled through acoustic tunnels created by baffle screens.

A particularly extreme approach was adopted by the producer Mutt Lange when he was working with the heavy rock band Def Leppard. Apparently he recorded the notes of some of the heavy power chords one string at a time, resulting in rumours circulating that it was taking weeks of studio time just to record a single guitar part! Presumably everyone involved felt it was worthwhile when the resulting album, *Hysteria*, became one of the biggest sellers of the 1980s.

SPEAKER SIMULATORS

While few serious guitarists would be happy about having their signal plugged directly into the mixing desk, technology has made possible an increasingly popular, and acceptable, alternative – the speaker simulator. Connected between the speaker output of the amplifier and mixing desk, this is a processing effect, some models even having additional onboard processing in order to create the effect of a variety of speaker configurations.

Using the speaker simulator has some distinct advantages – not least of which is the reduction of excess noise – especially in home-recording situations. Powerful valve amplifiers need to be used at high volume to achieve their essential overdrive, and in an enclosed environment this may result in unwanted feedback as well as deafening volume. You not only bypass these problems when you record via a speaker simulator, you can also monitor accurately the sound that is being recorded.

PLAYING LIVE

Over the last 30 years or so, recorded music, especially in the form of the album, has for many represented the yardstick of a musician's capabilities. But for thousands of others, playing live is a far more potent – and often the only possible – way of communicating with audiences. Yet merely appearing on stage for the first time can be a daunting prospect for the beginner that throws up a host of new issues. Being a good performer does not necessarily mean the same thing as being a good musician, or being a good studio player. As well as adjusting to different technology in often alien surroundings, the stage novice has to face the same issues that are common to all performers, such as confidence, image projection and, inevitabley, stage nerves.

EQUIPMENT

The main factors that will determine the type of equipment you will need when playing in public are the kind of music you play and the size of the venue. The main requirement, except perhaps for when you are playing the very smallest clubs or bars, is a public address (PA) system. A basic PA might just comprise a single microphone for vocals connected to an amplifier and speaker, whereas at the other end of the scale a big-name act is quite likely to use a system that appears to be as complex as a fully-equipped recording studio.

SETTING-UP IN SMALL VENUES

Quite often when playing in very small venues, each of the musicians will provide his own amplification, which he controls themselves from the stage though the drums and brass don't even need to be miked-up at all, they are loud enough already. If your act has a separate vocalist, an additional amplifier and microphone will probably be required, although it can be possible to manage by simply plugging a microphone into a spare channel on the

guitar amplifier, not that this is very satsfactory. In any case, without a mixing desk and external engineer controlling the sound, the balance between the instruments is bound to be a bit haphazard. The other problem with this kind of arrangement is that you won't be able to hear yourself playing very well, but don't try to keep turning up the volume to compensate – that will only result in the others in the band doing the same, and the audience getting deafened at the same time!

It's worth trying to organize more effective sound control, even though there might be some attraction in the basic simplicity of working like this. For a start, try to find someone who would be interested in acting as your sound engineer – lots of new young bands seem to have extra "hangers on" who want to be involved in one way or another at rehearsals and gigs.

A simple PA system of reasonable quality can be put together for very little money. All you need is a six-channel mixing desk, a moderately powerful stereo amplifier (500 watts per channel should be ideal for small venues), bass speakers, horns and crossovers, and a few microphones – try and get as many of these items as you can secondhand. Your own PA system will not only make you self-sufficient when playing gigs, it can also be a boon when rehearsing – hearing yourself sounding good for the first time can be a big inspiration.

Playing live, leave as much as possible of the non-playing side to your sound engineer, keeping the band free to concentrate on performing. Think about using DI boxes or speaker simulators, so that the overall volumes of the bass, guitars, keyboards and vocals are balanced by the engineer. Although he or she might be an unknown quantity to the audience, a good sound engineer familiar with your material is a valuable member of the band.

MONITORING IN LARGER VENUES

In most commercial venues, the PA system is likely to be either a permanent fixture in-house or hired in for the occasion. These kind of systems will use a lot of technology, such as multiple speaker and amplification systems and rack-mounted digital effects that you find in a recording studio. As well as the drums being miked up, all of the instruments will have their own dedicated inputs or microphones. An engineer working at a large mixing desk, usually located behind the audience at the back of the hall, controls the individual sound levels of each instrument.

THE BACKLINE SYSTEM

Many guitar-based bands, even at the highest level, still like to work with "backline" amplification, keeping control of their own amplifier settings and having the signal relayed to the front-of-house PA via a microphone. There are some effects that are impossible to achieve without this backline system, even though more advanced DI solutions can keep amplifier characteristics, allowing a greater degree of external control. The acoustic phenomenon of feedback is probably the most familiar effect.

During the late 1950s and early 1960s, some electric blues players began to integrate this into their sound when they realized that it could be an interesting effect in its own right. It takes a lot of skill in understanding the volumes and EQ to set up specific configurations of guitar and amplifier to use controlled feedback properly, not to mention a good instinctive feel when combining it within a general playing technique. You will find that your position on stage in relation to the amplifier will actually determine the effectiveness of the sustain.

This will vary from one stage to another, depending on the acoustics of the surrounding environment. Guitarists who use controlled feedback in a big way often move about the stage

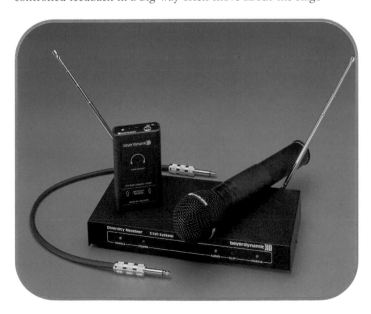

during a soundcheck to locate the best feedback and then mark these positions with tape or chalk.

TRANSMITTER SYSTEMS

Even among semi-professional guitarists, radio or "wireless" transmitters are becoming an increasingly popular device on stage. A transmitter attached to the guitarist's belt or guitar strap is plugged into the guitar instead of plugging directly into an amplifier. A VHF receiver positioned alongside, and plugged into the amplifier or mixing desk, picks up the signal from the guitar, allowing the player more freedom to move about the stage without the risk of tripping over guitar leads.

When the transmitters were first introduced, they were plagued by radio interference – as satirized in the movie *Spinal Tap* – but frequency-switching has now been developed to make this virtually a thing of the past.

ACOUSTIC GUITARS

Problems surrounding the mixing of electronic and acoustic instruments together on stage have been an issue in the life of sound engineers since the first development of electrical instruments and amplification.

Controlling the volume and sound is the main difficulty when working with acoustic guitars on stage. The player has to stay in absolutely the same position if a consistent signal is to be heard when an acoustic guitar is miked-up using regular studio techniques, and any move away from the microphone alters both the volume and tonal balance. This doesn't really present a problem in, for instance, classical, folk or flamenco music, but is a more tricky issue in the context of a rock or pop performance. Dealing with high-pitched feedback caused by the microphone picking up its own sounds from the PA, or preventing external sounds drifting into the microphone and causing a muddy sound, are a constant source of concern.

This problem is not easily solved, although compressors and noise gates can help when used carefully. Some guitarists side-step the problem by playing electro-acoustic instruments; these are normal acoustic guitars with built-in pickups that can be played acoustically, or plugged into an amplifier. Although they sound weaker when heard in isolation, for most uses in a group they allow the musician to achieve a reasonable acoustic sound. Fitting a magnetic pickup or transducer microphone to the sound hole of a regular acoustic guitar is another alternative, with similar vices and virtues.

LOOKING AFTER YOUR GUITAR

One of the reasons why it is always recommended that you buy the best guitar you can afford is because, unlike most modern musical instruments, a high-quality guitar of any kind is unlikely to depreciate much in value. But even if you're not looking for a precious investment, a few sensible measures such as cleaning the components, changing strings, checking the way it has been set up, and storing and transporting with care, will help you to get as much enjoyment and a reliability as possible from your instrument.

STRINGS

Although referred to as "catgut", the strings on the earliest guitars were usually made from sheep intestines. Steel and nylon strings were not introduced until the 19th century, steel strings being used on electric, flat-top, and arch-top acoustic guitars, and nylon mainly for classical and flamenco instruments.

TYPES OF STEEL-STRING

The differences among steel strings are a question of what we call "string wrap." The top two strings – and often the 3rd in the case of ultra-light-gauge strings – are normally a single thread of wire, while the other strings are made of a wire inner core with a second piece of wire wound tightly around the outside. The sound and playing quality of the strings is directly influenced by the nature of this wrapping. There are three common types of winding, with each type having its own characteristics, roundwound, flatwound and groundwound.

WEAR'N'TEAR

Strings, like most things, wear out or break. This can result from applying too much tension, for instance if you bend them a great deal, use altered tunings, or tune above concert pitch. They also lose their stretch over a period, often being caused by build-ups of salt from sweating fingers, which makes the strings rust.

Cleaning strings after each use will make them last longer. Another way some players get rid of build-ups of dirt and grime from the underside and windings of the strings is by "snapping", which involves pulling the strings away from the fingerboard and letting them snap back into position. Also removing the strings and boiling them in water for around ten minutes is a favourite method of musicians who want to save some money, getting rid of grease and grime while improving the tone.

Roundwound strings, which are wound using conventionally shaped round wire – thus giving the characteristic ridge-like feel – are the strings that are most commonly used on electric and acoustic instruments.

Flatwound strings are most often found on arch-top guitars, and involve a core enveloped by a flat ribbon of metal. This gives a feel as smooth as that of the treble strings, when tightly wound, also allowing the fingers to move along the strings without creating an acoustic "squeak". The downside of this type of string is that the sound they produce is a litte bit duller in tone than that achieved with roundwound strings, and they are also the least long-lasting of the three types, having as they do a natural tendency to crack.

Groundwound strings utilize conventional round windings which are then ground down so that the surface is partially flat, attempting to provide the tonal advantages of roundwound with the playing advantages of flatwound.

GAUGES

As well as coming in a variety of materials, strings also come in different sizes, this too having a major impact on the way in which you play and the sound you produce.

String widths, known as "gauges", are usually expressed as decimal fractions of an inch. How you view the pros and cons of the various types is largely a matter of personal taste. On the one hand the lighter strings are easier to hold down and bend, and are gentler on the fingers, but on the other they are characterized by a lower volume and shorter sustain, and the extent to which they can stretch makes keeping them in tune more difficult. And some players are also of the opinion that heavier-gauge strings simply give a better sound.

While you normally buy strings as complete sets, grouped into various gauges from heavy (the largest) down to ultra-light (the smallest), they are usually available individually, and a lot of guitarists experiment with using strings from different sets, and sometimes even using different windings.

CLEANING

A wide variety of agents are available for cleaning the different parts of the guitar. Any regular household sprays or creams can be used, with care, for most modern guitars which are finished in cellulose or other types of synthetic varnishes. Any cleaning agents that contain silicone or wax, however, are to be avoided, as using them can often result in discolouration to the finish, giving the instrument an unpleasant, tacky feel. And never, ever, even think of using abrasive cleaning fluids, as these will seriously damage the finish.

When dealing with high-quality classical guitars, many of which have a French-polished finish as opposed to a synthetic varnish, extra care needs to be taken. You should never treat these instruments with regular polishes, instead surfaces should simply be wiped down regularly with a lightly dampened cloth, followed by buffing with a dry cloth.

CLEANING STRINGS

Your strings will last a lot longer, and the guitar will feel a great deal more pleasant to play, if you keep your strings clean. Take a dry, lint-free cloth, pull it between the strings and fingerboard, and then drag it the full length of the strings between the bridge and the nut – this is simply the most effective cleaning method. Also, some guitarists prefer to use special string-cleaning fluids, but remember that these are not suitable for cleaning nylon strings.

CLEANING THE FINGERBOARD

You can clean fretboards that have a synthetic varnish in the same way as the body. A great many guitars have oiled ebony or rosewood fingerboards, and these need to be cleaned thoroughly each time you change the strings. A handy method for this is to apply some lemon oil to the wood, leaving it for about five minutes before cleaning it off with a dry cloth.

CLEANING FRETS

Dirt from the fingers often builds along the edge of the frets. This should be removed with a gently pointed object, such as a nail file or toothpick. The grime should come away quite easily, so don't scratch too hard, otherwise you will damage the fingerboard.

STORING THE GUITAR

You should give some thought to the way in which you keep your guitar stored if you are not going to use it for any length of time. As well as protecting the instrument from accidental damage, the prime consideration is to try and avoid the guitar being exposed to wide fluctuations in temperature and humidity. Acoustic instruments are particularly at risk, where an abrupt change of climate can alter the action, distort the wood, impair glued joints, and cause cracks to appear in the finish. If only for this reason, you should avoid storing a guitar in a loft or basement, or near radiators or hot water pipes.

It's obviously common sense to store your guitar in a sturdy case, and before storing the instrument, always give it a thorough cleaning to prevent tarnishing or rusting of the metal parts. Also, always detune the strings to avoid any tension stress being placed on the joints between the neck and the body of the guitar.

TRAVELLING

When your guitar is being transported in a car, van, or by rail, it can be open to all kinds of risk. The instrument should always be kept in its case, and laid down lengthways, either on its back or on its side.

Any musician who travels around a lot with his guitar should seriously consider taking out insurance cover. This can be expensive – traditionally insurance companies get the horrors when they see the word "musician" on an application – but it can help to protect your valuable investment.

FLIGHT CASES

In order to give your guitar the most basic protection, it should be carried in a flight case. Available in a wide variety of shapes and sizes, the simplest cases, made from padded plastic or fabric, zip around the outside of the guitar. They are very cheap and offer just a minimum of protection – in fact, wrapping your guitar up in an old thick blanket can be just as effective.

Sturdier cases have a hard shell, usually made from plywood or strong plastic, with the inside being padded to hold the instrument in place, and lined with fake fur to protect the body finish. Cases like this are usually sufficent for normal, routine use.

CHANGING YOUR STRINGS

Because of the various string-fixing mechanisms found on different guitars – at the bridge and at the headstock – there are a number of slightly different string-changing techniques. In all cases new strings need to be "stretched" when fitted, regardless of which type of instrument you use. This is done by pulling the string a few inches away from the fretboard and then releasing it. If it has dropped in pitch, retune it and repeat, and carry on doing this until the string stays more or less in tune. This has to be done for all the strings. You should be in a position to restring any type of instrument using the techniques described below and opposite.

ELECTRIC GUITARS

On every steel string you will find what is referred to as a "ball end", a tiny disk of metal around which one end of the string is wrapped and secured. The opposite end of the string is threaded through a hole located behind the bridge, pulled through and held in position by the "ball". Except for locking-nut systems (see right), on the majority of electric guitars the strings are held in place by an independent tailpiece (which you will find on most Gibson models), or are passed through the body of the instrument from the back into an all-in-one-bridge unit (as with most Fender guitars – see below).

The same type of system for securing strings at the machine head is to be found on most electric and steel-string guitars. The strings can be passed through a hole in the side of the capstan to which they are attached, which usually stands out vertically from the headstock. The end is then moved around and under, being trapped in place when we tighten the machine head, and the loose string can then be cut back, leaving less than an inch (2.5 cm) spare. Some capstans also have vertical holes, in which case the string is cut to length, the end being inserted into the tip of the

capstan. We then bend the string to one side and wind it around. This way the string endings are left neat and tidy.

LOCKING-NUT SYSTEMS

Changing strings can be a lot more time consuming on locking-nut systems, such as Floyd Rose tremolo units. With the aid of an Allen key, the strings are simply clamped in place at the bridge saddle. To do this the ball ends have to be removed, this being best done with a pair of pliers. On tremolo systems, where the tension of all of the strings will alter when one string is removed, it's advisable to fix in place something like a block of wood or pack of cards beneath the bridge mechanism, thus preventing it from rocking back and forth.

At the other end, the strings are wound onto the machine heads in just the same way as on any other electric guitar. Once all the strings are in place, the block supporting the bridge has to be removed. Make sure you don't overtighten the string before this stage, otherwise the string will be in danger of snapping when you move the block. You can then tune the strings with the machine heads in the usual way. They are then locked in place at the nut with an Allen key, fine tuning being done by using the individual adjusters located on each bridge saddle.

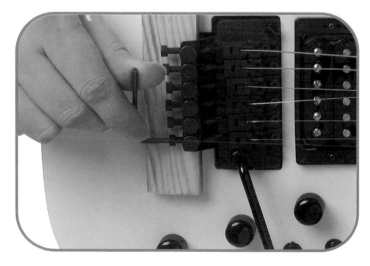

WHEN TO CHANGE

How often strings should be changed is basically a matter of personal taste. Some top professionals restring their guitar every time they perform or record, while others will leave strings in place literally for years, or at least until they break. When any new set of strings is fitted, they do have to be "worn in" – this will be achieved satisfactorily after just a few hours of playing.

STEEL-STRING ACOUSTIC GUITARS

Most steel-string guitars feature vertical bridge pins that go into the bridge itself, the ball end of the string being passed through the hole behind the saddle. The strings are trapped in place when the pin is then inserted firmly into the hole.

CLASSICAL GUITARS (BRIDGE)

Nylon strings are fitted using a tied loop, as they do not have ball ends. The end of the string is passed through the bridge hole, passed back over the bridge, knotted behind the saddle, and the slack is then passed under the string on the bridge. The other end of the string is pulled to tighten the loop behind the bridge, thus holding the string in place.

CLASSICAL GUITARS (HEADSTOCK)

Pass the string over the nut and insert it through the hole in the capstan, then bring the end of the string over the capstan and pass it underneath itself. The end of the string will be trapped in place when you begin to tighten the machine head.

TIME AND ENERGY SAVERS

Having to turn machine heads until a string becomes tight can be both time-consuming and tiresome. To make life easier, you can do the operation much more quickly with the aid of a plastic or wooden string winder which fits over the machine head. An even more advanced alternative is to take the end of the string winder – that is the piece that comes into contact with the machine head – and saw it away, attaching it to the bit of an electric screwdriver. This way you will be able to wind on your strings at the flick of a switch!

SET UP

Various alterations that can be made to any guitar, either to suit the playing style and preferences of the individual musician or following mechanical problems with the instrument, are illustrated on the following two pages. While some of these adjustments can be made by the player, more complicated work would need to be put in the hands of a specialist. Experts in guitar technology and custom guitar makers might even study the playing style of a client before deciding how his or her guitar should be set up.

THE ACTION

The "action" of the guitar, which describes the height of the strings above the frets, is a basic adjustment that every guitar player can tackle. What is known as a high action – when the strings are high above the frets and need more pressure from the left hand – is not usually recommended. A low action is better suited for fast solo work, although an action set too low will create fret buzz. In order to keep the slide from scraping against the frets, a lot of bottleneck players set the action higher than they would do for normal playing.

You can easily measure the action by putting a finely graded steel rule on top of the 12th fret, measuring the gap between the fret and the bottom of the string. In setting the action, guitarists usually opt for the lowest possible action that doesn't create fret buzz – it's not a matter of absolute precision, and is largely a question of trial and error. But there are guidelines we can observe: average readings are likely to be between 0.08–0.12 inches (2–3 mm) for an acoustic guitar and 0.05–0.09 inches (1.5–2.5mm) for an electric instrument.

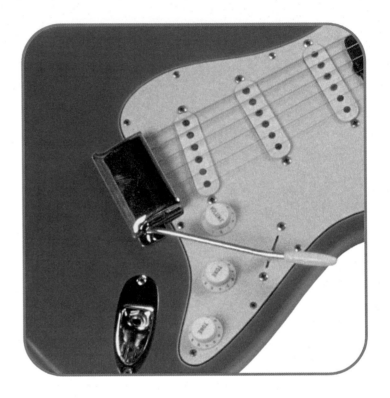

CHANGING THE ACTION

We adjust the height of the strings by altering the height of the bridge. On electric guitars, each string usually has its own saddle, which is heightened by turning a small screw in a clockwise direction.

On acoustic guitars, the bridge saddle is usually made from bone, often with screws at the side with which we can raise the whole platform at either side, which may be all you require. But to make adjustments to individual strings, the saddle would have to filed down, something you would certainly need to leave to a specialist guitar technician.

INTONATION

Any drastic adjustment of the action is, in effect, a change in the distance between the nut and the bridge, and however subtle it might be this modification can have a significant influence on the intonation of your instrument. The effect might be such that the guitar might not play in tune without your making further changes. The reason for this is that the distance between the nut and the 12th fret has to be *exactly* the same as the distance between the 12th fret and the precise position where the string touches the bridge saddle.

The intonation of your guitar can be tested by playing an open string and then a note on the 12th fret, which should be *precisely* one octave apart if your guitar isn't going to be out of tune further along the fretboard. Another way to check is to play an open string followed by the harmonic on the 12th fret, which should be exactly the same.

If you find that the note at the 12th fret is sharp, the string needs to be lengthened by moving the saddle back, as it is too short. On electric guitars we will usually find adjustable string saddles which can be controlled with a small screwdriver or Allen key, the saddle being moved closer to the nut by a clockwise turn of the screw.

LEAVE IT TO THE EXPERTS

Some guitar adjustments are definitely best left to the experts. If the ordinary guitar player attempts them it is usually asking for trouble, and there's the time and effort involved.

NECK CURVE

As a a result of the tension caused by the strings, all guitar necks have a very slight curve, which is usually centered on the 7th or 8th fret. When heavy strings are used the curve can become more extreme, and this in turn makes the strings more difficult to press down onto the frets because the action in the area of the mid-fingerboard is higher than at either end of the fingerboard.

There is an adjustable metal bar that passes through the length of the neck called a "truss rod" which controls the curve of the neck. Turning it clockwise tightens the truss rod and therefore reduces the curve, and this can be done using a small spanner or screwdriver. If the fingerboard begins to warp or twist, or the curving becomes too extreme, the entire neck might have to be removed and refitted, or even replaced.

FRETS

As can be imagined, frets can wear out, with grooves appearing where the strings have worn away the nickel. Fret buzz can result when these grooves become too pronounced. The fine tuning required to bring a new fret down to the correct height is best in the hands of an expert, even though removing and replacing a fret may be relatively simple. A set of replacement frets can give a well-used instrument a new lease of life.

DEALING WITH ELECTRICS

The electric guitar's circuitry is so simple it is very unlikely to ever actually break down, the more usual problems being associated with crackling noise coming from the tone and volume controls and pickup switches – which can usually be solved by spraying switch-cleaning fluid along the contact points – or a loose jack socket.

There sometimes comes a point, however, when you may have to replace the component, but anyone who can use a soldering iron should be able to replace any of the individual parts, as the electronic circuitry on electric guitars is relatively straightforward.

There are very few components to worry about – usually two pickups, a switch, a socket, four volume/ tone controls, and two capacitors – so even for the technical amateur, it's a simple job. A good idea is to mark the wires in some way in order to make sure they end up being soldered to the same points on their replacement parts.

You can usually gain access to the circuitry by removing a perspex panel on the back of the guitar. Alternatively, there is a front panel which can be unscrewed and lifted off the body, under which the entire circuitry is fitted, on certain models.

THE CHORD DICTIONARY

Probably the most useful asset that a guitarist can acquire is a comprehensive chord vocabulary, and a good understanding of the way in which chords are actually constructed. As well as giving composers and songwriters a more sophisticated palette of "colours" from which to draw, in understanding the way different voicings and inversions work it also provides arrangers with valuable skills.

The Chord Dictionary following is a useful reference guide for playing 33 chord types in all twelve keys.

There are two alternative positions for each voicing, and a total of 1,188 different chord voicings illustrated. Many of the chords should be familiar to you by now, but as you work your way through the dictionary you will probably come across some of those weird chords that you've heard on records a hundred times but not been able to figure out. In addition, it will hopefully introduce you to some rather more unusual and exotic sounds. But you must remember when playing through the dictionary that it is not always possible to achieve an acceptable voicing for every chord in every key. In some cases the inversions will be such that the sound produced will just seem rather odd, even though all the notes are in place.

ENHARMONIC KEYS

For reasons of simplicity, the enharmonic keys – that is those with two names – are referred to in the way most commonly used, so we talk about the key of B♭ rather than A♯. In the same way the keys of C♯, E♭, F♯, and A♭ are used instead of D♭, D♯, G♭, and G♯ respectively.

The notes on the chord diagrams, however, are named enharmonically correctly, so you will sometimes come across a less familiar identity for a certain note. The chord F7-9, for example, has a flattened ninth which (as it is in the key of F), reduces the ninth note from G to G♭. So G♭ is the correct label, even though the note is far more commonly referred to as F♯.

USING THE CHORD DICTIONARY

The chord diagram illustrates an overhead view of the fingerboard, with circles indicating the finger positions. The unmarked circles show that the note is optional. The name of the note being played is marked by each string. Any string coloured gray should not be played. The standard music notation and guitar tablature for the chord is also illustrated: two more inversions of each chord are shown in tablature form, showing how the same chords can be played in different positions on the fingerboard.

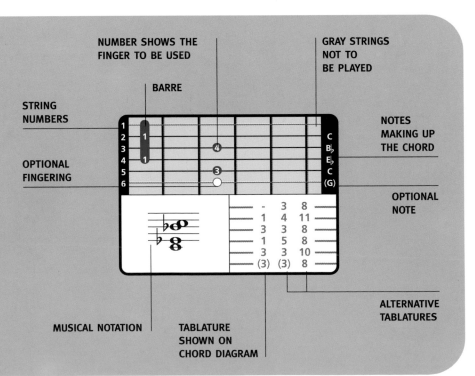

NUMBER SHOWS THE FINGER TO BE USED

GRAY STRINGS NOT TO BE PLAYED

BARRE

STRING NUMBERS

OPTIONAL FINGERING

NOTES MAKING UP THE CHORD

OPTIONAL NOTE

ALTERNATIVE TABLATURES

MUSICAL NOTATION

TABLATURE SHOWN ON CHORD DIAGRAM

SCALE DEGREES

The table on the right, which illustrates the components of each chord type, will help your understanding of the way the chords are built. The crosses on the matrix link the chord names to the scale degrees utilized in any key.

AUGMENTED AND DIMINISHED CHORDS

We need to draw attention to the unique features of two chord voicings. The notes of augmented (aug or +) and diminished (dim or °) chords are so related that we produce different inversions of the same chord by moving the same shape along the fingerboard.

The chord A diminished uses the notes A, C, E♭, and G♭. By moving the chord shape three frets along the finger-board, you will hear a C diminished chord, which is actually made up of the same notes—C, E♭, G♭, and A. The diminished chords in G♭ and E♭ also use these four notes. In the same way, the diminished chords in B♭, D, E, and G all use the same four notes, as do those in B, D, F, and A♭.

The augmented chord is a little different in so far as it only makes use of three notes. However, you also create the same augmented chord if you move the augmented shape four frets along the fingerboard.

Once again, we can use all the notes that make up this chord as the root for different inversions of the same chord.

CHORD TYPE	ABBREV.	I	ii	II	iii	III	IV	v	V	vi	VI	vii	VII	I	ii	II	iii	III	IV	v	V	vi	VI
Major	maj	•				•			•														
Minor	m	•			•				•														
Dominant Seventh	7	•				•			•			•											
Minor Seventh	m7	•			•				•			•											
Major Seventh	maj7 or Δ7	•				•			•				•										
Suspended Fourth	sus4	•					•		•														
Seventh Suspended Fourth	7sus4	•					•		•			•											
Sixth	6	•				•			•		•												
Minor Sixth	m6	•			•				•		•												
Diminished Seventh	dim7 or °	•			•			•			•												
Augmented	aug or +	•				•				•													
Seventh Diminished Fifth	7-5	•				•		•				•											
Seventh Augmented Fifth	7+5	•				•				•		•											
Half-Diminished Seventh	m7-5 or ø	•			•			•				•											
Minor/Major Seventh	m/maj7	•			•				•				•										
Major Seventh Augmented Fifth	maj7+5	•				•				•			•										
Major Seventh Diminished Fifth	maj7-5	•				•		•					•										
Ninth	9	•				•			•			•				•							
Minor Ninth	m9	•			•				•			•				•							
Major Ninth	maj9 or Δ9	•				•			•				•			•							
Seventh Augmented Ninth	7+9	•				•			•			•					•						
Seventh Diminished Ninth	7-9	•				•			•			•			•								
Seventh Augmented Ninth Diminished	7+9-5	•				•		•				•					•						
Sixth/Ninth	6/9	•				•			•		•					•							
Ninth Augmented Fifth	9+5	•				•				•		•				•							
Ninth Diminished Fifth	9-5	•				•		•				•				•							
Minor Ninth Diminished Fifth	m9-5	•			•			•				•				•							
Eleventh	11	•				•			•			•				•		•					
Minor Eleventh	m11	•			•				•			•				•		•					
Eleventh Diminished Ninth	11-9	•				•			•			•			•		•						
Thirteenth	13	•				•			•			•				•						•	
Minor Thirteenth	m13	•			•				•			•				•						•	
Major Thirteenth	maj13 or Δ13	•				•			•				•			•						•	

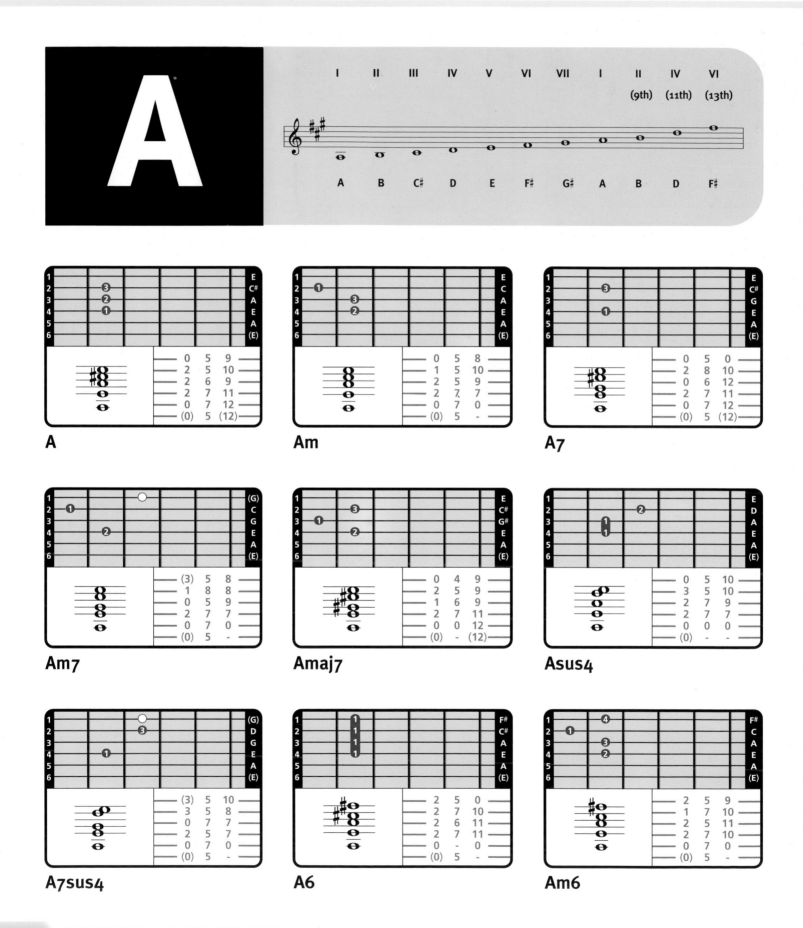

A

Am

A7

Am7

Amaj7

Asus4

A7sus4

A6

Am6

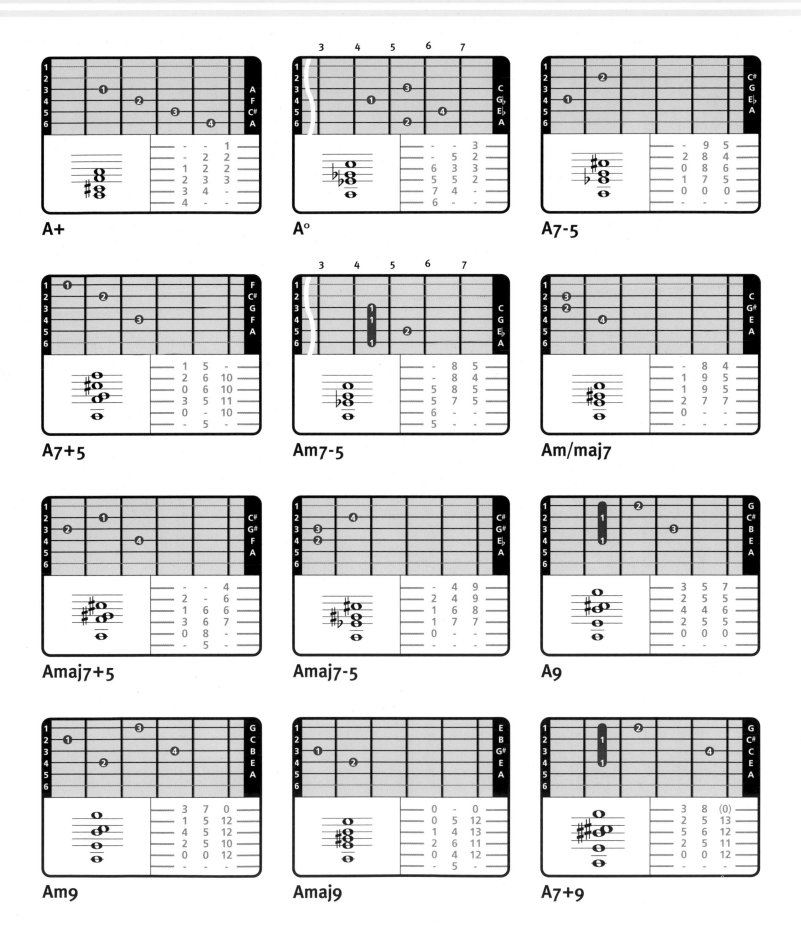

A+

A°

A7-5

A7+5

Am7-5

Am/maj7

Amaj7+5

Amaj7-5

A9

Am9

Amaj9

A7+9

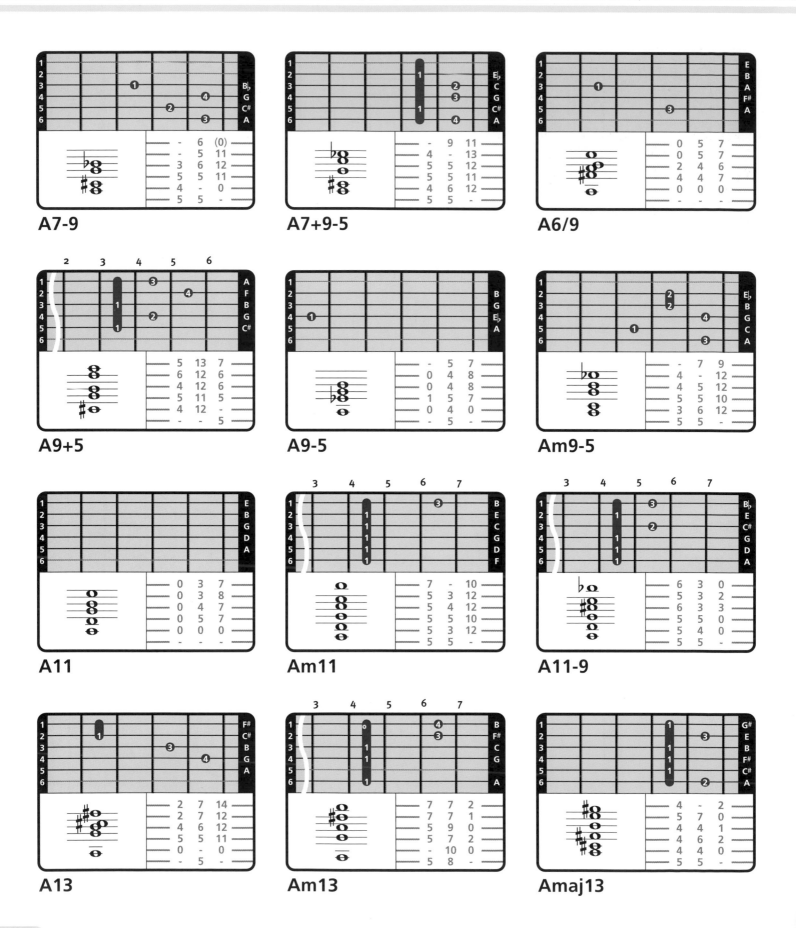

A7-9

A7+9-5

A6/9

A9+5

A9-5

Am9-5

A11

Am11

A11-9

A13

Am13

Amaj13

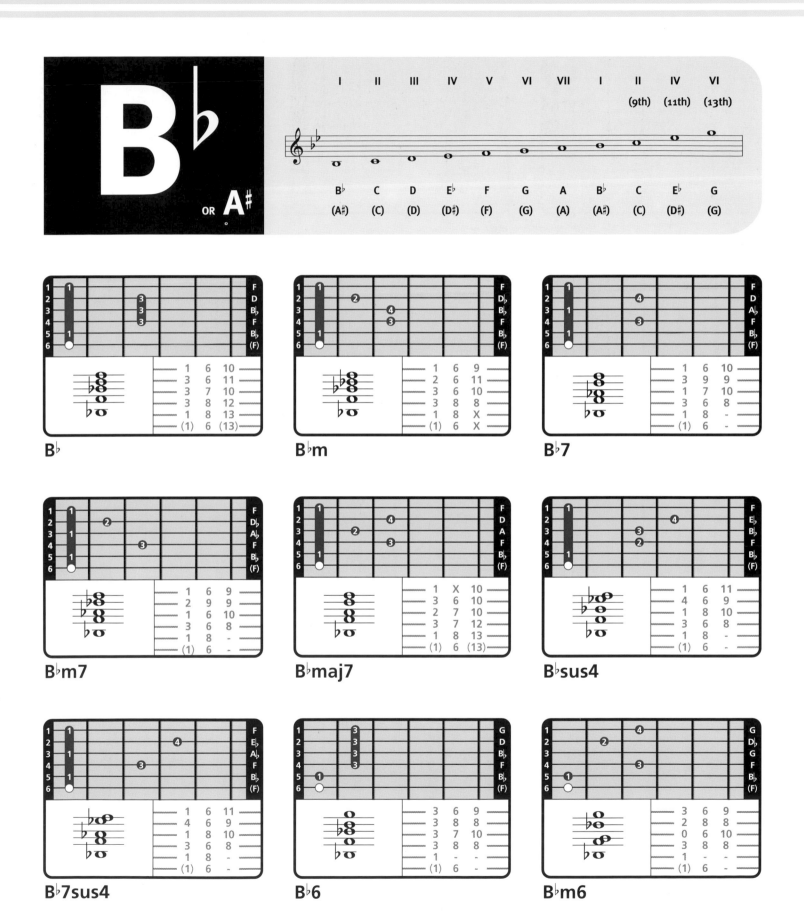

B♭

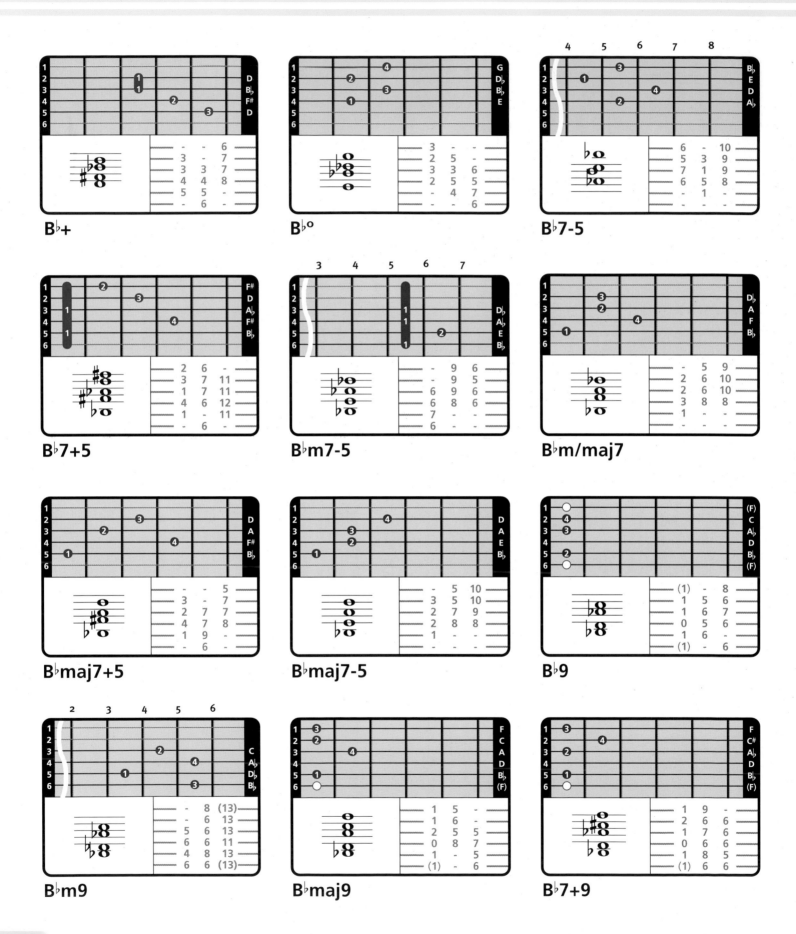

B♭+

B♭o

B♭7-5

B♭7+5

B♭m7-5

B♭m/maj7

B♭maj7+5

B♭maj7-5

B♭9

B♭m9

B♭maj9

B♭7+9

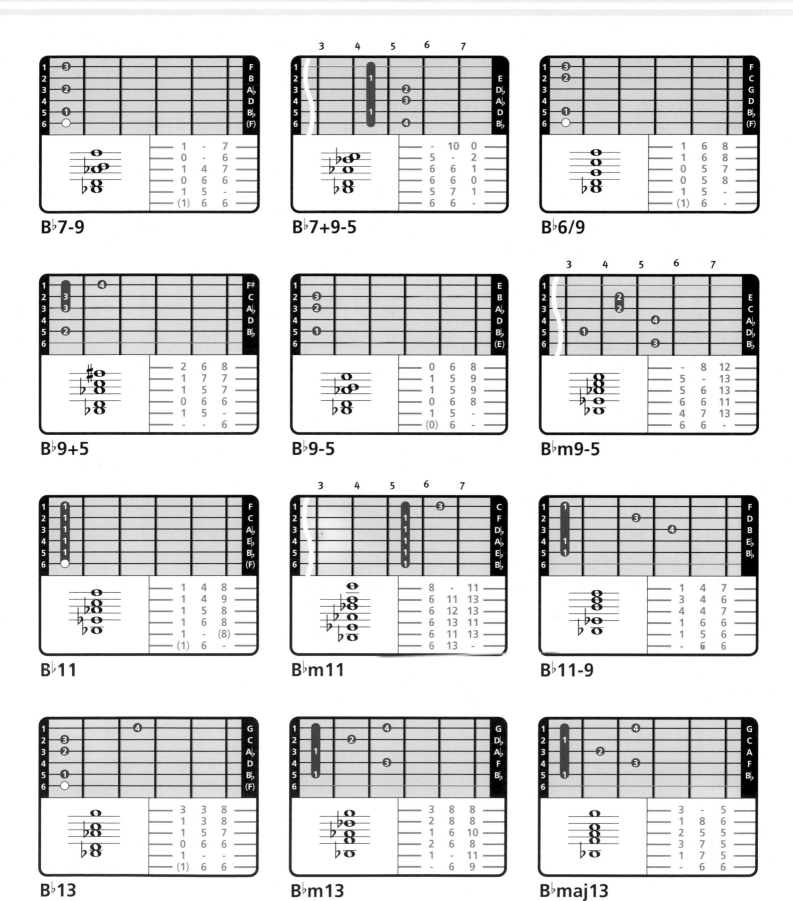

B♭7-9 B♭7+9-5 B♭6/9

B♭9+5 B♭9-5 B♭m9-5

B♭11 B♭m11 B♭11-9

B♭13 B♭m13 B♭maj13

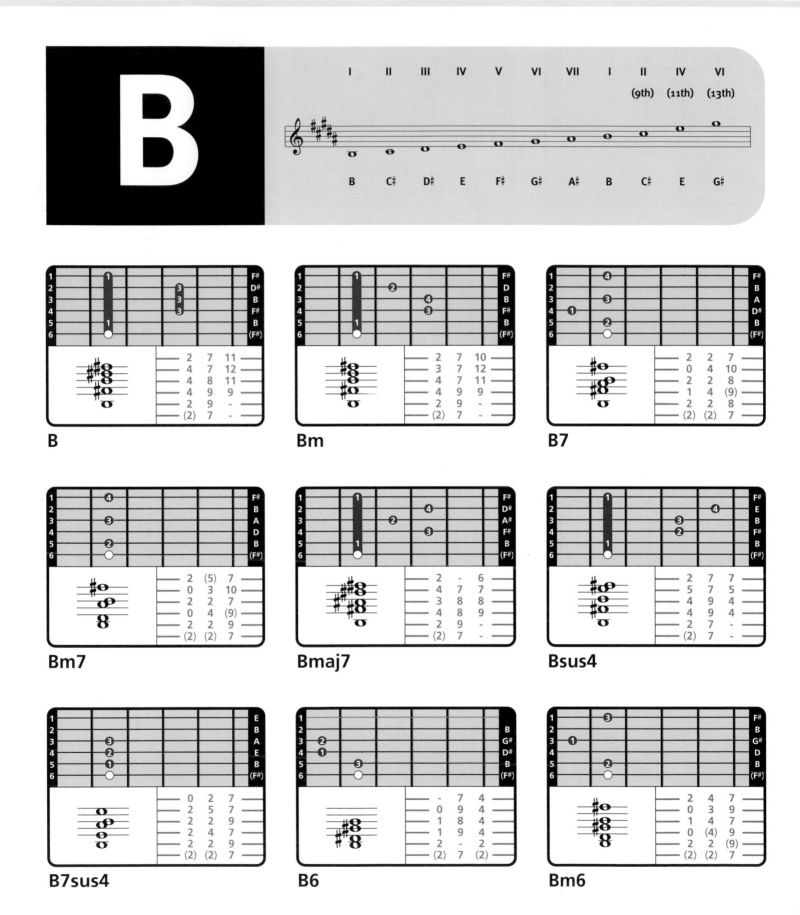

B

I	II	III	IV	V	VI	VII	I	II (9th)	IV (11th)	VI (13th)
B	C#	D#	E	F#	G#	A#	B	C#	E	G#

B

Bm

B7

Bm7

Bmaj7

Bsus4

B7sus4

B6

Bm6

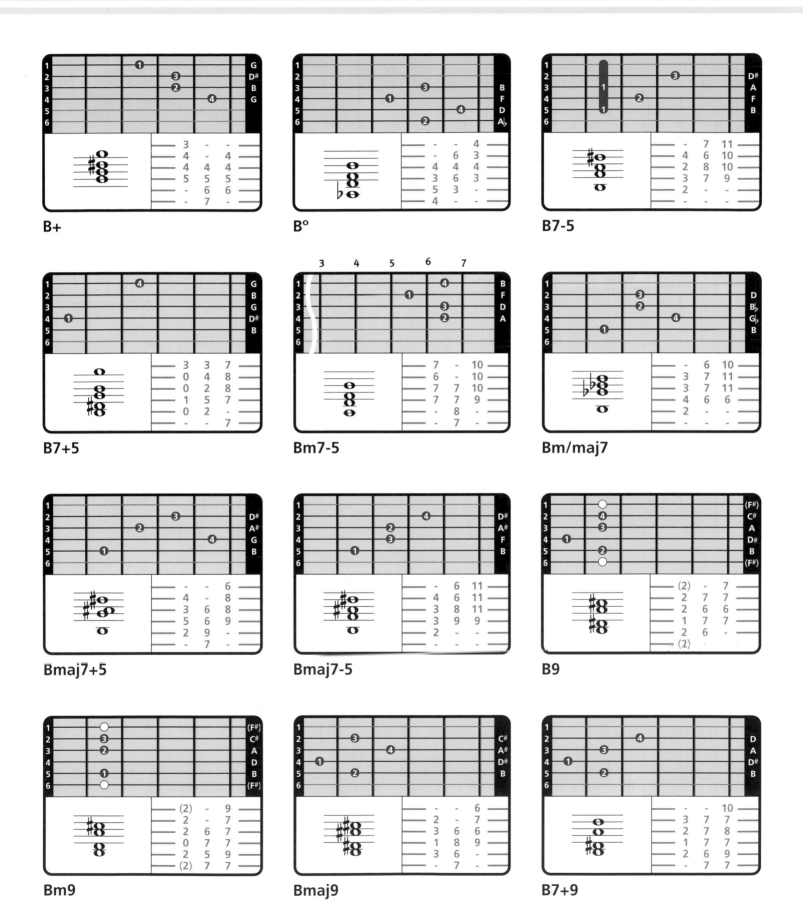

B+

B°

B7-5

B7+5

Bm7-5

Bm/maj7

Bmaj7+5

Bmaj7-5

B9

Bm9

Bmaj9

B7+9

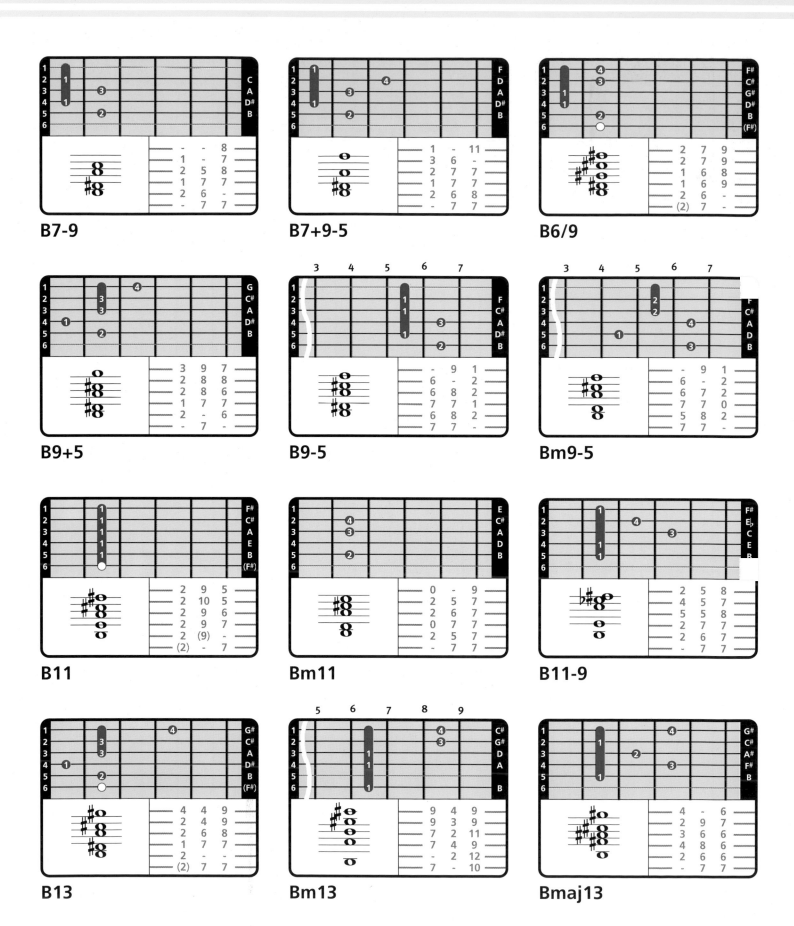

B7-9

B7+9-5

B6/9

B9+5

B9-5

Bm9-5

B11

Bm11

B11-9

B13

Bm13

Bmaj13

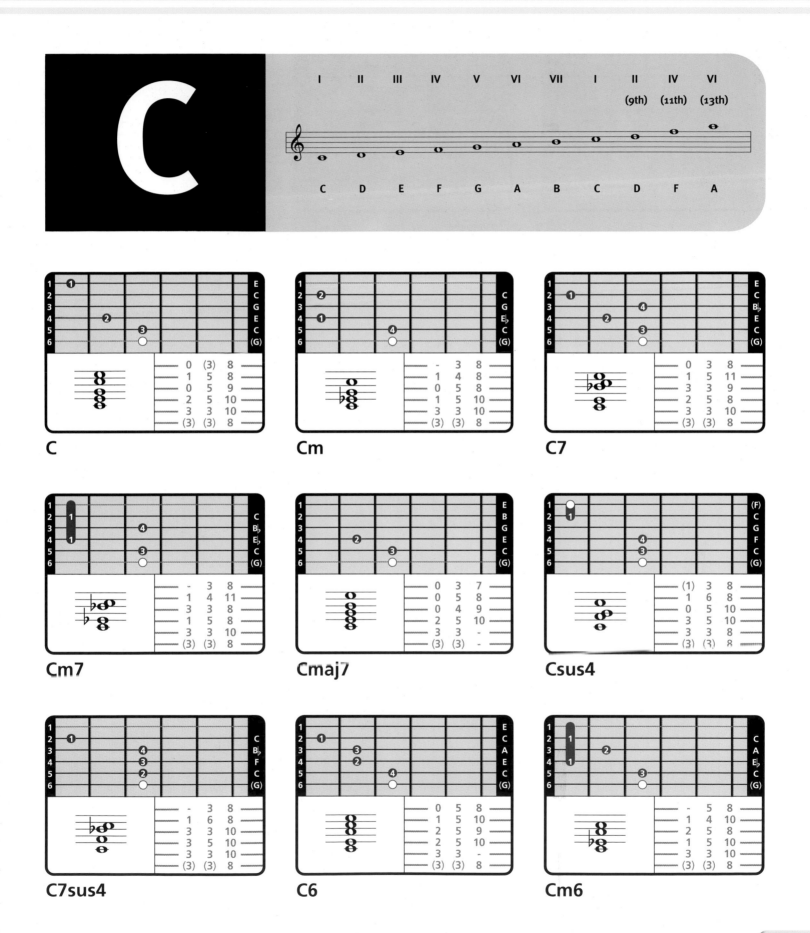

C

I	II	III	IV	V	VI	VII	I	II (9th)	IV (11th)	VI (13th)
C	D	E	F	G	A	B	C	D	F	A

C

Cm

C7

Cm7

Cmaj7

Csus4

C7sus4

C6

Cm6

C

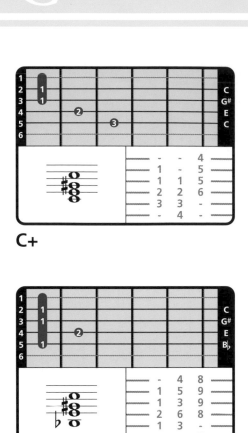

C+

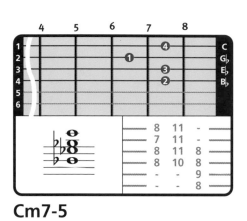

C°

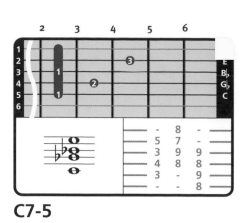

C7-5

C7+5

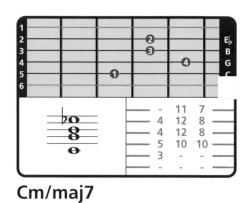

Cm7-5

Cm/maj7

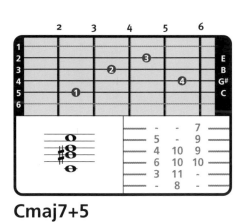

Cmaj7+5

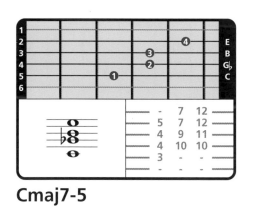

Cmaj7-5

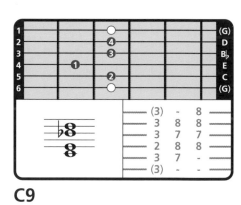

C9

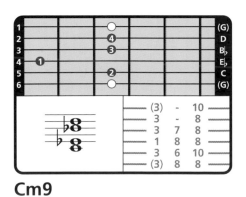

Cm9

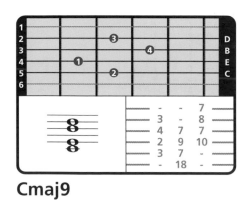

Cmaj9

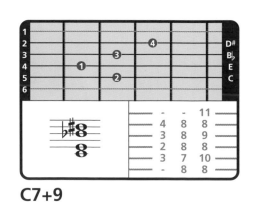

C7+9

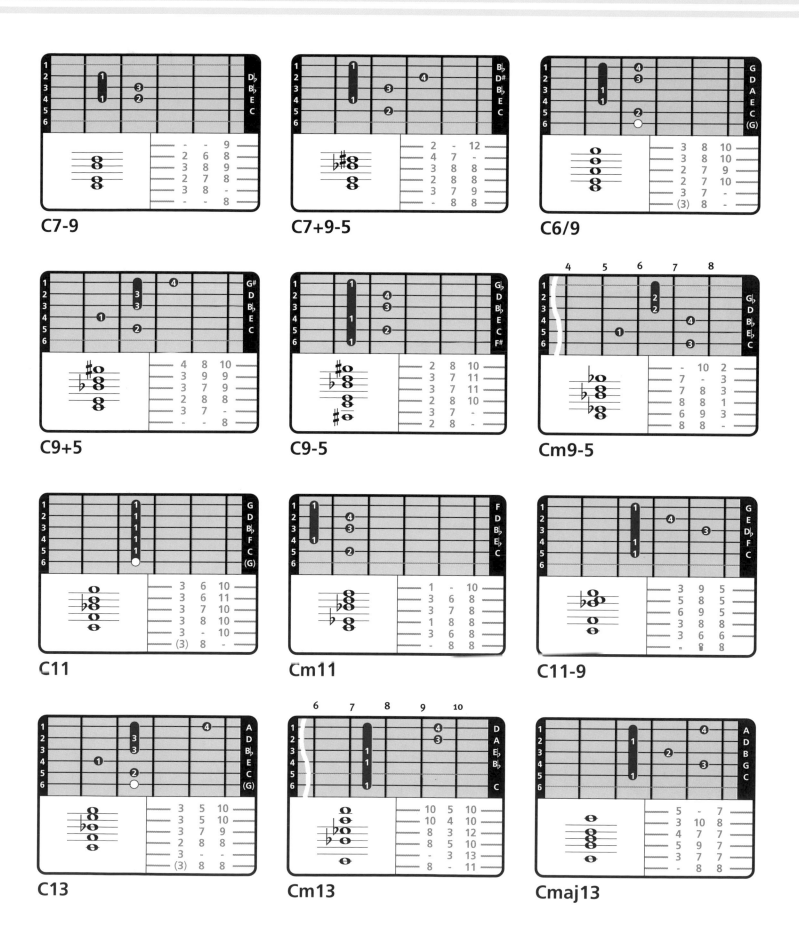

C7-9

C7+9-5

C6/9

C9+5

C9-5

Cm9-5

C11

Cm11

C11-9

C13

Cm13

Cmaj13

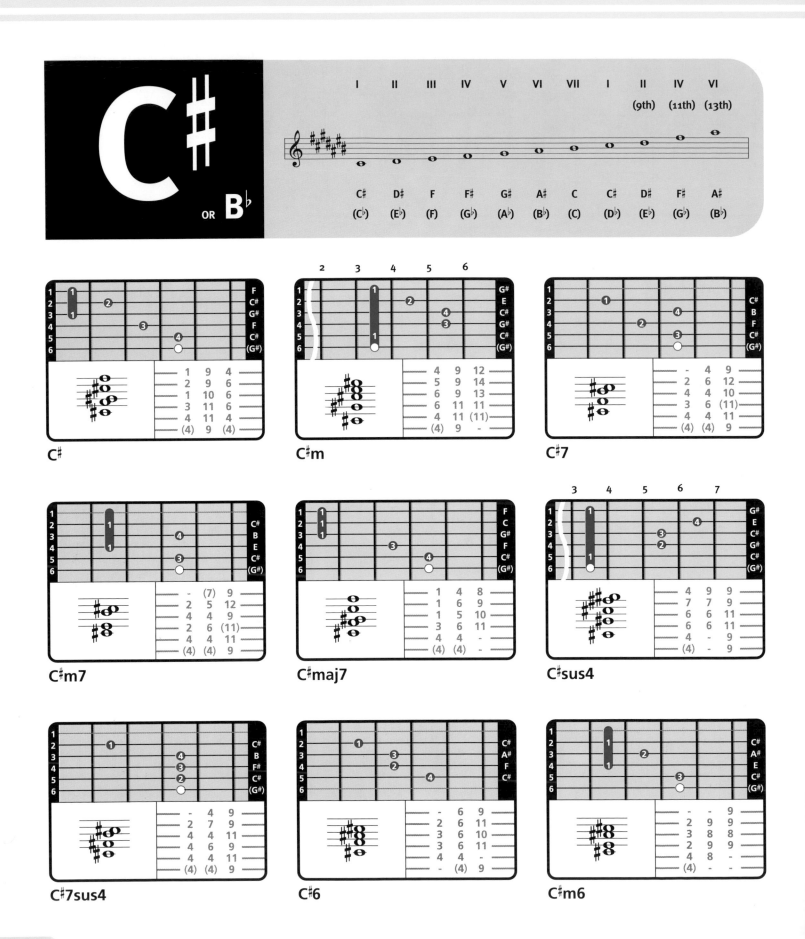

C#

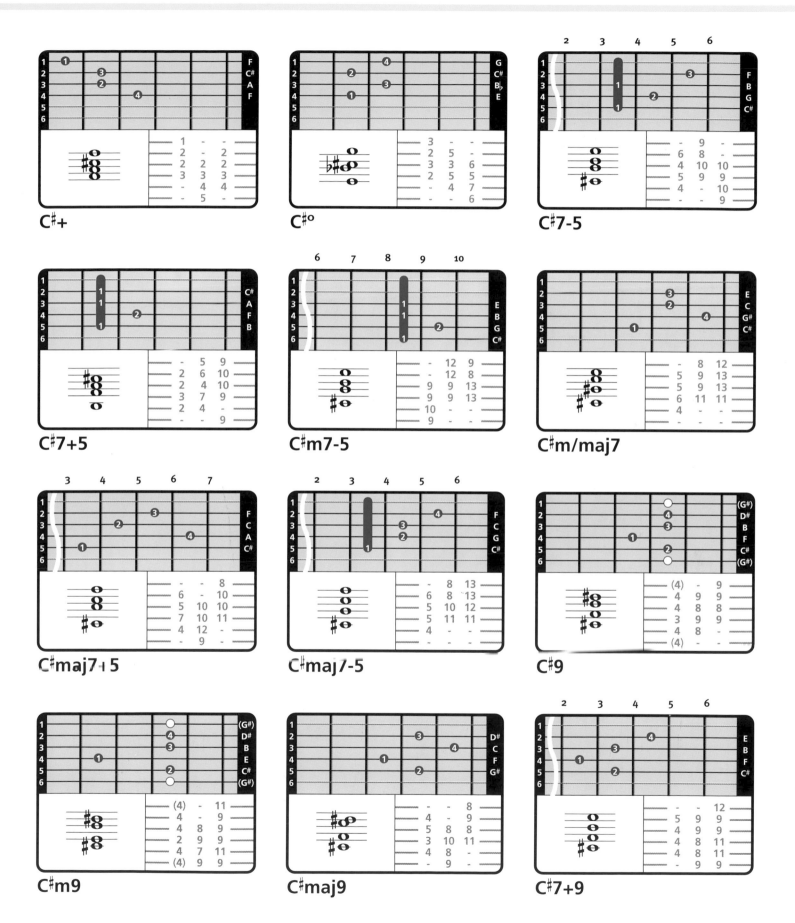

C#+

C#o

C#7-5

C#7+5

C#m7-5

C#m/maj7

C#maj7+5

C#maj7-5

C#9

C#m9

C#maj9

C#7+9

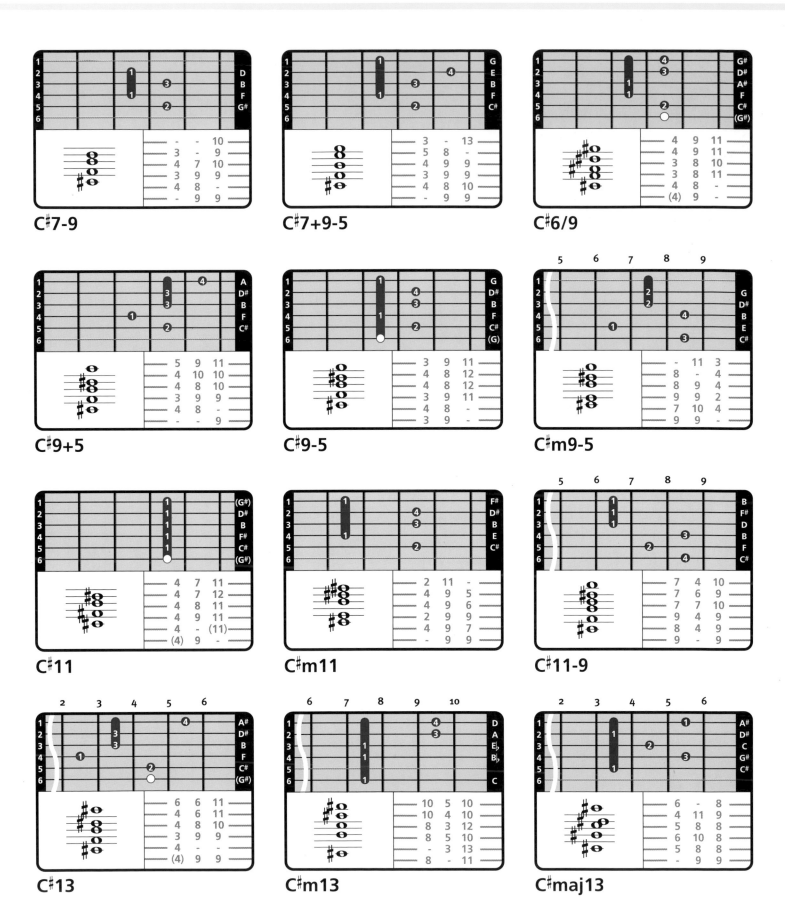

C#7-9

C#7+9-5

C#6/9

C#9+5

C#9-5

C#m9-5

C#11

C#m11

C#11-9

C#13

C#m13

C#maj13

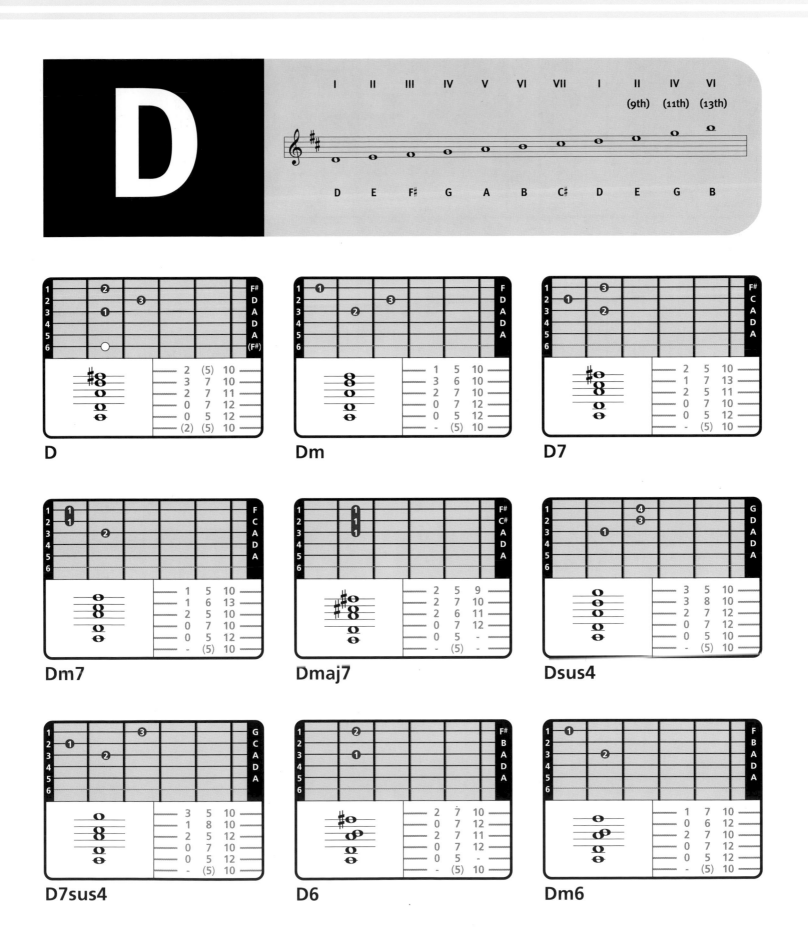

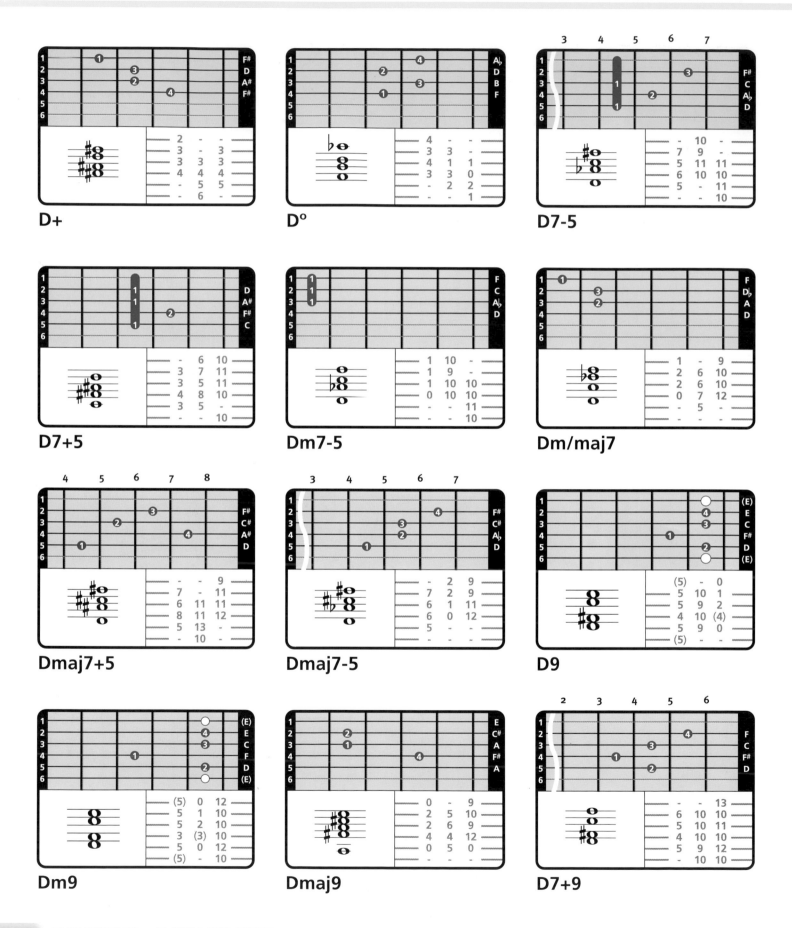

D+

D°

D7-5

D7+5

Dm7-5

Dm/maj7

Dmaj7+5

Dmaj7-5

D9

Dm9

Dmaj9

D7+9

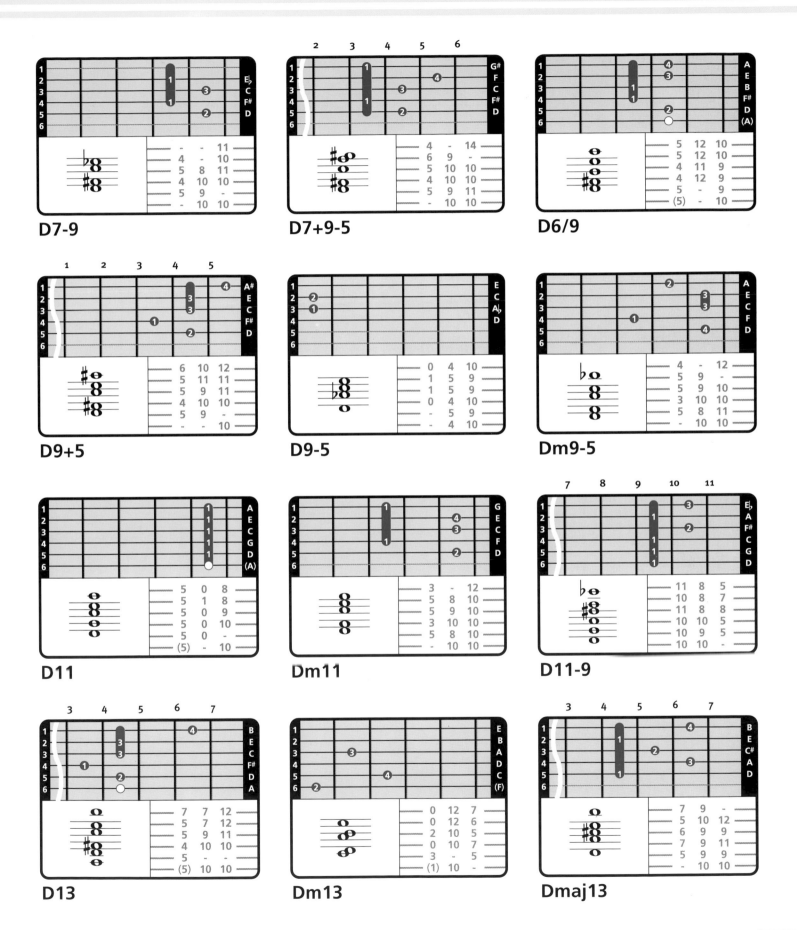

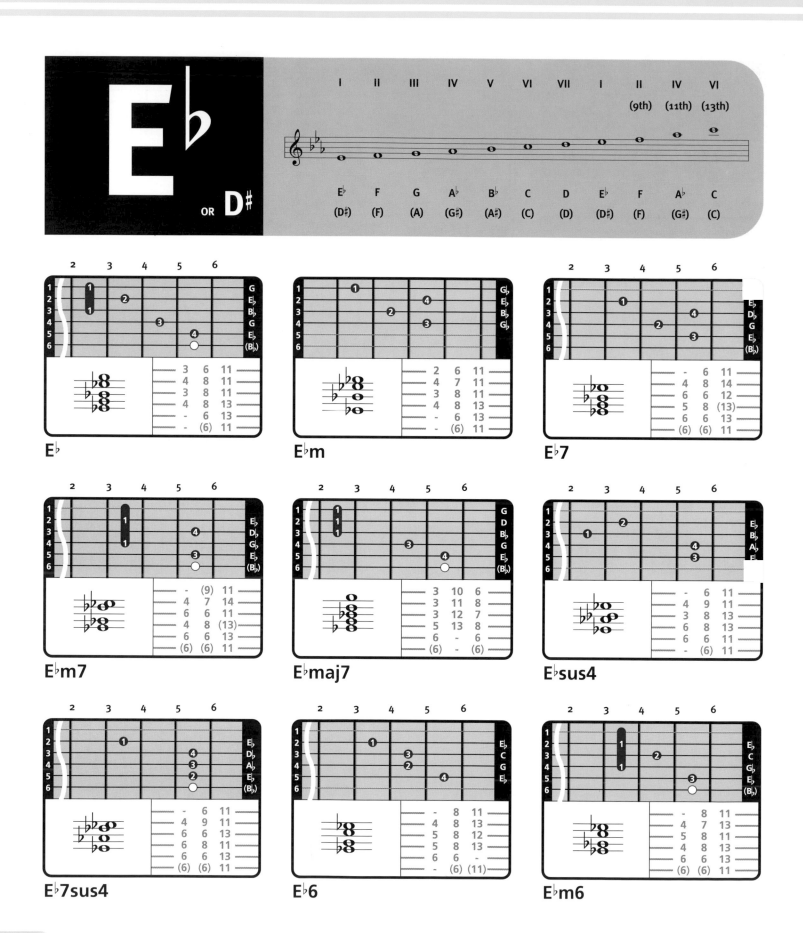

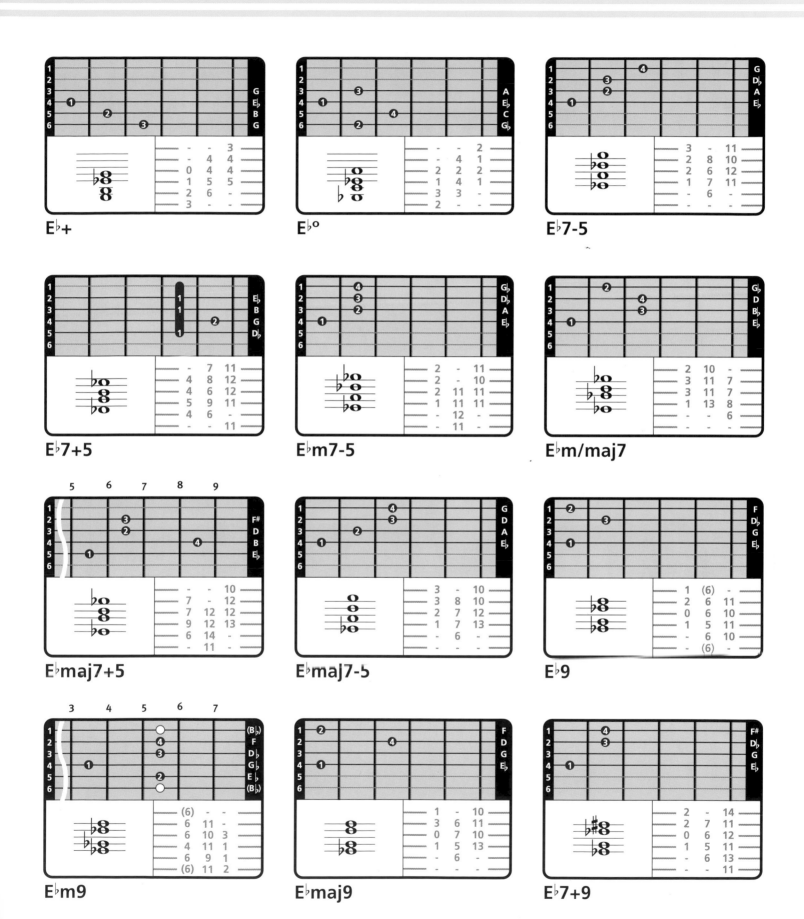

E♭+

E♭o

E♭7-5

E♭7+5

E♭m7-5

E♭m/maj7

E♭maj7+5

E♭maj7-5

E♭9

E♭m9

E♭maj9

E♭7+9

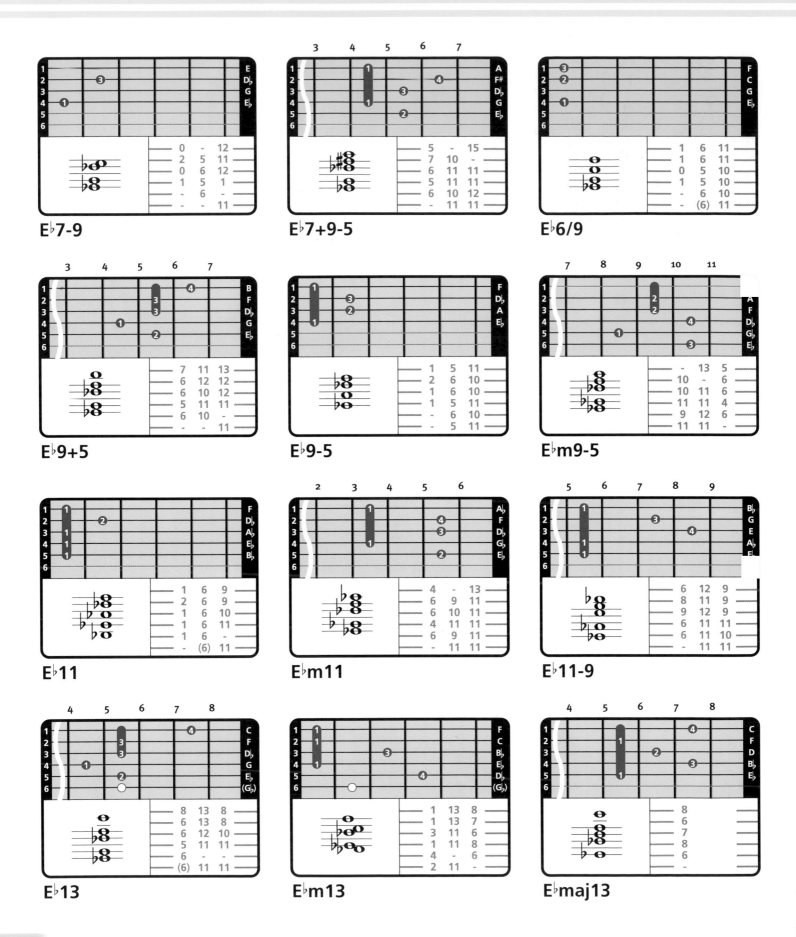

E♭7-9

E♭7+9-5

E♭6/9

E♭9+5

E♭9-5

E♭m9-5

E♭11

E♭m11

E♭11-9

E♭13

E♭m13

E♭maj13

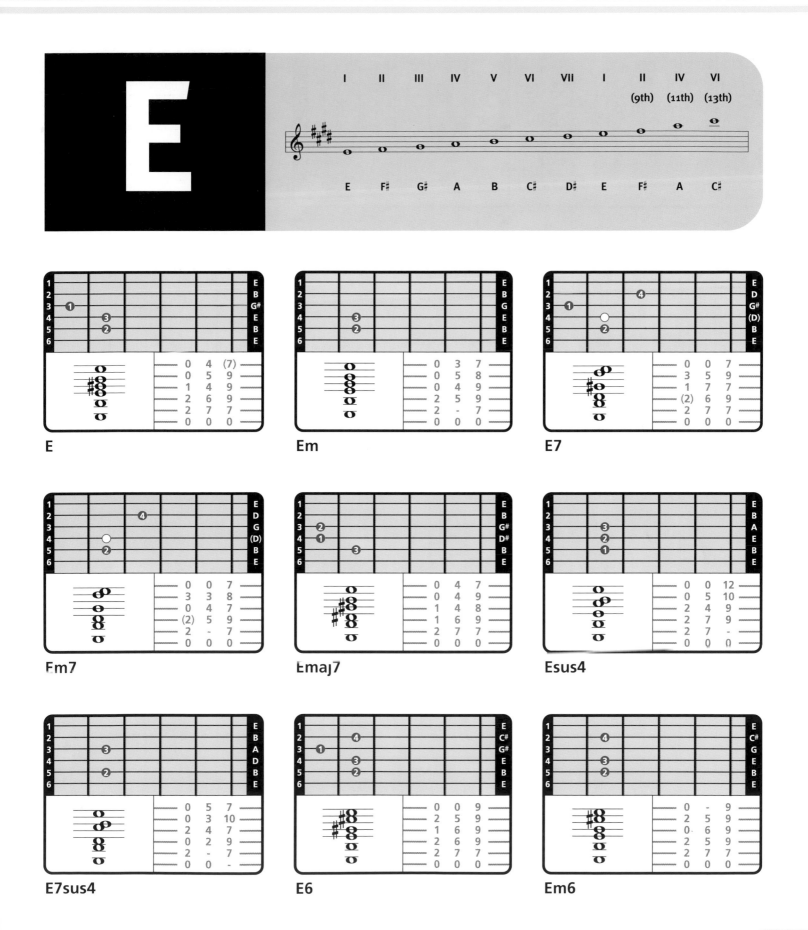

E

Em

E7

Fm7

Emaj7

Esus4

E7sus4

E6

Em6

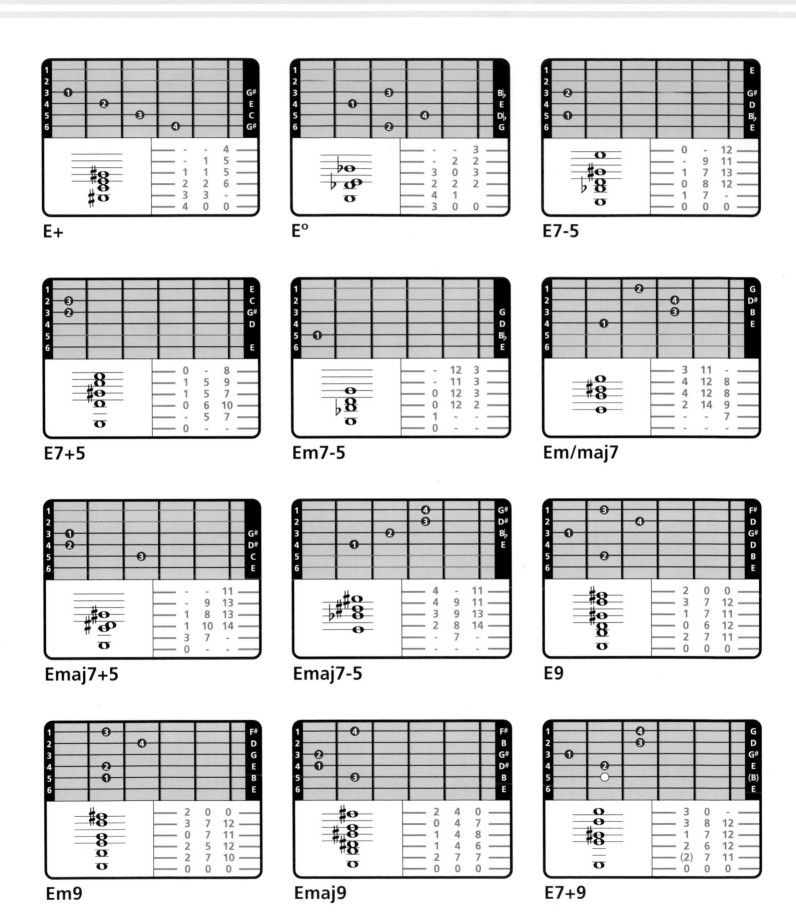

E+   E°   E7-5

E7+5   Em7-5   Em/maj7

Emaj7+5   Emaj7-5   E9

Em9   Emaj9   E7+9

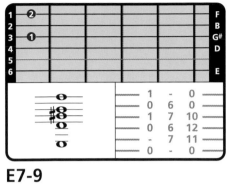

E7-9

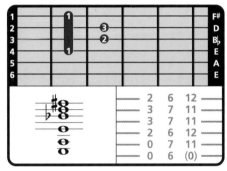

E7+9-5

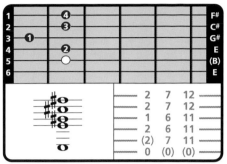

E6/9

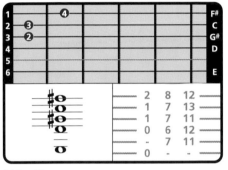

E9+5

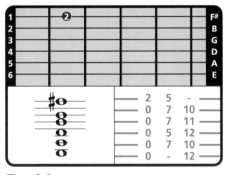

E9-5

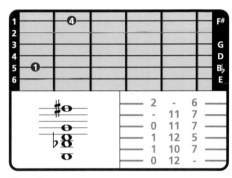

Em9-5

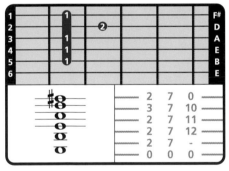

E11

Em11

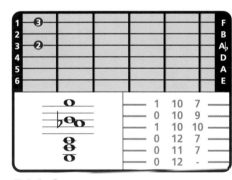

E11-9

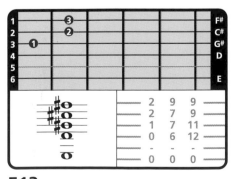

E13

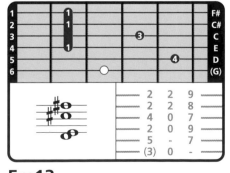

Em13

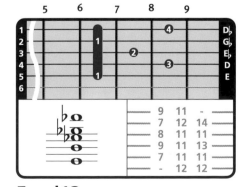

Emaj13

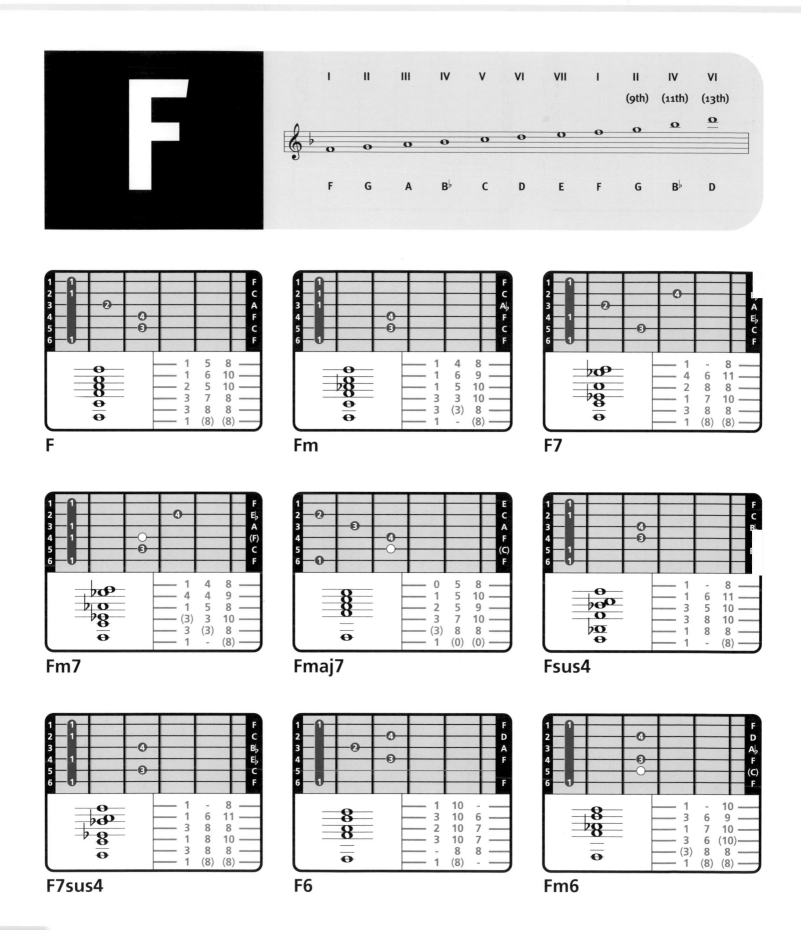

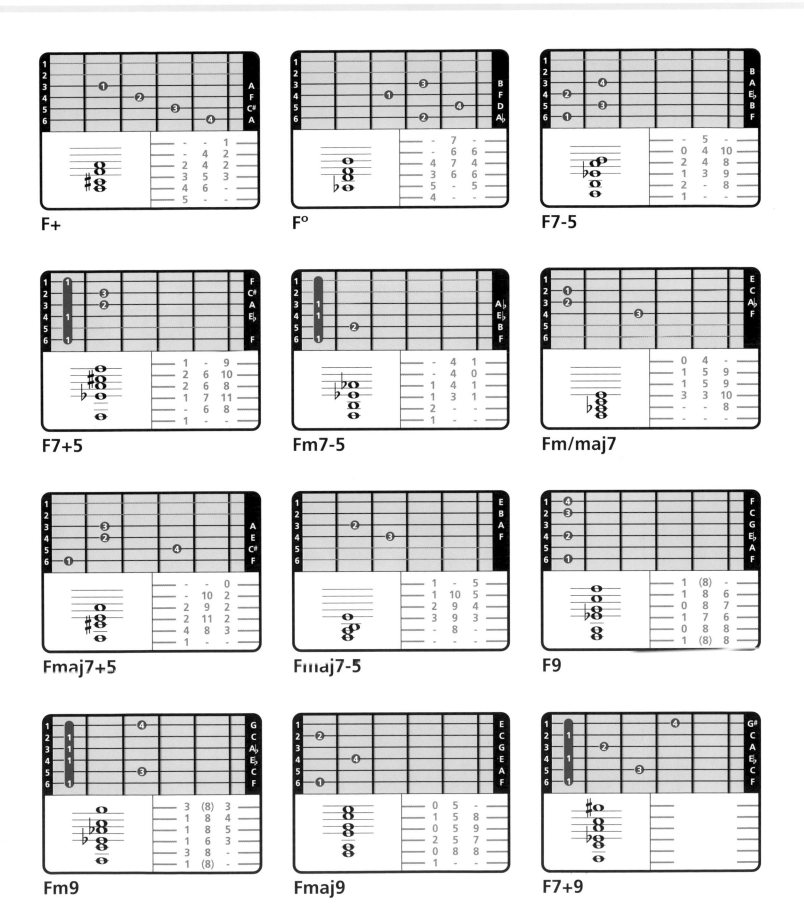

F+

F°

F7-5

F7+5

Fm7-5

Fm/maj7

Fmaj7+5

Fmaj7-5

F9

Fm9

Fmaj9

F7+9

F

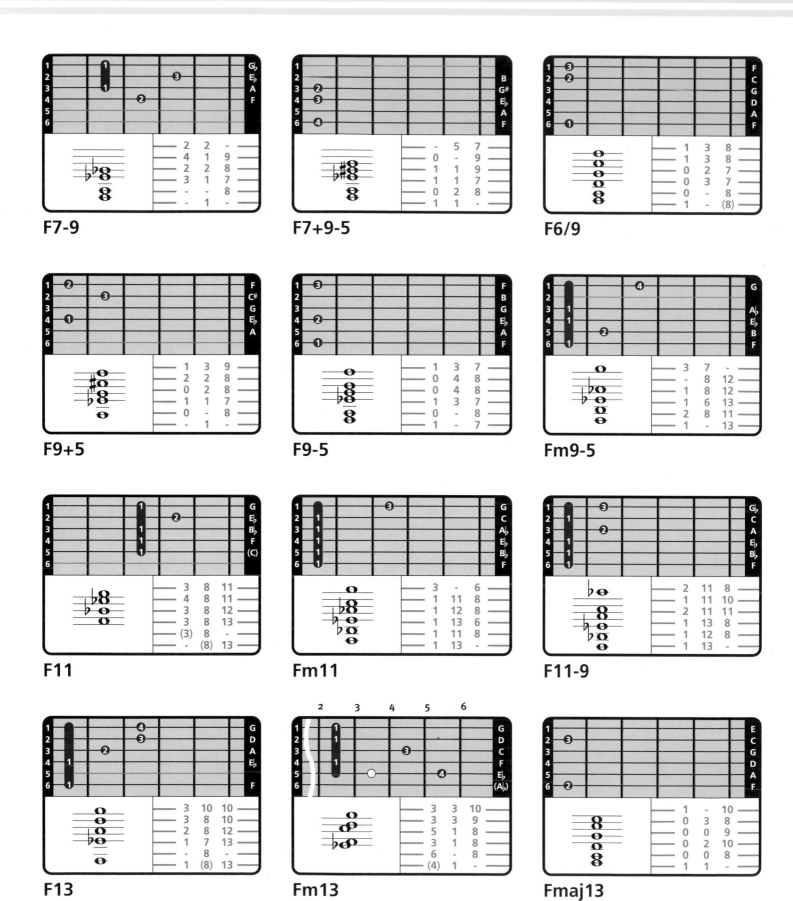

F7-9

F7+9-5

F6/9

F9+5

F9-5

Fm9-5

F11

Fm11

F11-9

F13

Fm13

Fmaj13

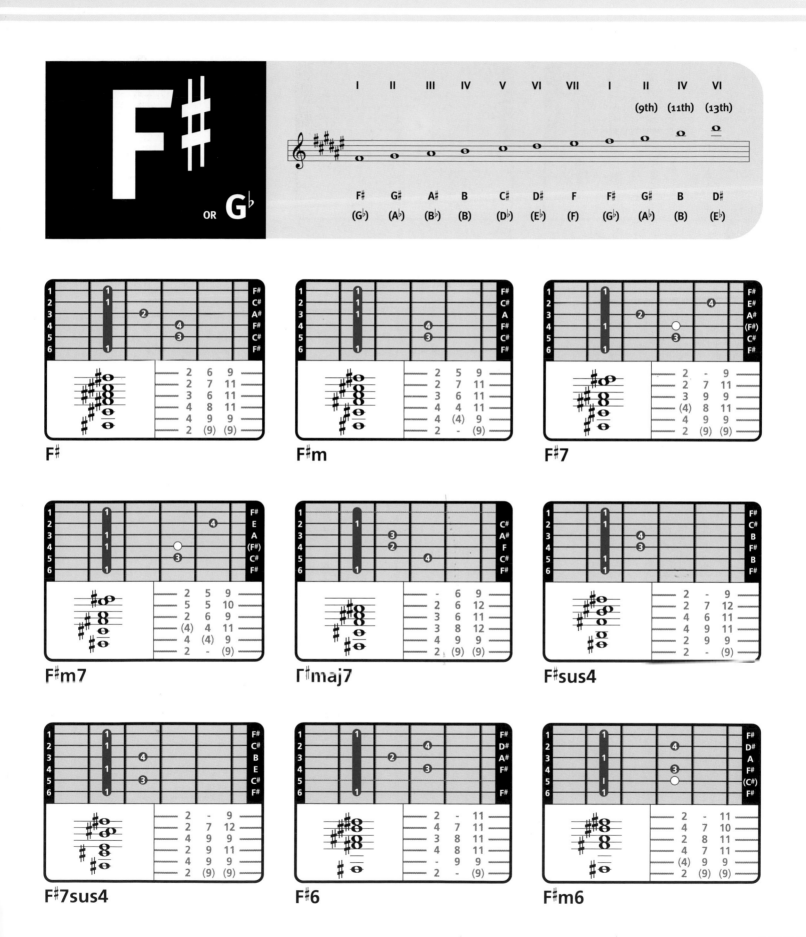

F#

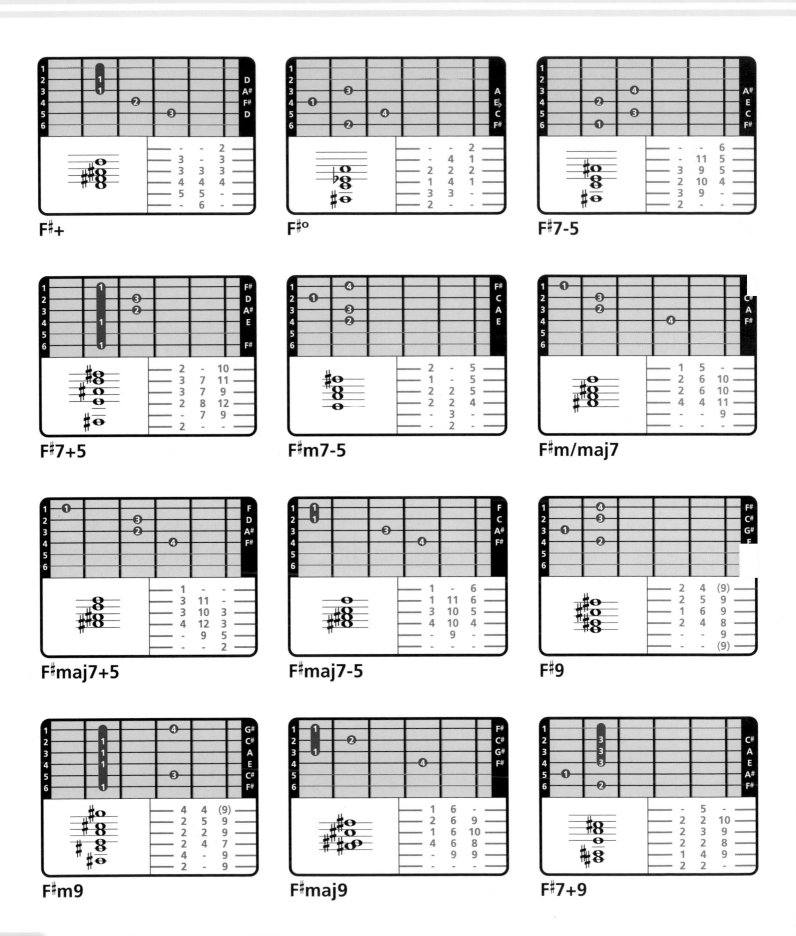

F#+

F#o

F#7-5

F#7+5

F#m7-5

F#m/maj7

F#maj7+5

F#maj7-5

F#9

F#m9

F#maj9

F#7+9

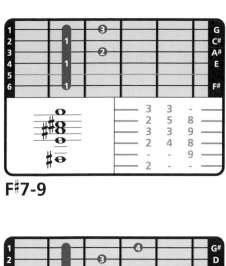

F#7-9

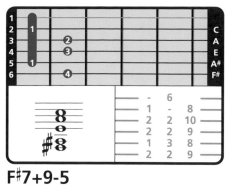

F#7+9-5

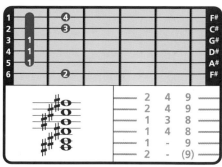

F#6/9

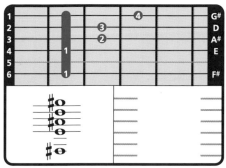

F#9+5

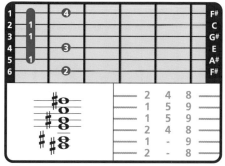

F#9-5

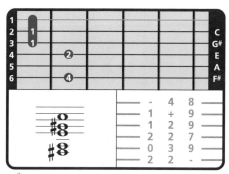

F#m9-5

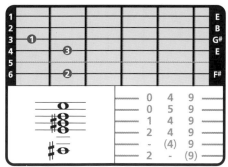

F#11

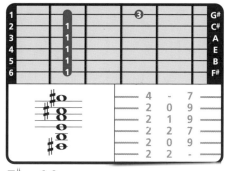

F#m11

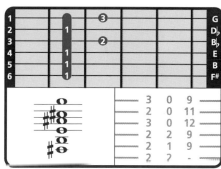

F#11-9

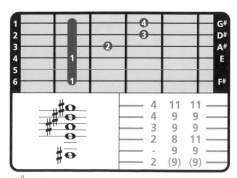

F#13

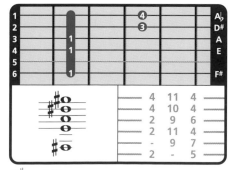

F#m13

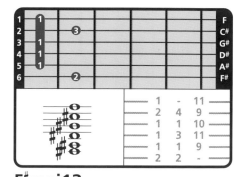

F#maj13

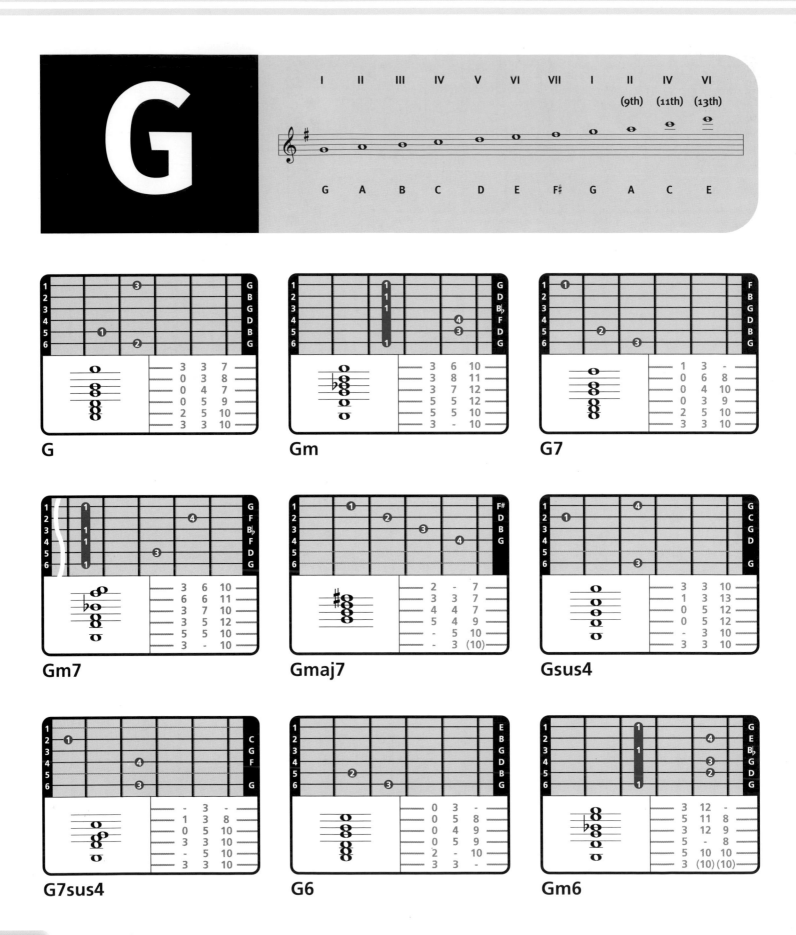

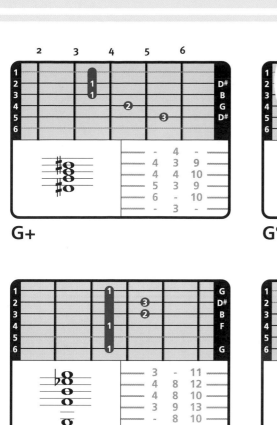

G+

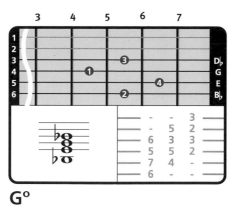

G°

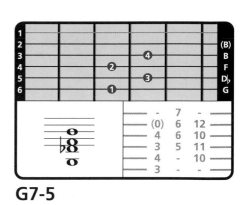

G7-5

G7+5

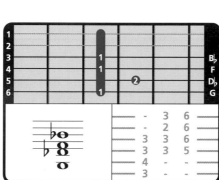

Gm7-5

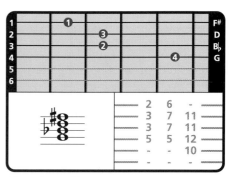

Gm/maj7

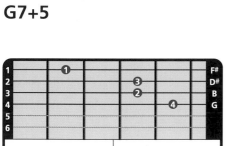

Gmaj7+5

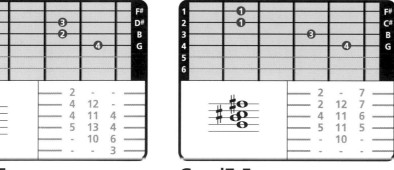

Gmaj7-5

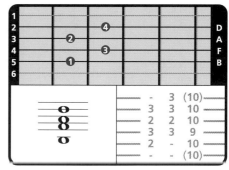

G9

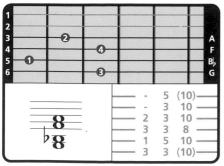

Gm9

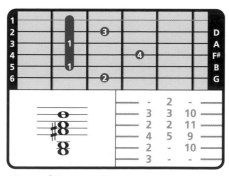

Gmaj9

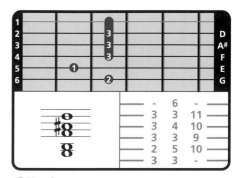

G7+9

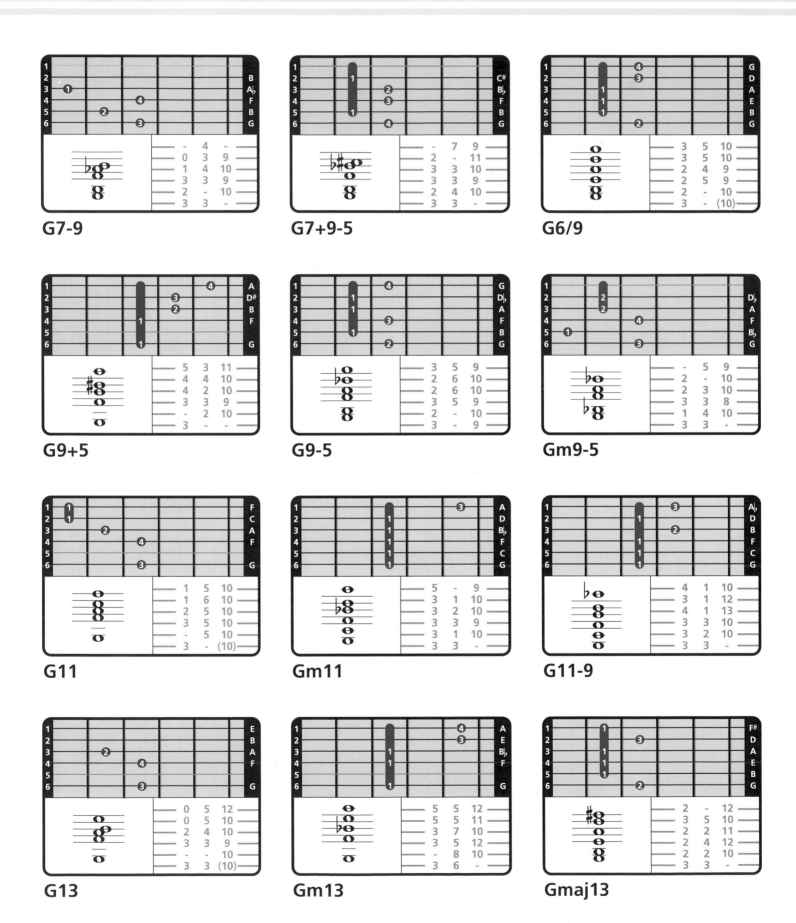

G7-9

G7+9-5

G6/9

G9+5

G9-5

Gm9-5

G11

Gm11

G11-9

G13

Gm13

Gmaj13

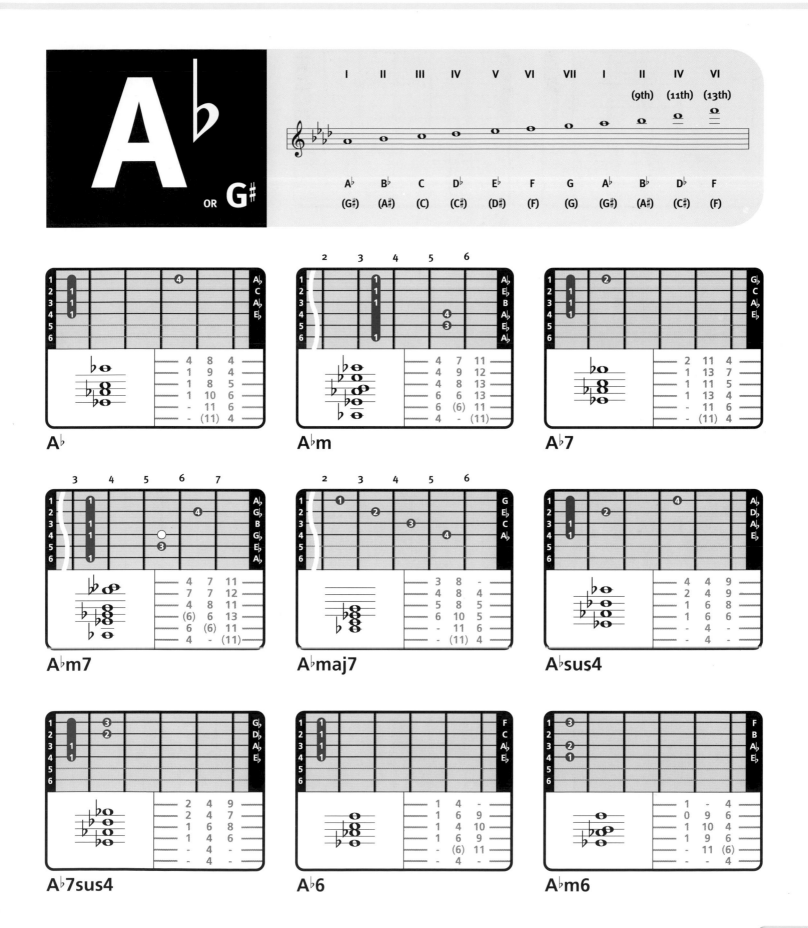

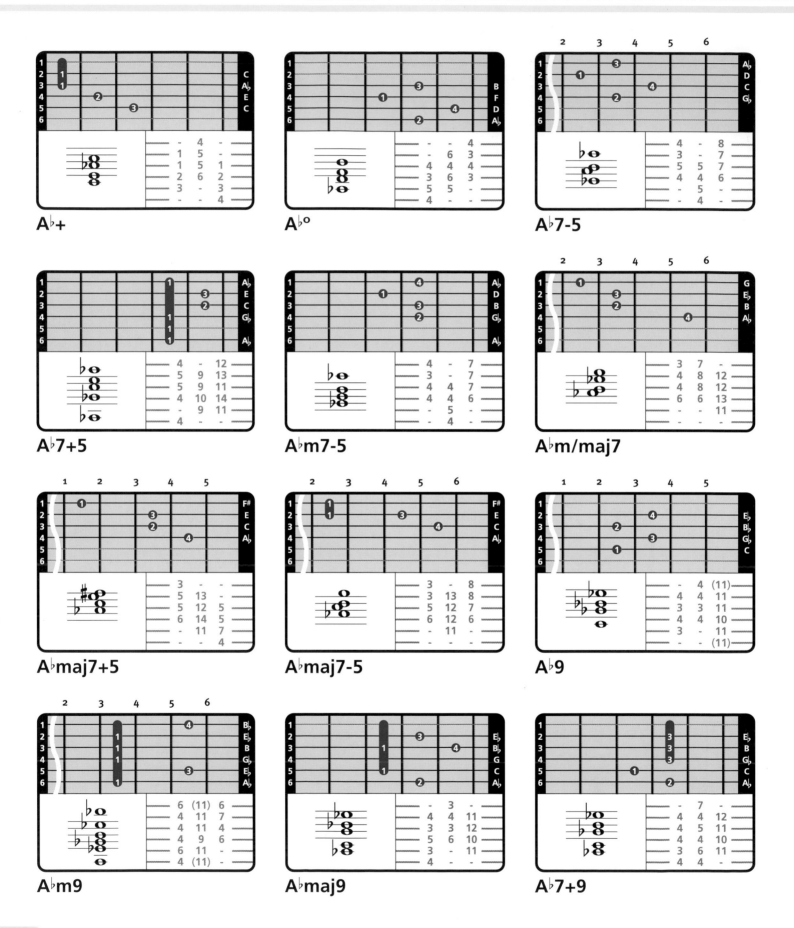

A♭+

A♭º

A♭7-5

A♭7+5

A♭m7-5

A♭m/maj7

A♭maj7+5

A♭maj7-5

A♭9

A♭m9

A♭maj9

A♭7+9

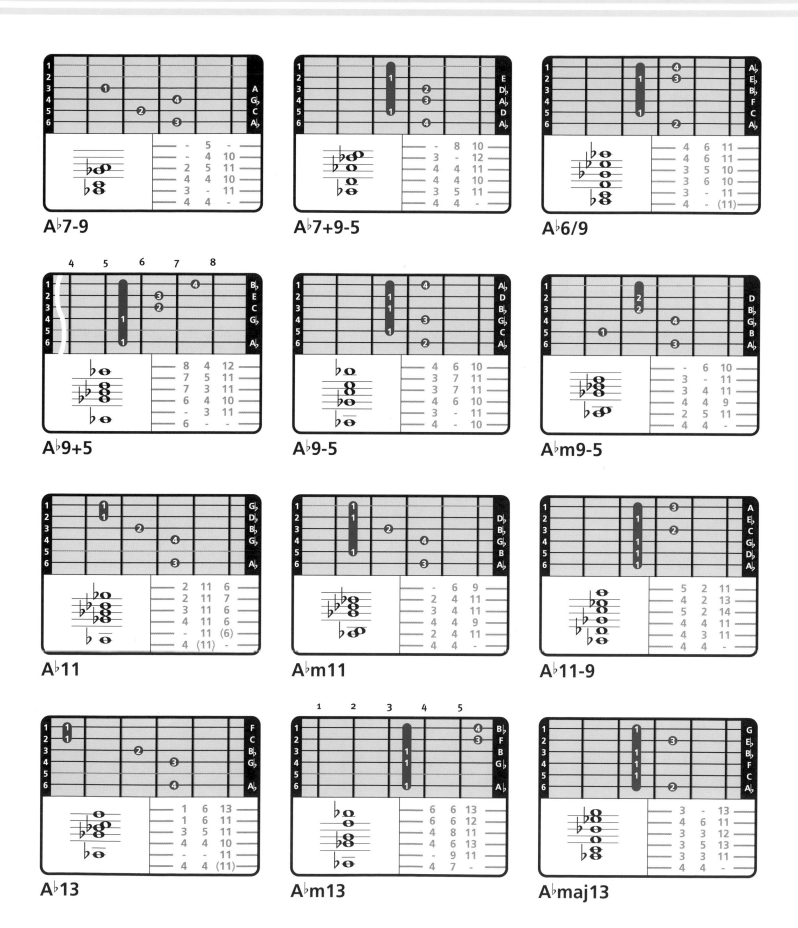

A♭7-9

A♭7+9-5

A♭6/9

A♭9+5

A♭9-5

A♭m9-5

A♭11

A♭m11

A♭11-9

A♭13

A♭m13

A♭maj13

INDEX

CREDITS

The publishers would like to thank the following sources for their kind permission to reproduce the pictures in this book:

AKG London

Arbiter Group plc

ArenaPAL

Backbeat UK/Outline Press Ltd

Steve Barber

Beyer Dynamic (GB) Ltd

Bridgeman Art Library

Terry Burrows

© Christie's Images Ltd

Corbis

Justin Downing

Edinburgh University Collection of
   Historic Musical Instruments

ET archive

Exclusive Distribution

Focusrite Audio Engineering Ltd.

Fotomas Index

Andrew Galindo

Getty Images

Gibson

Jean-loup Charmet/A. Bellet

KGA

The Kobal Collection

The Lebrecht Collection

London Features International Ltd

Marshall Amplification plc

Mary Evans Picture Library

CF Martin Guitar & Co Inc.

Osborne Creative Services

Pictorial Press Ltd

POD Pro photograph courtesy of Line 6 UK. All Rights Reserved.

Royal College of Music, London

Sylvia Pitcher Photo Library/Sylvia Pitcher

Redferns

Retna

Rex Features Ltd

Rickenbacker

S.I.N.

Solid State Logic/Richard Davies

Sound Technology plc

Sound Valley Distribution

Eva Vermandel

Every effort has been made to acknowledge correctly and contact the source and/copyright holder of each picture, and Carlton Books Limited apologises for any unintentional errors or omissions which will be corrected in future editions of this book.